W9-CLG-148

Educational Change

From Traditional Education to Learning Communities

Clifford H. Edwards

ROWMAN & LITTLEFIELD EDUCATION
A division of
ROWMAN & LITTLEFIELD PUBLISHERS, INC.
Lanham • New York • Toronto • Plymouth, UK

Published by Rowman & Littlefield Education
A division of Rowman & Littlefield Publishers, Inc.
A wholly owned subsidiary of The Rowman & Littlefield Publishing Group,
Inc.
4501 Forbes Boulevard, Suite 200, Lanham, Maryland 20706
http://www.rowmaneducation.com

Estover Road, Plymouth PL6 7PY, United Kingdom

British Library Cataloguing in Publication Information Available

Library of Congress Cataloging-in-Publication Data

Edwards, Clifford H.
  Educational change : from traditional education to learning communities /
Clifford H. Edwards.
      p. cm.
  Includes bibliographical references.
  ISBN 978-1-60709-987-1 (cloth : alk. paper)—ISBN 978-1-60709-988-8
(pbk. : alk. paper)—ISBN 978-1-60709-989-5 (electronic)
  1. School improvement programs. 2. Educational change. I. Title.
  LB2822.8.E36 2010
  371.2'07—dc22
                                                              2010034982

☺™ The paper used in this publication meets the minimum requirements of
American National Standard for Information Sciences—Permanence of Paper
for Printed Library Materials, ANSI/NISO Z39.48-1992.

Printed in the United States of America

For Shon, Steven, Jeffrey, and Eric

Contents

Preface

Historically suggested curriculum innovations have vacillated between an emphasis on structure and integrity of the various subjects and a greater emphasis on student involvement in making decisions about what they learn and regulating their own classroom behavior. Some innovations that were attempted tended to be short-lived. This is due in large measure to their featuring simplistic solutions and failing to really consider what ails education. In addition, most innovations have not been carefully researched, particularly in terms of the many implications associated changes embrace.

Rather than basing changes on carefully articulated principles and sound educational philosophy, which have the advantage of accompanying research, modifications are usually made based on political expediencies and simplistic biases. It is evident many times that those who recommend various changes are not well enough versed in educational theory and philosophy and knowledgeable about associated research to make sound choices about what schooling should be. This is particularly evident in the No Child Left Behind Act set forth by the federal government.

Not only have curriculum and instruction in education been composed of elements that hamper desirable learning outcomes, the discipline strategies for minimizing classroom disruptions have also been out of sync with human nature and children's needs. The result has been for teachers to exercise excessive control over students' classroom behavior. Many of the discipline models that are employed rob students of the potential to become more responsibly self-governing. This is true even regarding those discipline approaches that advocate more human, democratic teaching and learning.

To create a properly run classroom, teachers often have to contend with influences from the home and society that adversely affect classroom operations. Dysfunctions in children's homes as well as societal conflicts and issues often promote school disruptions and reduced learning. Because of these problems, teachers tend to blame many of the difficulties they experience in their classrooms on these outside factors. In reality teachers create many of these problems themselves. Imperatives imposed by school administrators and state school officials also promulgate some of the problems.

One of the difficulties that beg for resolution is the nature of school evaluation. Currently most evaluation focuses exclusively on student achievement, and a significant part of this is in the form of high-stakes tests. These are imposed by many state education departments to acquire monetary benefits that are available when they adhere to specified conditions sponsored by the federal government. The validity of these tests along with their negative influence on school curricula requires immediate attention. The excesses these efforts have inspired in terms of the behavior of teachers and administrators as well as their negative impact on students are unacceptable. The adverse moral implications of various decisions are manifestly clear.

Long-standing evaluation procedures also need to be revised. Grades have long been held as a respectable way to denote students' academic accomplishments. Their purpose ordinarily was to provide a way to sort students for entrance into college. It is even claimed that they motivate students. However, their deleterious effects are overlooked even though an enormous body of research seriously questions their use. The rationale that grades are needed to motivate students is not valid, and their use for sorting students for college cannot be justified given the enormous negative impact they have on some students. In recognition of this problem, grades have gradually become inflated. Unfortunately, inflating grades only adds to the problem.

Given the problems commonly associated with schools as they are, it is evident that changes are necessary. However, these changes should not be of the kind that have ordinarily taken place. Most of these changes never solved the real problems. Deficiencies continue, such as students experiencing poor intellectual development and decision-making capabilities. They are also lacking in the necessary skills to equip them for life in democratic communities along with needed moral development. These and other deficiencies define current school operations.

What has become a more prevalent suggestion from educators and researchers is that schooling should be organized so that it genuinely prepares students for life in a democratic society. The instructional program that is encouraged is a learning community in which students help to direct their own learning. The basic learning format is to engage in inquiry-based research regarding critical problems and issues, which helps students acquire a comprehensive understanding of the most fundamental concepts and which helps them to develop lifelong skills for learning and knowledge apprehension.

In learning communities, instruction would be consistent with the way humans naturally learn. This involves constructivist learning theory. It means students would be empowered to become responsibly autonomous and find legitimate ways to satisfy their basic needs so that they do not react negatively to what happens in school. When students' needs are met in school, they are far more motivated to learn than when need fulfillment is thwarted by the many obstacles that are rampant in current school practices. Children would become involved in fulfilling social relationships and in the process learn how to communicate with others more effectively while developing the life-enhancing aspects of creative endeavors in the classroom.

Evaluation in democratic learning communities is not confined to determining what facts students remember from their lessons. It is much more comprehensive. Thus, it takes many more concerns into account than the simple recall of information as emphasized in common school testing programs. Schooling in democratic learning communities does not lend itself to traditional testing strategies. Rather, the quality of education is determined by assessing a broad spectrum of constituents.

While traditional testing focuses on outcomes, evaluation in learning communities also examines the learning process. Moreover, students' moral development is assessed along with need satisfaction, motivation, leadership, teacher and administrator effectiveness, patterns of thinking, problem-solving capability, inquiry research skills, relationships, communications, creativity, teacher commitment, as well as discipline and other factors.

In learning communities, discipline is an outgrowth of the instructional process. It is implemented in the same way the instructional program is put into effect. Thus, students help to formulate their own principles with which to guide classroom behavior. Teachers refrain from dealing with discipline problems as they occur. Instead, students are invited to consider the implications of these problems as well as potential ones and decide what should be done about them. The teacher helps students to avoid punishing each other or imposing fabricated consequences. Instead students are empowered by helping to figure out how classroom problems can be avoided through a concerted effort by all to accentuate the learning of fellow students.

Teachers and their colleagues are also involved in democratic learning communities along with school administrators. Using this format, teachers are engaged in leadership responsibilities and decision making about their classroom learning communities. In professional learning communities, teachers help each other find the most effective ways to employ learning community principles in their own classrooms. Through their genuine participation in decision making in the school, they acquire more commitment for teaching and become researchers in their own classrooms. This is the surest way for teachers to find a voice in their professional life and accentuate the authentic development of their skills.

Parents should also be involved in learning communities. Their role might be confined to periodic interactions with teachers and discussions with their children, but it might also involve learning along with their children and helping to make decisions about the operation of the schools. A parent with a particular expertise can be of considerable help to the successful operation of a learning community.

In changing to a learning community approach to education there are many obstacles. Foremost among these are the difficulties that can predictably be encountered in helping to deprogram students who have been shaped up to respond as directed to the coercive practices of traditional schools. They will have become conditioned to grading and other reward procedures and likely will be weighed down by ineffective motivational encumbrances. Many will have acquired negative views of schooling and have developed debilitating notions about their own capabilities and aspirations.

Teachers will also be required to change. First of all, their control propensities will have to be moderated so that they feel more inclined to empower student decision making. Their own experiences as students may stand in the way. They also need to believe that with expert guidance, students can learn how to make responsible decisions and work effectively with other students in accomplishing far more than is possible in a traditional schooling format.

Most administrators are committed to top-down decision making. They see their job as distributing administrative directives with which others are expected to comply. They may also visualize their responsibility as imposing the directives from the state education department unquestioningly. However, in learning communities, shared leadership is necessary. The administrators' most important responsibility is to ensure that shared leadership not only takes place in professional learning communities but in classrooms as well. They must also effectively protect learning communities from unwarranted intrusions that threaten to hamper their effectiveness. In addition, it is critical that the resources needed for the smooth operation of all learning communities in the school are acquired in a timely way and appropriately distributed.

The main focus of this volume is to help educators understand those elements that threaten effective education. Its purpose is to provide a more effective strategy for curriculum and instruction and associated discipline, and to help teachers and school administrators learn what is necessary for making appropriate changes. The need for change has been a long-standing debate, with different options periodically implemented. Most changes have had limited success because they fail to address the problem in a sufficiently comprehensive way. A learning community approach to education provides a means for effectively solving most of the problems that have been identified in educational research.

Chapter One

Philosophical Issues Regarding Curriculum and Instruction

An examination of the history of education reveals patterns of change and various philosophical differences regarding what constitutes appropriate schooling for children. An understanding of these historical changes is essential in determining what education should be. There have been a number of significantly different emphases regarding schooling, each with strenuous support but without accompanying research to justify them. Each of these approaches makes different assumptions about acceptable school outcomes and the nature of learning, as well as appropriate instructional processes.

Some of the emphasized educational philosophies require strict control of the curriculum and instructional processes. Others focus on democratic principles with the purpose of helping children learn to live productively in democratic communities. These various orientations to education have vastly different purposes and schooling procedures. Historically the emphasis on structure or student interests has vacillated back and forth repeatedly. At present the struggle between featuring structure or democratic principles in education continues.

The purpose of this work is to properly characterize both emphases and show the critical importance of carefully examining traditional educational practices and dutifully considering change to more democratic principles to guide schooling. In a democracy it is important not to lose sight of the need to help children become responsible citizens rather than pawns of a system that exercises excessive control and in the process may rob children of many of the moral aspects of an enlightened society.

Not only will important aspects of curriculum and instruction be considered, but also the accompanying processes of classroom decorum and discipline. Both of these aspects of schooling must be considered because learning greatly depends on properly organized instruction along with a learning environment in which effective instruction and learning may proceed without undermining disruptions.

Many educators consider discipline and instruction to be entirely different in a tactical sense and to be based upon different sets of principles. However, discipline and instruction can't be separated from one another any more than the curricular plan can be divorced from its instructional implementation. Not only do they depend on each other to achieve clarity of purpose and action, they dictate and integrate these classroom functions into a consistent whole. Otherwise discontinuity exists, creating confusion not only for teachers, but also for their students.

Historically there is almost a complete dearth of discipline considerations in the various curricular proposals and innovations. Also, there have been conflicts between philosophical directions and objectives and the way various curriculum proposals were implemented in the schools. This has enormous implications for current curricular matters as well as associated discipline theory. Through all of this, very little research was conducted to assure the curriculum developers that the changes implemented were in fact effectively achieving the results they sought (Tanner & Tanner, 1975).

The historical changes in the schools that started around the early 1900s have led some to liken them to a swinging pendulum, going from an emphasis on the structure and integrity of the various subjects and the perpetuation of the cultural heritage to an extreme emphasis on child development and self-direction. From this latter perspective children were thought inherently capable of directing their own learning experiences. They were often compared to the natural opening of flower petals.

Those who fostered greater structure supported various programs that were concerned either with transmission of the cultural heritage through so-called "classical writings" or with maintaining the structure of the various subjects in the form in which they were developed by university scholars. While educators were exploring these differences, almost nothing was being considered regarding what discipline implications existed for different curricular programs.

The various schools of thought regarding curricula primarily addressed student learning based on disparate conceptions of the nature of children along with what they should eventually become. The major issue centered on whether it was best for children to acquire classical knowledge from the past from which to live their lives, which was assumed to be dependable generation after generation, or if they should learn in a way that would result in the reconstruction of society in forward-looking ways that help create a society that could be defended as consistent with inevitable changes. It is ironic that none of these proposed changes included a comprehensive consideration of discipline issues.

However, through this period it appears that corporal punishment was assumed to be necessary. Obviously greater attention should have been dedicated to examining this assumption given the fact that the purpose of corporal punishment was to "beat the devil out of children and restrain their wills," an apparent holdover from certain Protestant religious views. For many years it had been assumed that the source of children's unruliness was from devilish influences rather than the environment in which they lived (Gordon, 1989).

The issues that separated various recommended curriculum orientations around the beginning of the twentieth century have continued on to the present. They may be represented by different patterns of schooling, but they still reflect the ever-present issue of student autonomy versus teacher control. Because discipline should reflect the same principles as curriculum and instruction, an examination will be made of some of the issues and the way curricula have evolved over time. It is interesting to note that discipline practices have not received the same attention. Recommended modifications in discipline practices came along much later.

HISTORICAL PERSPECTIVES ON EDUCATIONAL PHILOSOPHY AND SCHOOL CURRICULA

Different philosophies of education have quite different views of how children should be educated. For example, perennialist conceptions of curricula hold that schooling should consist principally of "permanent studies" including the rules of grammar, reading, rhetoric and logic, and mathematics for elementary and secondary education and a study of the greatest books of the Western world, beginning at the secondary level of schooling (Hutchins, 1936). Perennialists consider modern scientific studies irrelevant due to the changing state of knowledge. They contend that certain subjects have the uniquely inherent power to cultivate the intellect, making it unnecessary to routinely incorporate new knowledge into school curricula.

The educational philosophy of essentialism supports the inclusion of five essential areas of disciplined study: (1) command of the mother tongue and the study of grammar, (2) mathematics, (3) sciences, (4) history, and (5) foreign language (Bestor, 1956). Knowledge in these areas is to be acquired by students and stored for future use. Essentialists believe that studying these subjects disciplines the mind despite the fact that mental discipline had been refuted by the findings of educational psychologists in the early decades of the twentieth century. These researchers found that there was no strengthening of the mind nor transfer of abilities from one subject to another in the absence of common content or methods of study. For there to be any benefit of so-called transfer of training, there had to be identical elements in content or methods (Thorndike, 1906).

One of the movements during the same time period was an effort to create a curriculum synthesis. Various subjects were to be studied together in terms of some organizing principle. Thus, all the sciences were to be studied together in a single course in terms of their relationships to each other. In the area of social sciences learning had an anthropological orientation. Humanity was to be studied in relation to the physical and social environment. Emphasis would be given to the influence of communities on their members, and history would be integrated by referring to the written records of human evolutionary processes. Geography would be added as it related to the growth of civilization via the movement of individuals and communities for various purposes. This effort helped to solve two critical problems for the schools: an overcrowded curriculum and the exponential increase in knowledge.

As these curricular emphases were unfolding, progressive education was already making inroads on the educational scene. As far back as the late 1870s, ideas about a more child-centered curriculum were being circulated among educators. Teachers were encouraged to individualize their teaching and to make sure student interest was an essential component of instruction. It is essential to note that despite the emphasis on interest, it was differentially defined. Those who supported the philosophy of German philosopher Johann Friedrich Herbart saw interest as something external that teachers add to subject matter to make it palatable and enticing to students.

Followers of John Dewey, on the other hand, defined interest as something inherently present where the goals of instruction were important to a child. Thus, interest was intrinsic to the activity itself rather than extrinsically supplied by the teacher. This is a particularly important distinction to make and constitutes an ongoing debate among educators about how to maximize the outcomes of instruction.

Dewey made further clarifications regarding interest in response to what is commonly referred to as "romantic progressive education." Though the romantic progressive education movement claimed connections to Dewey, he was careful to make critical distinctions between their recommended practices and various aspects of curricula as he saw them. To Dewey, it is the responsibility of the teacher to identify and cultivate those interests that are inherent in the subject, prized by the community, and that lead in the direction of society's demands (Dewey, 1934).

On the other hand, romantic progressives felt that all learning should be left up to the student's idiosyncratic desires. Dewey rejected this orientation and indicated that children tend to snatch at transient or accidental interests rather than enduring ones when they are simply asked by teachers what they would like to do. He further concluded that spontaneous pupil activity mitigates against freedom because it subjects children to haphazard conditions that produce superficial learning experiences lacking in intelligently directed thought.

Dewey supported curricula that promoted reflective thinking. To him, thought had to be connected to action. This involved genuine problem solving that involved students testing out their ideas and discovering their validity for themselves (Dewey, 1916). This was in contrast with educators who emphasized the memorization of information.

During the late 1800s and early 1900s there were numerous efforts to shape curricula to conform to a variety of philosophical bases. In all of these, the primary issue involved the degree to which children could legitimately direct their own learning. Those convinced that students could not validly govern their own learning supported curricula with considerable structure and teacher control. Those who supported the opposite extreme allowed children to learn what they wanted at their own pace.

A number of programs featured various combinations of these two philosophies. Some were judged contradictory in their purposes and procedures. Most failed to conduct appropriate research. The one exception was the Progressive Education Association's Eight-Year Study. In this research, the support of three hundred colleges and universities was enlisted to admit students without regard to traditional entrance requirements. Secondary schools involved in the study were released from these requisites for a period of five years.

In the Eight-Year Study students from thirty secondary schools were selected for study. These schools made efforts to employ student-directed learning. When compared with their traditionally schooled counterparts, these students were found to have higher grade-point averages; received more academic honors; were more precise, systematic, and objective thinkers; and were more intellectually curious during their college experiences. They were more actively concerned about what was happening in the world, earned more nonacademic honors in college, and were more resourceful in meeting new situations. This was especially so among schools that departed the most from traditional curricula.

Some schools during this time attempted to find ways to break down barriers between subjects so that the real meaning of the fields of knowledge could be made more apparent to students. This was a particularly difficult task and usually resulted in curricula with a laminated appearance rather than full integration, even when one subject was allowed to provide the organizing center. This eventually led curriculum developers to reject such integration efforts in favor of using social problem solving as the organizing principle.

It is singular to note that this mimics the very way in which scholars learn. Increasingly scholars have found it necessary to visualize problems and solve them within their innate complexity by using various fields of study to arrive at valid solutions. These schools also focused on student self-direction and individual guidance (Chamberlain, 1942).

In the mid-1950s and the decade of the 1960s, essentialism was superseded by what is referred to as the disciplines doctrine. Educators with this curricular orientation rejected the traditional conception of knowledge as fixed or permanent as defined in essentialism and focused on disciplined inquiry within the boundaries of the established disciplines. Interestingly, advocates ignored the need for interdisciplinary study even when the problems faced by students in their learning required that kind of approach.

In applying the disciplines doctrine to curricula, the nature of learners along with their needs and interests was expressly avoided. Rather, learners were viewed as miniature versions of university scholars. By the end of the 1960s, in reaction to excessive control, students began rejecting this curriculum orientation and demanding more curricular relevance. The result was to give credence to curricular efforts not unlike those advocated by progressive educators decades earlier (Tanner & Tanner, 1975).

It is important to understand that Dewey, progressive education's so-called primary advocate, was routinely misunderstood. Instead of schooling experiences based entirely on student preferences, Dewey advocated a curriculum that exemplified reflective thinking. To him, reflection should not be confined to the specialized domains of knowledge but extended to social problem solving. In addition, thought was not to be divorced from action, but rather tested through application. Educational experiences involved students integrating their personal interests with general social expectations (Dewey, 1916).

Unfortunately the argument about what the curriculum should be is usually presented as a dichotomy and given only two mutually exclusive, contradictory emphases. Thus, a dualism is accepted that supports either structured knowledge or social power through problem solving. This dualism is supposedly irreducible and unreconcilable. However, as Dewey (1916) has indicated, the inability to reconcile these different curriculum orientations is erroneously taken as intrinsic and absolute when in fact the issue is simply historical and political. The dichotomy is artificial and promotes an unreasonable confrontation between ideas that in fact can be complementary.

Dewey integrated these presumed dissimilar elements by creating a curriculum of personal-social problem solving. He advocated using the various intellectual disciplines for solving social problems that were personally relevant to students as well as society as a whole. The cultural heritage as represented by the fields of knowledge and social improvement come together in this process.

It is particularly insightful to recognize the nature of the historical debate regarding curriculum, because it is essentially the same conflict that is currently disputed. And predictably the same controversy prevails when it comes to discipline theories—teacher control versus student self-direction. Perhaps the best resolution of the dissonance is the creation of learning communities in which teachers help students recognize the legitimacy of community expectations of which they are an integral part and their related personal desires. With the teacher's help students can bring the social and the personal desires into a state of balance.

The current debate regarding curricular matters and discipline centers on the recognized need to prepare students for life in democratic communities versus having them meet defined standards that are assessed with standardized test batteries. These tests are usually designed to measure information recall rather than determine students' ability to function in complex democratic communities. However, simply transferring the maximum quantity of knowledge to the growing generation is inadequate. The aim must be the training of independently acting and thinking individuals who believe that service to communities is the highest life problem (Einstein, 1950). The only sure method of social reconstruction is when individual activity involves a responsible sharing of social consciousness (Dewey, 1964). Learning communities provide the surest way to accomplish this.

THE SCHOOL CURRICULUM AND DISCIPLINE PROBLEMS

The transitory nature of curriculum development has contributed to poor discipline theory in a very significant way. Without a consistent philosophy to guide curriculum construction, there has been an accompanying inconsistency regarding discipline. In fact, until the mid-1900s educators did little to address discipline problems, preferring instead to continue, by default, with traditional punishment methods. Essentially discipline was ignored while various educational practices were employed without consideration of their discipline implications.

Teaching without a Proper Context

One significant but common failure that contributes to poor understanding, and that consequently promotes discipline problems, is teaching without a proper context. Children's need for a recognizable context in which to learn is usually ignored while educators teach concepts as abstract, self-contained entities, disconnected from practical reality. Outside the school, children are accustomed to learning within a real-life context and applying what they come to understand to a variety of new situations and experiences. As conditions change, they find it necessary to make adjustments in how they approach and solve problems. Real-life conceptual contexts provide an appropriate orientation for this to take place.

However, schooling tends to be static and oriented to the past. Past knowledge is often assumed to be the key to solving future problems, when in fact societal changes produce conditions requiring new approaches. In addition, knowledge in and of itself may not be useful for solving problems and adjusting to new conditions. Knowing the process of problem solving is much more essential.

In reality, children have three contexts for learning to which they need to apply themselves: past, present, and future. Each of these has several components: the child's current set of experiences in connection with maturity and brain development, the family, the immediate community, and various levels of existence—city, state, country, and the world. Each of these must take into account various cultures and political realities.

As students enter school, they are limited in their comprehension to their own immediate past history and the context it produces. However, an unfamiliar context is thrust upon them that is alien to their present mode of understanding. This new context cannot be instantly adopted by students. Therefore, the challenge for teachers is to supply a context for instruction that does take children's past experiences into account. In most school settings this does not happen. The students' personal contexts are ordinarily given no credence in the classroom.

In addition, it is generally accepted that students can and should immediately acquire the school learning context. This, of course, is impossible. Yet as children start school, they are immediately involved in acquiring society's store of knowledge within an abstract construct that holds little meaning for them. However, though the knowledge acquired over the centuries by society should be greatly valued, its importance should not be allowed to dictate a curriculum devoid of components that articulate with students' personal backgrounds and learning propensities. This is a serious educational mistake. Personal constructs are the only beginning point children have from which to learn when they enter school. No child has a valid school context at that early age.

There is no doubt that a broader and more inclusive conceptual orientation would help children better understand the world as they learn, but if they do not have it, teachers should not simply pretend that they do. It is the teacher's responsibility to discern a child's history and provide learning experiences that are consistent with that particular context. Actually there are approaches to learning that make it unnecessary to discern each child's background and experiences. They involve greater self-determination by students regarding what they learn. Thus, their conception of their own history can help to guide them into more meaningful learning.

This doesn't mean that society's historical context should be ignored. Rather, teachers should gradually help to broaden students' perceptions of the world so they see how their own experiences fit the larger context. This must be done in connection with practical experiences rather than just in the usual abstract sense. During instruction, teachers can help children form an enlarging context of the present. But they must keep in mind that it is a growing context, not one with which children are already familiar. Teaching must gradually advance in the sense of changing the context in which students learn to the reality framed by their new academic experiences.

Not only do schools usually fail to orient instruction toward students' personal contexts, the learning orientation is ordinarily divorced from reality. Instead, children are expected to manipulate symbolic information and apply it in ways that are detached from the real world. Thus, the school's reality is different from the social as well as work conditions students will find when they leave school. This outcome has forced employers to engage in their own training programs to bring children up to speed in the world of work (Gose, 1997; Nagle, 1998).

Under these conditions, children fail to make proper associations and are unable to apply what they learn to problems they face each day (Resnick, 1987). Not only are they less able to comprehend what is taught, they do not see its usefulness. Consequently they become frustrated and see school as unrelated to life. Because they find no meaning in what they are forced to learn, they repeatedly ask their teachers why they have to do it and often sabotage the learning of classmates.

Discipline problems are the usual outcome of this mismatch between students' conceptual preparation and the experiences provided in most schools. This is because the rote-learning ambience contained within an unfamiliar context fails to aid meaningful understanding along with shortchanging students in terms of their needs for affiliation, autonomy, and cognitive challenges (Kohn, 1999).

One way to help students obtain a more complex context in which to understand is service learning. In service learning, students learn in practical settings. At the same time they acquire important social, scientific, and communication skills. In these programs, students have been involved in the cleanup of hazardous waste sites, passage of crucial environment laws, planting trees, community improvement, building restoration for the homeless, solving sewage problems, helping in day care centers, working in retirement centers, and the like (Lewis, 1991; Nathan & Kielsmeier, 1991).

In service learning situations, students may also work in a doctor's office, insurance agency, factory, or other location that can enlarge their world context. Researchers have learned that these service activities not only enhance and broaden students' academic performance, but they contribute greatly to the social and psychological development of participants (Conrad & Hedin, 1991).

Children achieve a greater readiness for learning in school if their experiences are infused with problem-solving opportunities. One excellent example of an instructional program that helps students learn within a proper context is Science Technology Society (STS). In this program, students are helped to identify social problems that have both scientific and technological implications. Students may, for example, choose to work on a specific pollution problem in their community, using their science skills to take measurements of various pollutants and track their effects. After the problem has been carefully studied, the students make recommendations to appropriate community groups. Occasionally students have been helped to obtain legal assistance to initiate litigation to correct pollution problems (Bybee, 1985).

STS employs inquiry-based learning, which is compatible with a learning community approach to schooling. This strategy will be elaborated in detail in chapter 6. The STS instructional approach can be applied to many different subjects and is a particularly potent means for helping students frame their learning within a familiar context. It also provides a way to create a wholesome learning atmosphere devoid of the usual disruptions.

The future context is not known, although it is sometimes predicted. Students should be allowed to create their own predictions as well as examine those supplied by others. Herein is the crux of social problem solving. It is hoped that students will learn to adapt to inevitable changes as well as becoming architects of their own futures as they anticipate what they will need to know and be able to do later. Schools categorically fail to promote the development of a future context for students. They tend to be too enamored with the stock of knowledge ascertained in the past, which it is believed can simply be transmitted to children and successfully used by them, while ignoring the necessity of engaging students in forward-looking problem solving.

Failure to Teach Thinking Skills

The problems that children face in life often overwhelm them because they are unprepared to solve them systematically. They are unsuccessful in solving problems because this important skill is not sufficiently emphasized in their school experiences. Schools have historically been devoid of instruction designed to teach children problem-solving skills. As already mentioned, they instead focus on forced recall of information. This leaves children without the requisite skills to think through problems. They are unable to successfully use the various elements that help in problem solving, such as examining and validating assumptions and applying proper criteria.

Unless children are encouraged to engage in higher-order thinking skills as part of their school experience, they are likely to be limited in their cognitive abilities and suffer from the effects of unsolved problems at home, in school, and elsewhere. Increasingly, cognitive psychologists encourage learners to generate their own conceptual structures within a familiar context using problem-solving strategies (Jones, 1988).

The traditional knowledge-assimilation approach used in most school experiences is resisted by students. Instead, they insist on adding to their own conceptual structures only that information that makes sense to them personally (Osborne & Wittrock, 1983). Thus, they tend to learn only what fits in with what they already know and is consistent with their current learning context. Consequently the most acceptable way to provide instruction that students will accept as genuine is personal research and problem solving. Knowledge that is simply transmitted to students fails to be assimilated.

When students are engaged in higher-order thinking processes, they naturally build more valid conceptual structures of their world that they can then more successfully use to solve problems in a world with ever-increasing complexity. Memorized lessons do not provide children with the skills necessary to understand and deal with the modern world.

It is interesting that children most lacking in thinking skills are the ones singled out to receive remedial work regarding their presumed lack of basic skills, while their more advanced classmates are more likely to be given meaningful thinking experiences (Shavelson, 1985). Thus, some students miss out on critical experiences from which they would have greatly benefited in addressing the challenges they face in a modern society.

Nonacceptance and Grading

One of the challenges teachers face is how to convey a sense of acceptance to all their students. However, only a portion of their pupils typically acquire this important affirmation. There are various reasons for this, not the least of which is the requirement for teachers to provide competitive grades. It is difficult for teachers to convey approval when they administer grades that some students undoubtedly find aversive. In fact, students likely find all but high grades repugnant.

Typically, students' respect for their teachers can become emotionally connected to the grades they receive. In addition, an individual's sense of worth can be threatened by the usual belief that the value of a person depends on the ability to achieve in school and that lack of success results in loss of love and approval. Though it may seem incomprehensible, in our society there is a tendency to equate achievement with human worth. Thus, children come to think of themselves only as worthy as their socially valued school achievements (Covington & Beery, 1976).

It has been found that no single thing contributes as much to a student's sense of positive self-esteem as a good report card, nor shatters it so profoundly as do poor grades (Rosenberg, 1965). This fact adds to the personal deprivation often felt by children who receive low grades. It is difficult for many students to accept the assessment of low competence and consequent poor self-worth. For them it becomes necessary to denigrate teachers who give them low grades in order to acquire some sense of self-respect or to react in some other futile, disruptive way.

Early in their school careers children may try very hard to achieve what they consider satisfactory grades, but many are unsuccessful. This leads to the harsh moral logic of childhood that getting high grades is more important than trying hard. Trying hard eventually acquires no particular virtue because it is commonly unrewarded. Children who try hard but are unsuccessful come to believe that only outcomes count. When they get low grades, it is difficult to accept the cause as low ability, yet they have little recourse but to admit to themselves that this is the case. This tends to be so even though there is very little difference between the actual abilities of most children.

The same is true of their initial school achievements. However, the achievement gap widens dramatically during their twelve years of schooling. Ironically children respond to their initial failure to achieve high grades by keeping their real ability a secret, and often achieve at lower levels than their true ability should dictate. This is accomplished by nonperformance and intentional failure. They have learned that if they succeed on any school task, the same performance may perpetually be expected of them. However, because they feel unable, they do not think continual excellence is possible. Deliberate failure is their answer to this dilemma. If inadvertently they are successful, they can always blame it on luck or fate or the good will of their teachers.

It is easy to see how children may become confused about the difference between ability and worth. They come to believe that their school performance is equated with worthiness. Interestingly, they may then try to cover up the shameful implication that they lack ability by setting up various strategies to orchestrate their own failure. Given their school experiences, students may be unable to avoid failure as they define it, but they can at least attempt to avoid the sense of failure (Covington & Beery, 1976).

Another strategy children use to protect their self-worth is to hide how much effort they put forth on a task. This is done so others will think they have high ability. For example, an individual may not tell their peers that they studied hard for a test. If they then do well, they can attribute it to high ability. Children also engage in self-handicapping patterns of behavior to protect their self-worth. They may, for example, procrastinate studying for an exam. Then low performance can be attributed to low effort (Covington, 1992).

Failure is inevitable by definition within the ABCDF grading system (Englander, 1986). This system assumes that student achievement follows a normal curve. This means that about 68 percent of the students should receive C grades, 14 percent B's, 14 percent D's, 2 percent A's, and 2 percent F's. If tests produce different results, they are to be statistically manipulated to create a grading curve consistent with the assumption of normality. However, test scores of most groups of students do not produce a normal distribution. This may lead teachers to modify test items in an attempt to satisfy this assumption, when in fact such an assumption is unwarranted.

In students' minds, an F is not the only failing grade. Failure is attributed to any grade less than that to which they aspire. To some students a B grade represents failure. It is ironic to note that strictly speaking, when using a norm-based grading system in a class of twenty-five students, there would be no A's nor F's (Lorber, 1996).

Some schools have modified the traditional ABCDF system in recognition of the need to make grading more reasonable and less destructive of students' self-worth. One such system, called criterion-referenced grading, attempts to grade on competency. In this case, all students in a particular class could conceivably obtain A grades if their achievement level is adequate. Of course, one of the problems with this system is that grading can become arbitrary and excessively subjective. Teachers could define achievement levels in whatever way they wish and assess student achievement without due regard to quality or consistency. Conceivably the standards could be so high that no student could achieve excellence, or so low that little effort is required for all students to obtain A grades. Obviously, validity as well as reliability then becomes an issue.

It is not easy to determine what a valid level of achievement is for a particular group of students. Add this to the fact that ABCDF grades are used by university admissions officers and others to compare students on their relative achievements and there can be considerable confusion. Universities expect comparative grading so they can accept only those students they believe are genuinely at the top of their class. A norm-referenced system, despite its proven detrimental consequences to students, is unquestioningly accepted by universities as the most valid indicator of relative merit (Kohn, 1999).

Another aberration in student assessment is grade inflation. This has been done ostensibly in an effort to soften the negative impact that grading inflicts on the self-concepts of students. Actually inflating grades is unlikely to help maintain good self-worth. Higher grades won't make children suddenly believe they are achieving at higher levels. When grades are inflated, students are under the illusion that they are far more qualified than they actually are with the result that they fail to attain their potential while in school.

It is particularly disconcerting to discover that though grade inflation is designed to promote better self-esteem, it in fact has the opposite effect. It has been learned that an excessive focus on self-esteem actually promotes pessimism and depression. This occurs when individuals do not have to meet challenges, overcome frustration, or demonstrate persistence to be successful (Seligman, 1995).

The usual standards of achievement as dictated by standardized tests and inflated grades should not be taken as an appropriate standard of performance. A true sense of well-being can be acquired only when students' efforts represent their best work and are consistent with high, self-imposed standards of excellence. Their achievements can be superior to expectations prescribed by tests and grades.

Standardized Achievement Tests

Standardized achievement tests are commonly used to determine whether or not students have met school expectations. They have been considered important from the standpoint of comparing students' academic performances. This is evidenced in the move to have more competency testing, mandated curricula, and federal initiatives such as No Child Left Behind. The idea behind these moves is to force schools to achieve particular standards. Supposedly, whatever curricula are in place, along with current teaching strategies, have not sufficiently helped attain hoped-for achievement levels.

It is believed that low achievement can be corrected through the use of standardized achievement tests. It is erroneously assumed that these tests are valid both in terms of the current curricula and in the kind of educational experiences that would be the most beneficial to children. It is also assumed that teachers can somehow get their students to learn what is needed to score high on these tests. In addition, it is assumed that children everywhere should learn the very same things. Of course such efforts say nothing about the needs and interests of students.

Historically, failure to consider students' interests has not been successful. For example, the discipline-centered curricula employed in the late 1960s and 1970s was a dismal failure according to Jerome Bruner (1971), one of its primary architects. Bruner explains that it was the failure to take students' interests into account that led to its demise. The result was lack of learning, as well as open rebellion by students. Teachers not only need to take students' needs and interests into account, they also must ensure that learning activities appropriately map onto students' natural learning styles.

School experiences should also prepare students for life in democratic communities. This involves acquiring problem-solving skills for solving present problems and preparation to deal with future problems. Standardized testing in contrast emphasizes coercive, autocratic teaching practices. Students spend their time memorizing what they often consider irrelevant information they are required to remember for test purposes.

The schools have not done well with meeting student needs and interests. This is because neither is generally taken into account during learning experiences. Instead the tests themselves become the primary focus. Unfortunately most tests are designed to measure information recall rather than attend to important life skills (Meier, 2002).

Failure of Need Fulfillment

There is a consensus among researchers regarding basic human needs that must be satisfied by students while they are in school. All agree that satisfying these needs is essential to effective learning. The failure of schools to adequately satisfy student needs is likely the most potent deterrent to school achievement and the origin of discipline problems. This is so because needs cry out to be fulfilled while students hold most other considerations in abeyance.

Most human behavior consists of efforts to achieve personal needs (Glasser, 1998). Initially students may engage in an intense pursuit to satisfy their needs. However, if they are unsuccessful, they may give up their search. But others often find aberrant ways to satisfy their needs, which teachers have difficulty interpreting. For example, it is difficult to understand why children would act contrary to their own best interest. Yet they routinely do when their efforts to satisfy their needs are thwarted, even if their struggles have little or no chance of really accomplishing what they wish.

Aberrant behavior fails to satisfy needs because it doesn't ordinarily help accomplish the results for which students hope, as well as turning their teachers against them. Unfortunately, when children are unable to satisfy their needs through deviant actions they begin to think disparagingly of themselves but keep on being disruptive. Others react by withdrawing (Glasser, 1998). This latter group of students is commonly ignored by their teachers. Thus, students may fail to get their needs satisfied whether they act out or just withdraw.

Chapter Two

Issues Regarding Discipline

It is critical to realize that classroom misbehavior from most any theoretical perspective is assumed to be a function of the "pathology" of the student. Thus, many potential causes of student disruptiveness are ignored. For example, the problem may really be related to the particular curriculum being implemented, the faulted pedagogical approaches of the teacher, the complex culture of the classroom, the classroom environment, bureaucratic administrative procedures, punitive classroom rules, discipline approaches, bullying, racial issues, and so on. However, these probable causes of discipline problems tend to be ignored, even though modifying them could conceivably help to eliminate student disruptiveness.

With all potential causes of classroom problems remaining unexamined, students are considered exclusively culpable and in need of modification. Similarly, ethical questions regarding how students should be treated have been ignored or narrowed in scope in most discussions regarding classroom discipline. Thus, the fact that punishment may promote anger and a disruptive inclination is usually ignored. It is erroneously assumed that punishing students is necessary and does not put them at risk or promote negative reactions.

It is enlightening to note that discussions about punishment are almost exclusively framed in procedural terms, not ethical ones. Even when discussing curriculum and instruction, such terms as "delivery systems," "on-task behavior," and "learning as changing behavior" set the stage for assuming the need for external control and the inappropriateness of democratic teaching principles. These terms create a mind-set about teaching and learning that tends to dictate control-oriented practices and obscures the consideration of more democratic teaching and discipline. In doing this, dependence upon authority, linear thinking, social apathy, passive involvement, and hands-off learning is implicitly taught (Beyer, 1998).

To many educators, school discipline and instruction are based on different sets of principles. Commonly there is an almost complete dearth of discipline considerations in the various curricular proposals and innovations. This has enormous implications for current curricular matters as well as associated discipline theory. Little or no research is devoted to the issue of articulating discipline and instruction so that appropriate compatibility exists.

HISTORICAL CHANGES IN INSTRUCTION AND DISCIPLINE

As mentioned earlier, the changes in school curricula that have taken place since the early 1900s have varied from an emphasis on the structure and integrity of the various subjects and the perpetuation of the cultural heritage to an extreme emphasis on child development and student self-direction. From this latter perspective, children were thought inherently capable of directing their own learning experiences.

While the differences between subject-oriented and student-oriented approaches were being explored by educators, almost nothing was being considered regarding what discipline implications existed for these different curricular orientations. Curriculum and instruction matters were exclusively considered. At present, discipline tends to be ignored in favor of imposing standardized testing on schools as a means for curriculum improvement. This has led educators away from a consideration of student interests and needs and the causes of student discipline problems.

This harkens back to what was happening in the late 1800s and early 1900s, where discipline considerations also took a backseat to curriculum concerns. During this time punishments of various kinds were administered to deviant students to bring them under control. Corporal punishment was routinely imposed. Its purpose was to "beat the devil out of children and restrain their wills," an apparent holdover from certain Protestant religious views. For many years it had been assumed that the source of children's unruliness was devilish influences rather than the environment in which they lived (Gordon, 1989). By this time, punishment had a long tradition and was assumed to have the desired effects.

Early Discipline Models

It wasn't until the 1950s that various more humane discipline alternatives became more common. It was at this time that two separate and distinct emphases emerged. The first employed the work of B. F. Skinner and focused on carefully applied contingencies of reinforcement (rewards) to modify students' disruptive behavior (Skinner, 1953). A second general approach was championed by Carl R. Rogers. He supported a teacher role of encouragement, trust, and facilitation. Whereas Skinner believed student behavior must be carefully controlled, Rogers advocated a process called actualization. He believed children could be helped to become more responsible through teacher encouragement and guidance. Using this process, teachers could help their students become self-disciplined (Rogers, 1969).

Behavior Modification

Behavior modification was one of the earliest approaches to classroom discipline. Although not expressly prohibited, in applying behavioristic principles, punishment was not encouraged except in exceptional cases, such as regulating the behavior of autistic children. The use of reinforcement (rewards) is the preferred procedure. In applying behavior modification, teachers are to recognize the difference between reinforcing and punishing stimuli in terms of their effects. It is necessary for them to understand different kinds of reinforcement as well as various schedules of reinforcement that achieve different effects.

Ways to extinguish unacceptable behavior must also be appropriately applied to properly manage students. To effectively use behavioristic principles, teachers must be able to properly categorize student behavior in connection with their responses so they know if they are punishing or reinforcing unacceptable behavior. It is common for teachers to believe they are punishing inappropriate behavior when in fact they are reinforcing it. Any behavior, good or bad, that increases in frequency in consequence of teachers' actions has been reinforced (Walker & Shea, 1999).

In behavior modification a variety of reinforcements can be applied and delivered in various ways. Students might be given tangible rewards such as edibles, gold stars, or useful objects such as marbles, coloring books, and tape players. Or they might be provided with activity rewards such as watching TV, listening to music, being the teacher's aide, or playing educational games.

Specific rewards can be given to students when the teacher determines that they are behaving as previously instructed. This is most effective when done immediately. Teachers can also administer tokens that students can use like money to exchange for a variety of available backup reinforcers. Because a variety of rewards can be offered in a token reinforcement system, the strength of the reinforcers is greatly enhanced.

Assertive Discipline

Assertive Discipline, which was developed by Lee Canter, is another behaviorist approach. However, rather than featuring reinforcement, it focuses on a well-organized punishment strategy along with a less systematic application of rewards. In this approach, rules are carefully specified by the teacher, as are punishments. When students misbehave, their names are written on the chalkboard as a warning. If further disruptions occur, check marks are placed on the chalkboard next to the offending student's name, indicating the accrual of an increased level of punishment severity. The purpose of this is to increase pressure on students and force compliance with classroom rules.

Usually the most severe punishment consists of a meeting with the principal and the offending student's parents. This might occur after the accumulation of something like four check marks. In addition, Canter advocates the use of positive consequences and also encourages teachers to work with parents and the administration to curb discipline problems (Canter & Canter, 2001).

Rather than solving discipline problems, punishment is more likely to encourage increased rebellion. Although there is little or no support from research for punishment in the schools, it is still the most common procedure used to deal with discipline problems. From 80 percent to 90 percent of school rule violations are handled punitively (Englander, 1986).

Logical Consequences

Rudolf Dreikurs developed a more humanistic approach to discipline called Logical Consequences. He believed students must be helped to understand the motives for their misbehavior and learn to behave in more acceptable ways to satisfy their motives. He concluded that students' motives included gaining acceptance, exercising power, exacting revenge, and displaying inadequacy. The motives are arranged above in the order in which students sequentially try to satisfy them. If children failed to gain acceptance, they were likely to initiate behavior calculated to fulfill the next motive in the sequence, and so on.

Dreikurs believed that students' behavior was purposeful, inherently sequential, and directed toward inherent motives. To employ Logical Consequences, teachers must recognize the motives of students by the kind of disruptive behavior they exhibit. Once they have done this, they should try to help students acknowledge their motives and the unacceptable consequences they may bring. After they admit the undesirable results of their actions, students are encouraged to modify these mistaken goals (Dreikurs, 1968; Dreikurs, Grunwald & Pepper, 1982).

Teacher Effectiveness Training

An even more student-oriented discipline approach called Teacher Effectiveness Training was created by Thomas Gordon. He found in his research that when teachers exercise power-based control, children react with various coping mechanisms. They resist, rebel, retaliate, break rules, throw tantrums, lie, blame others, bully others, engage in apple-polishing, withdraw, make others look bad, become fearful, and cheat.

Gordon indicated that teachers must learn how to differentiate problem ownership when children misbehave. If it is a student-owned problem, he advocates active listening. In this process, students are allowed to solve their own problems, with the teacher providing encouraging responses to help them move forward. These responses acknowledge that the teacher understands what the student is saying rather than giving input to solve the problem.

When a teacher-owned problem is identified, like when students destroy school property, the teacher sends confronting I-messages. This involves stating the problem, identifying the effects, and then expressing how the teacher feels about it (Gordon, 1989). If students balk at this strategy, it is recommended that the teacher switch to active listening so as not to come across as imposing personal preferences.

Control Theory/Choice Theory

Control Theory/Choice Theory represents the work of William Glasser. It is characterized by techniques teachers may use to increase student self-direction and responsibility while reducing discipline problems. Reality therapy is employed by helping disruptive students to identify and state their inappropriate behavior. They are then directed to determine all the potential consequences associated with their misbehavior. After this, they are encouraged to make a value judgment about their behavior and its consequences and then develop a plan that guarantees no further disruptions. Glasser assumed that student misbehavior is a function of their efforts to satisfy their needs for receiving love and acceptance, exercising control, obtaining freedom, and experiencing fun. His solution to student disruptiveness is to help students identify appropriate ways to satisfy their needs and thus make it less likely they will try to fulfill them in misguided ways.

Glasser is an advocate of what he calls quality schools. In quality schools, teachers and administrators provide lead management instead of boss management. Learning should involve cooperation between students. Students must understand what quality work is and not be satisfied with school accomplishments that are of low quality. Academic excellence would be emphasized and would exclude fact memorization.

Students who experience difficulty complying with classroom rules are sent to a time-out room called the connecting place, to receive counseling. This procedure is designed to help them get back to class and work productively without disturbing others. Before being allowed to return to class, a student must prepare a written plan that outlines his intended appropriate behavior. He or she must also be interviewed by the teacher and receive permission to return.

Glasser advocates a program for preventing discipline problems. He believes this can be accomplished in classroom meetings. Discussions are held regarding specific ways to prevent discipline problems. This involves establishing the goals for instruction, formulating classroom rules, and examining teaching procedures and classroom operations with the objective of making learning more enjoyable and productive (Glasser, 1992, 2005).

Judicious Discipline

Forrest Gathercoal created a discipline approach called Judicious Discipline, patterned after the U.S. judicial system. The First, Fourth, and Fourteenth Amendments to the U.S. Constitution provide the basis for this discipline procedure. From these, students are taught their rights along with what is termed compelling school interests. They learn that their individual rights are protected so long as they do not interfere with legitimate school requirements.

Compelling school interests are in reality requirements for the protection of the entire school community and consist of the following: (1) protection from property loss or damage, (2) safeguarding legitimate educational purposes, (3) securing health and safety, and (4) avoiding disruption of educational processes. Individual rights are to be protected except when the rights of the entire school community take precedence over them.

With Judicious Discipline, school operations and expectations are based on democratic principles. Rules and definitions of inappropriate student behaviors are clearly stated in terms of how they violate compelling school interests. Any student violation of rules results in the application of logical consequences rather than punishment. Students have the right to appeal any action taken to regulate their classroom behavior (Gathercoal, 1990, 2001).

Jones Model

Fredric H. Jones created a control-oriented discipline model that employs unique instructional strategies and student seating as well as discipline strategies. According to Jones, it is important to make seating arrangements that allow the teacher to get to any student location in the classroom quickly. Thus, from any student's desk, the teacher should be able to move in any direction rather than being restricted to just moving up and down rows of desks.

Instructional strategies are also critical. Teachers should avoid universal helping interactions where they spend too much time with an individual student while other class members wait for excessively long periods of time. Instead, they should use the praise/prompt/leave technique. This involves a short statement of praise for what the student has already accomplished, a short prompt to help the student begin the next phase of his or her work, and then leaving. This is essential because many students try to monopolize the teacher's time unnecessarily and open the classroom up to excessive disruptions by individuals who are waiting for the teacher's help.

In the Jones model, discipline involves limit setting. This consists of a series of strategies that place the teacher increasingly close to misbehaving students. These procedures advance only until the student stops misbehaving and goes back to work. Students sometimes react negatively when this technique is employed, but it is ordinarily successful in stopping disturbances.

The first step is to simply stop instruction and turn and look at the offending student. If this does not stop the disruption, the teacher is to calmly walk to the student's desk and stand looking at him or her. Next, the teacher is to lean on the student's desk on his or her elbows. Finally, the teacher can take up a position at the side of the student's desk and kneel there.

The Jones model also includes a process called responsibility training. This is an incentive system that utilizes negative reinforcement. Students are awarded an amount of preferred activity time (PAT), which can be gradually eliminated in consequence of disruptiveness. Preferred activities are chosen in advance of instruction and ordinarily consist of enjoyable classroom learning experiences. During any instructional sequence the teacher starts a clock whenever there is a disruption. The clock runs until the disruption ceases. The amount of time expired is taken from PAT.

Jones also employs a series of backup systems that are used when other techniques are not successful. Letters may be sent home describing students' unruliness, or students may be subjected to time-out and removed from the class temporarily. Students may also suffer detention, lose privileges, or be involved in a parent-teacher conference. They may also have to attend Saturday school, be delivered to their parents at work, have a parent sit with them at school, or be expelled (Jones, 1987a, 1987b, 2001).

Transactional Analysis

Eric Berne, a psychiatrist, is credited with creating Transactional Analysis. Berne believed that every individual has three ego-states that are recorded during childhood: Parent, Child, and Adult. The Parent ego-state is a collection of experiences from the first five years of life that includes pronouncements made by parents and other adults. It is the repository of all the verbal admonitions, rules, and laws issued by adults along with tone of voice and facial expressions.

The Child ego-state is recorded simultaneously and consists of responses children make to what they see and hear. Most of these reactions are related to the feelings experienced. These might include rejection and various frustrations as well as delightful feelings. Negative experiences result in "not okay" feelings, which create significant adjustment problems.

While the Child and Parent ego-states consist essentially of emotional content, the Adult ego-state is the rational part of personality. To maintain an orderly classroom, Berne recommends teaching children about Transactional Analysis and encouraging them to operate out of their Adult ego-states as well (Berne, 1964; Harris, 1967).

The three ego-states also provide an insightful explanation regarding impediments to communication that may interfere with the smooth operation of learning communities. The ego-states are referred to in chapter 6 as the means for understanding the origin of many statements individuals make inadvertently that may be contentious and thwart effective interaction and how each individual can make appropriate improvements.

Kounin Model

One of the early researchers in the area of discipline was Jacob Kounin. To effectively control student behavior, Kounin believed teachers must display the attributes of withitness and overlapping. Teachers who have withitness are said to have "eyes in the back of their heads." They have the uncanny ability to always know everything that is taking place in the classroom. They consistently target and respond to the right situation and time their actions expertly.

Overlapping refers to teachers' ability to deal with more than one discipline problem at a time. The most effective teachers know what is going on in the classroom all the time, properly target disruptive students and time their interventions, handle more than one problem at once, and display an appropriate level of firmness and clarity in making their desists.

Kounin also discovered that better discipline was exhibited in classrooms where students make transitions from one activity to another with a minimum of noise and misbehavior. Effective teachers were more able to maintain a proper focus during instruction and avoid reacting to relatively unimportant things while teaching. They also refrained from making irrelevant announcements and thus kept the continuity of their lessons intact.

Good teachers avoid overdwelling, or continuing a learning activity beyond the point of usefulness. Kounin believed that good discipline involved teaching excellence. To him, lessons must be meaningful and challenging and have sufficient variety so that students don't end up bored (Kounin, 1970a, 1970b; Kounin & Gump, 1961, 1974).

Of the above discipline models only Reality Therapy/Choice Theory contains student involvement in determining the methods of instruction. Classroom meetings are held in which students have an opportunity to talk about the instructional process. However, students do not help determine the curriculum nor are they involved in evaluation. Both the Jones and Kounin models include teacher-controlled instructional processes. These are used by the teacher to manage student behavior. The rest of the models are limited to discipline techniques.

NEW DEMOCRATIC DISCIPLINE METHODS

Most of the newer discipline approaches are touted as democratic and geared to develop responsibility and citizenship. Critics such as Alfie Kohn take issue with this. He says that many of these programs are remarkably autocratic, urging teachers to lay down the law. They are wrapped in rhetoric about motivation and responsibility, dignity and cooperation, and self-esteem but have a striking resemblance to "standard old-time discipline" with its focus on rewards and punishment (Kohn, 1996).

Some of the programs Kohn specifically names as not truly employing democratic procedures despite claiming to do so include Cooperative Discipline, 21st Century Discipline, Positive Discipline, Discipline with Dignity, and Discipline with Love and Logic. Short descriptions of some of these programs are presented below.

Win-Win Discipline

Win-Win Discipline is designed to help students make responsible decisions and develop long-term life skills, not just control behavior. To help prevent disruptive behavior, it is recommended that an effort be made to help students satisfy their needs legitimately. Also, the curriculum should be made more interesting and challenging, with cooperative learning being applied. In addition, teachers must make sure that their expectations and procedures are understood by their students and students given choices about what and how they learn. Finally, rules are provided consisting of class agreements that meet both teacher and student needs. These are posted in a prominent place in the classroom.

If children misbehave, they are first provided a gentle reminder by the teacher. If the disruptive behavior persists, the teacher identifies one of the following positions and asks students to suggest responsible ways to meet needs associated with that position: seeking attention, avoiding failure, being angry, seeking control, being energetic, being bored, and being uninformed. The teacher then makes statements to support the student's choice of responsible behavior. After this, if the misbehavior persists, a follow-up strategy is employed, such as having the student explain what a responsible person would do, or identify a behavior to replace the disruptive one. For a long-term solution the teacher works with students to help them plan for self-improvement.

There are specific strategies for each of the seven student positions identified. For students trying to get attention, the teacher may use physical proximity, hand signals, eye contact, or I-messages. This can be followed up with a one-on-one meeting to help students learn how they can get attention in a positive way. To help students avoid failure, teachers are to provide instruction that matches their learning preferences better and play down the finality of making mistakes. Students are taught how to manage their anger if they have that problem. This includes conflict resolution conferences and class meetings.

If students are disruptive while seeking control, teachers should provide opportunities for more decision making in class. Energetic students need breaks and relaxation time. They need distracting elements removed and help in pursuing their interests. Bored students need their teachers to restructure learning and involve them more in making plans for activities. If students' misbehavior is connected to being uninformed, the teacher should try to give better directions, reteach if necessary, and let them work with peers.

Teachers are encouraged to respond at the moment of student disruptions by ending the disruption quickly and refocusing students back on the lesson. They should then tell students that the disruptive behavior is unacceptable and identify the reasons behind the problem. After this, teachers should work with students to find a mutually satisfactory solution. Steps should be taken to create long-term development of responsible behavior.

In the event students' misbehavior persists, teachers are encouraged to apply the following consequences in a more prescriptive way by making students apologize for misbehavior, provide restitution where appropriate, or suffer the loss of an activity. Teachers are encouraged to provide the following step-by-step sequence of consequences as necessary: (1) warning, (2) reflection time to think about inappropriate behavior, (3) creation of a personal improvement plan, (4) telephoning parents, and (5) visiting the principal (Kagan, 2001; Kagan, Scott & Kagan, 2003). In this program it is obvious that teachers exercise considerable control and that consequences of a punitive nature are applied. In addition, its orientation is reactive rather than preventive.

Inner Discipline

Coloroso states that Inner Discipline is designed to help students behave creatively, constructively, cooperatively, and responsibly without being directed by the teacher. Efforts should be made by the teacher to create a sense of community and to ensure that students are treated with dignity so as not to threaten their self-worth. Teachers should let students suffer the natural consequences of their behavior so long as it isn't potentially dangerous. Logical consequences should be applied when classroom rules are broken. In doing this, teachers should not give in to students' requests to avoid these imposed consequences.

Students commonly use three ploys to avoid suffering the application of logical consequences provided by teachers. First, they may beg, bribe, weep, and wail to avoid what the teacher is imposing on them. If the teacher gives in, students supposedly fail to acquire an inner sense of discipline. Second, students may respond with anger and aggression. Teachers tend either to become passive or to lash back. Instead they should simply state that the consequence will be enacted regardless. Third, students may sulk. This accompanies an attitude of "I'm not going to do what you say. You can't make me." Again, the consequence should be invoked in a matter-of-fact way (Coloroso, 2002, 2003).

Although students have an opportunity to give input in creating a list of consequences, the teacher has the sole responsibility of enforcing them. Again consequences that are potentially punitive are administered as directed by the teacher. The teacher is obviously the one in charge. The approach is reactive rather than preventive.

Cooperative Discipline

Linda Albert is the author of Cooperative Discipline. She believes that misbehavior comes about in response to students' motivation. These motivations include a desire for attention, power, revenge, and a display of inadequacy. She is also an advocate of using a wide variety of strategies to prevent discipline problems. Cooperative Discipline consists of three components: promoting capability, helping students connect, and helping students contribute. Capability is promoted by helping students realize that making mistakes is okay. Teachers try to build confidence by focusing on past successes, making progress tangible, and recognizing achievement.

Students are helped to connect by teachers' promoting acceptance and giving them genuine attention. In addition, teachers should show appreciation and give affection. They help students contribute by encouraging them to give of themselves not only in class but also in school generally and to the community outside the school. Of particular importance is the role of students contributing to each other through peer tutoring, peer counseling, peer mediation, and recognizing each other's accomplishments.

In Albert's system, students must adhere to a code of conduct. This code is jointly created by students and their teachers and consists of a conception of the nature of the class, including appropriate and inappropriate behaviors. The code is enforced by teachers first making sure deviant students understand the inappropriateness of their behavior. Their behavior is compared to the code of conduct. If there are disagreements, these are resolved in a student-teacher conference, a class meeting, or a conflict resolution process.

The code of conduct is posted where it can be referred to in correcting behavior. The offending student is asked to evaluate his or her behavior in terms of the code of conduct. If misbehavior is persistent, the teacher is to supply consequences. These should be directly related to the misbehavior as well as reasonable, respectful, and consistently enforced. The categories of consequences imposed by teachers include losing privileges; losing the freedom to interact with peers; being required to return, repair, or replace objects taken from others; being involved in school service; or being required to relearn appropriate behavior in a conference with the teacher. Difficult problems are to be taken care of privately with the teacher (Albert, 1989, 2003a, 2003b). With the Cooperative Discipline approach, when students misbehave the teacher takes charge and reacts to misbehavior rather than trying to prevent it.

Synergetic Discipline

C. M. Charles has created what he calls Synergetic Discipline. He believes teaching-learning should be a cooperative endeavor. This helps create synergy in the classroom where students enjoy learning and are productive. Quality teaching involves teachers helping students satisfy their needs for hope, acceptance, dignity, power, enjoyment, and competence. Teachers and students cooperatively establish a set of agreements about class functions and student conduct.

Insightfully, Charles believes that discipline problems reside not only in students, but in teachers and other school personnel as well. Student misbehavior is the result of unmet needs, trying to get out of doing assigned work, boredom, seeking excitement, trying to avoid embarrassment and failure, peer pressure, physical discomfort, lack of meaningful instruction, and low interest. Teachers contribute to student disruptions by using poor teaching techniques; being discourteous, inconsistent, or irresponsible; showing little interest in students; acting out frustrations; being provoked; being poor communicators; failing to anticipate various problems; and being coercive and punishing.

Teachers and students formulate a set of agreements that includes suggestions for learning activities, descriptions of what they like about teachers, statements of teachers' commitment to satisfy students' wishes regarding teacher behavior, and a definition of good and bad student behavior in the classroom. When students misbehave, teachers first remind them of expected behavior by pointing to a chart that lists what they have agreed upon. The cause of the misbehavior is then identified along with procedures regarding how to correct it. The cause of the misbehavior should be carefully identified.

If students dispute the cause of the misbehavior, the teacher should help them understand it (Charles, 2000). Although this approach has democratic elements, disruptions are the teacher's responsibility. In reality, the teacher is the perpetual director of what takes place in the classroom. As with previously described democratic models, this approach is geared to solving discipline problems once they occur rather than trying to prevent them.

Positive Discipline

Positive Discipline was created by Jane Nelsen, Lynn Lott, and H. Stephen Glenn. It features class meetings that help students acquire social skills designed to help them get along better in the classroom. Teachers try to show faith in their students and indicate that they really care about them. They also sponsor relationships among students that build confidence and independence. Students can choose to acquire greater responsibility for themselves or continue in traditional, control-based instruction.

In classroom meetings, teachers create an agenda, promote communication skills, help children learn about differences among themselves, and explain how to recognize others' motives. Teachers also inform their students that anytime consequences need to be administered for misbehavior they will be related to the offense, respectful to them as persons, and reasonable. Interventions by the teacher for misbehavior are to provide students with appropriate choices that are limited in number. Whenever there are disputes, teachers help students work through problems successfully. Students are informed about ways to interact with each other and find win-win solutions.

In working with students, teachers ask questions rather than lecturing them, and formulate questions that help them think about their behavior and redirect it. Teachers must be able to say no with dignity and respect. They should not give explanations for refusing what students request. They also must act more and talk less. They must use more hand signals and provide body posture and facial expressions to communicate their wishes.

Teachers should never try to find out who is behind an altercation between students. It is recommended that students be helped to make connections between opportunity, responsibility, and consequence. It is best if consequences are not used, because they communicate what happens when students misbehave rather than solving problems for the future (Nelsen, 1996; Nelsen & Lott, 2000; Nelsen, Lott & Glenn, 1993).

In this discipline model there are many democratically oriented elements, yet teacher direction is paramount. The teacher is the one designated to make sure various aspects of the program take place. Like the other democratic models, when it comes to student disruptions the teacher directs things and occupies a reactive role regarding disruptions rather than a preventive one. Though some obvious student roles smack of democratic procedures, underneath it all the teacher is really the individual who makes sure particular things happen. Students have no leadership responsibilities.

Equitable Learning Communities

Barbara Landau incorporates democratic principles within Equitable Learning Communities. She indicates that in democratic classrooms students are not in charge, nor are they allowed to make up rules without an acceptable framework. Instead, democratic classrooms must be mirrors of the structure of our society (Landau, 2004). She believes classroom rules should be based on a balance of individual freedoms and mutual responsibilities and reflect such common values as honesty, self-efficacy, respect, trust, and safety. Thus, rules are created to protect individual rights so long as they don't interfere with compelling school interests. This orientation, of course, is similar to Gathercoal's Judicious Discipline.

Landau believes that teachers should not just relinquish their power and control to students who lack the professional expertise to make appropriate choices and direct learning. Clearly the emphasis is on teachers maintaining control. It is true that students do lack expertise. However, to just leave it at that does not provide for the development of a democratic classroom. Considerable effort is needed to help children learn the skills, knowledge, and attitudes to operate in a truly democratic environment. One cannot simply declare that children lack the expertise and still assume that somehow teacher management, if it is sufficiently kind, can be equated with a true democracy.

To Landau, democratic classroom procedures include giving students clear instruction for tasks, developing an engaging curriculum appropriate for a wide variety of learning styles and needs, creating a welcoming classroom environment, basing assessment on student learning rather than on attitudes or behaviors, and using open and effective communication techniques. In the event of a power struggle between students and their teachers, Landau recommends sharing power. She explicitly follows Rudolf Dreikurs's procedures in administering logical consequences (Dreikurs, Grunwald & Pepper, 1982).

Logical consequences are administered because of Landau's belief that nobody is fully aware of why they behave as they do. Rarely do our intentions reach the conscious level. This is particularly true of children. They find it hard to explain their motives and usually rationalize while making excuses. Supposedly this justifies the teacher's responsibility of helping children understand their ambiguous motives. Landau believes that explanations of consequences need to be given to students so that they can visualize their intentions and understand the appropriateness of the consequences imposed on them.

Without the teacher's help, Landau believes students are unable to understand the real purpose of consequences. The following examples are provided: Suppose a child disrupts class. The teacher would say, "Since you have chosen to disrupt my class for this period of time, you can pay me back by staying after class." In another case, students have taken wet toilet paper and thrown it all over the restroom. The teacher would respond by telling them about the danger of slipping on wet floors and then ask them what they should do about it. Landau recommends such consequences as community service, apologies, time-out, loss of privileges, and counseling. Clearly, all of these can be interpreted by students as punitive and reactive rather than preventive.

In Landau's approach, some semblance of democratic participation is provided students in class meetings. Here students are allowed to air grievances, review rules, make decisions about ideas from the class suggestion box, and discuss what has been accomplished along with future directions. In addition, she recommends practices that do in fact promote a democratic orientation to learning. However, as with other new democratic strategies, there appears to be an advocacy for democratic learning communities, but when the particulars are described regarding what teachers should do in the event of student disruptions, teacher control is paramount.

Discipline without Stress, Punishment, or Rewards

Marvin Marshall advocates a discipline approach that claims to be free of rewards and punishment and that promotes democratic principles. When students are disruptive in class, the teacher asks them to complete an essay in which they explain (1) their disruptive behavior, (2) what they can do to prevent it, and (3) a statement of commitment to avoid disruptions in the future. Disruptive students are also required to fill out a self-diagnostic referral. The following items are on the form:

1. A description of the misbehavior.
2. Identification of the level of behavior with an explanation. The level of behavior is either anarchy, bossing and bullying, cooperation/conformity, or democratic.
3. Explain how the teacher's behavior is related to the student behavior.
4. Explain whether or not you want the teacher to treat you this way.
5. Explain what behavioral level you should apply to be socially responsible.
6. Explain how things would be different if you behaved responsibly.
7. Explain what you believe are solutions to your behavior problems.

If the self-diagnostic referral is unsuccessful, unruly students are required to prepare another one. This form is sent to the student's parents with a note explaining the problem the student has created. If a third referral is necessary, a "three strikes and you're out" approach is used. When this happens, all copies of the self-diagnostic form are mailed to the student's parents with an explanation that the teacher has exhausted every means to help the individual become socially responsible and that any future disruptions will be referred to an administrator. To stay in class, students must never display anarchy-level or bossing and bullying–level behavior. They must show a cooperation and conformity level or a democracy level.

Marshall encourages class meetings to promote better relationships between students and teachers and improve student behavior. In dealing with difficult students, teachers should tell students exactly how they wish them to behave without referring to their misbehavior in negative ways. Teachers should tell students exactly what they expect of them. They should provide students with choices among alternative learning assignments, ask reflective questions, acknowledge on-task behavior, change disruptive students' seats, assign responsible youths to act as buddies to those who regularly misbehave, and develop signals to communicate to students the need to redirect their behavior (Marshall, 2001).

It is clear that certain aspects of Marshall's discipline approach have democratic applications, but as with the other models that have been described, when students misbehave the teacher takes on a controlling orientation. Students have a minimal role in helping to manage classroom disruptions. As with all the other democratic discipline approaches, teachers are instructed to react to misbehavior rather than prevent it.

CRITICISMS OF CURRENT DISCIPLINE MODELS

As with other matters about schooling, the topic of discipline is full of controversy. There is, of course, the very prominent conflict regarding the extent to which children are capable of disciplining themselves. But there are also other more subtle concerns. In addition, the little research there is usually focuses upon a single discipline approach, attempting to show how it satisfies specified criteria, such as keeping children quiet. In the meantime, weightier matters such as whether or not children should be exposed to such treatments, or whether there are detrimental side effects, are ignored. These issues are philosophical and moral in nature, not just empirical. Even the few comparative studies that have been done generally fail to address these important considerations.

As might be expected, those who support the various discipline models are outspoken in their criticism of others. These criticisms include not only a denouncement of particular techniques for their lack of effectiveness, but also an examination of underlying flaws in their basic conceptions. Most of these critiques have centered on the degree to which children's behavior can be made appropriate for learning and instruction rather than on potential long-range harm or benefit.

It has already been mentioned that Alfie Kohn has categorically de-nounced the new democratic discipline approaches, claiming that they are full of rhetoric regarding community learning, development of responsibility, and promoting democratic citizenship when in fact they set aside such con-cerns when discipline problems surface. In one way or another the teacher is directed to take over and administer specified control techniques that Kohn charges are no different than traditional autocratic control laced with punish-ment and rewards.

Kohn suggests that when we are told that a particular discipline approach works, we need to ask, "Used for what?" And "works to accomplish what goal?" He adds that better discipline requires that we reconsider the way misbehavior is defined. He also believes that educators must accept the fact that children's basic needs include autonomy, relatedness, and competency, and that teachers need to create conditions to help their students satisfy these needs.

Many of the so-called democratic discipline approaches borrow from the work of Rudolf Dreikurs and Alfred Adler. Dreikurs attributed anything that went wrong in the classroom to children's unreasonable demands for atten-tion. He insisted that misbehavior can be explained by students' misguided efforts to achieve a fixed set of goals of which the children themselves are unaware. These same goals are used as a means for manipulating students through peer pressure by having the class publicly discuss the behavior of various children. Dreikurs's Logical Consequences approach also includes a dubious claim that behavior is significantly related to birth order (Kohn, 1996).

Kohn also criticizes Discipline with Dignity created by Curwin and Men-dler as well as Canter's Assertive Discipline. Both see students as the cause of all discipline problems, so there are no demands on anybody else in the system to change. He also explains that 21st Century Discipline fails to take student preferences into account. Rather, what the teacher wants is all that matters. This is so whether or not the teachers' demands are reasonable (Kohn, 1996).

In criticizing Albert's Cooperative Discipline, Kohn (1996) explains that students are held accountable for all their actions. He states that students choose to misbehave without reference to those conditions that actually pro-mote misbehavior. Thus, the educational structures that in reality promote discipline problems are assumed to be benign, laying the total fault for mis-behavior on children and their choices.

Kohn concludes that no system should allow teachers to consider them-selves and the system blameless, and children completely responsible for discipline problems. For example, a huge proportion of unacceptable behav-iors can be traced to the curriculum and instructional methods. What is learned may be either too difficult or too simple, or students may consider learning activities boring. Some students may not be interested in what is learned and see no way to use the information they are forced to memorize.

Butchart (1998a) draws the same conclusions as Kohn. He points out that most mainstream discipline approaches in one way or another gain student compliance through threats or rewards. Consequently, students do not learn of justice, community, or compassion. He astutely indicates that there is a curious contradiction in schooling at the present. Rather than emphasizing cognitive processes, reasoning, critical thinking, and reflection, all leavened with multiple pedagogical approaches reflecting greater sensitivity to differ-ent learning styles and multiple intelligences, the focus in the current curricu-lum is upon student behavior, noncognitive stimulus-response processes, un-reasoning obedience, and unreflective docility, all delivered by the teacher with no acknowledgment of differences in students' social backgrounds, learning styles, or intelligences.

In addition, teachers teach conceptual information in the academic curric-ulum but expect students to already know what is necessary and moral re-garding their personal conduct. It is interesting to note that since the 1950s the literature on discipline has fallen silent on the long-term social objectives of school discipline, stressing instead the immediate control of students. Short-term classroom order is emphasized rather than long-term responsibil-ity. Few approaches contain any clear conception of democratic social life, either as a short-term classroom goal or a long-term social objective. De-pending on the approach advocated, teachers are empowered to either punish students or rule with moral authority (Butchart, 1998b).

Most discipline theories have very little to say about the learning process. Almost without exception they do not articulate with constructivist learning theory, which is currently the most accepted explanation regarding how chil-dren naturally learn. Inquiry-based learning experiences are a central feature of constructivist learning, a strategy noticeably absent in the various disci-pline theories. Instead, it is commonly assumed that children can and should learn by rote and that the information they memorize will be useful. Both assumptions are seriously flawed.

In connection with this, Kohn (1996) points out that some discipline theorists conclude that students should not be allowed to do what they want, believing this is only an invitation to avoid doing what they are supposed to do. He further adds that an imposed curriculum is more likely to be a source of discipline problems than a solution to them.

There are other subtle problems in many discipline approaches that on the surface deny the use of rewards and punishments, but that in fact incorporate them plentifully. For example, Albert's Cooperative Discipline advocates publicly praising students. This is done obviously to get their peers to comply with teacher directions. There is also an advocacy for handing out gold stars and stickers along with pinning ribbons on children. In both Assertive Discipline and Discipline with Dignity, students are given rewards such as special classroom privileges. Teachers are also encouraged to catch students being good and praising them.

William Glasser, in describing his Control Theory/Choice Theory program of discipline, makes a strong case against behaviorism. He points out that humans have an inherent will that guides their behavior rather than being controlled by contingencies of reinforcement imposed by others or the environment. Despite his strong rejection of behaviorism, critics call him a behaviorist at heart (Henry & Abowitz, 1998). The question that must be explored regarding Glasser's views is the degree to which they foster the maintenance and improvement of democratic life.

Henry and Abowitz (1998) indicate that Glasser's approach hides a manipulative, individualistic pedagogy behind a concern for school spirit, cooperative learning, and a human workplace. They identify three fundamental flaws that keep Glasser's quality schools from being truly democratic. First, there is a focus in individual fulfillment of needs that undermines genuine community building. Second, Glasser equates a good worker with a good citizen. This undercuts the importance of public spheres of life where children live with each other as citizens, not as workers. Third, the focus on individual need fulfillment ignores the necessity of students achieving their social needs.

If public actions in school are seen solely as extensions of students' private needs, the classroom community is stripped of its power to prepare students for life in communities generally. In Control Theory/Choice Theory, though a boss-management orientation is discouraged, teachers still assume control and direct classroom activities. Students who misbehave are subjected to an interview with the teacher where they have to identify the inappropriate behavior as subtly defined by the teacher and work out a plan to avoid problems in the future. Compliance is promoted by teachers cajoling their students (Butchart, 1998a). These and other practices are control oriented and embody consequences and rewards that are consistent with behaviorism.

Though Glasser describes his approach as democratic, many procedures undermine whatever democratic elements are present. Thus, contradictory aspects of discipline are merged: for example, advocating that students learn to exert an optimal amount of energy trying to understand what the teacher wants them to learn instead of wasting time in various counterproductive activities they may choose.

This is an example of a management orientation in which students are seen as needing to be manipulated so that in channeling their energies in the ways prescribed by the teacher, they come to see themselves as working for their own goals, within a context where "motivation" is seen as a neutral, personally disconnected force. The hope is that students' time will be productive from a teacher's perspective so that their time will not be wasted. Deliberate or otherwise, this approach is calculated to create an illusion of student self-direction when in fact it is explicit teacher control (Beyer, 1998).

Even though in Control Theory/Choice Theory students are encouraged to perform academically to the best of their ability and not have their aspirations undermined by low teacher expectations, they still are graded. Glasser (1990) advocates a grading system that he claims is competency based rather than norm based. Thus, students supposedly are not compared to their peers for grading purposes. He believes that the lowest acceptable quality of student learning should be at the B level. However, for greater achievements, B+, A-, A, and A+ would be given. Consequently, he does in fact accept a grading system that in reality has comparative elements and is behavioristic in its orientation. Obviously, grades are distributed as rewards for various levels of comparative achievement.

One of the critical issues that tend to be ignored by various discipline theorists is the common practice of teachers defining what kind of behavior is appropriate and inappropriate in the classroom. The obvious question that should be raised is "appropriate to whom and why?" Unfortunately focusing on appropriateness forces teachers to direct their attention excessively on getting students to exhibit particular behaviors rather than promoting a variety of behaviors that are connected to each child's idiosyncratic thoughts and feelings, needs and perspectives, motives and values (Kohn, 1996). Because such an orientation may keep teachers preoccupied with control, the potential for the growth of independence and responsibility, along with moral and intellectual development, is diminished.

CONSEQUENCES VERSUS PUNISHMENT

Many discipline approaches advocate providing consequences instead of punishment. However, the line of differentiation between consequences and punishment is very thin. The discrepancy is in attributing particular outcomes to consequences that are claimed to be different from punishment when in fact they are not. Also, punishment is supposedly arbitrarily administered while consequences are a logical result of misbehavior that children will accept as justified without question. Thus, it is assumed that they will quietly and without resistance accept consequences because inherently they realize they merit them, given how they have misbehaved.

However, students don't always simply accept the consequences delivered by their teachers as appropriate and logically connected to their misbehavior. They tend to respond to logical consequences in the same way they do to punishment, because both send the same message, particularly when consequences are imposed by the teacher. Interestingly, this is also the case even when students have been involved in identifying supposed logical consequences. The only correct way to interpret the result of consequences is to observe how students respond when they are imposed on them.

Gordon (1989) says that logical consequences are simply a euphemism for external control by punishment. Commonly children are told that logical consequences and punishment are provided for their own good. However, it would be rare for children to feel good about receiving them (Curwin & Mendler, 1988). In reality it is still simply a matter of an authority figure exercising power over them and making their life unpleasant (Kohn, 1996).

The rhetoric regarding logical consequences is often wrapped in the language of choice. Most modern discipline programs advocate allowing children to make choices. However, offers to choose are ordinarily connected to covert efforts by teachers to control. For example, a child who is late coming in from recess may be given the choice in the future of either returning with the other children or standing by the teacher all during recess (Dreikurs, Grunwald & Pepper, 1982). The following are additional examples drawn from various discipline approaches that advocate applying logical consequences.

Children who have not completed an assignment on schedule may be told they can complete it now or during recess (Curwin & Mendler, 1988).

If a child leaves his toys lying around at home, his mother is advised to hide them. When asked by the child where they are, she responds with a lie by saying, "I'm sorry. I put them somewhere, but I don't remember right now." Or the parent might "accidentally" step on one of the child's favorite toys that has been left on the floor (Dreikurs & Grey, 1968).

Instead of sitting quietly, two first-graders are using their hands to rehearse a dance they will be performing later. The teacher makes them come to the front of the room and tells them they must demonstrate the dance to the rest of the class. Though the children were obviously embarrassed, we are told that it was a result of their own action and not because of any arbitrary judgment by the teacher (Dreikurs & Grey, 1968).

When a kindergarten boy bites other children, he is required to wear a sign around his neck that reads, "I bite people." The authors inform us that such a consequence shows ingenuity and also courage (Dreikurs & Grey, 1968).

A student who makes spitballs and flips them around the class is required by the teacher to make 500 more spitballs so that his throat becomes increasingly parched (Albert, 1989).

For various rule infractions, students are prevented from going to the library or eating lunch in the cafeteria. They are confined to the area of the principal's office and forced to miss a class field trip or required to write an essay on how they intend to stop breaking school rules (Curwin & Mendler, 1988).

When students have been noisy, the teacher gives an unannounced test with the most difficult questions possible. When the papers are returned, there should be as many low marks as it is possible to give, though the results are not placed in the grade book (Dreikurs & Grey, 1968).

Students who fail to adhere to class rules are isolated in a time-out area so they will experience a few uncomfortable moments. Repeat offenders are faced with more such isolation time (Albert, 1989). The isolation area can be made less punitive if it is called the happy bench (Nelsen, Lott & Glen, 2000).

Each student who violates a rule is required to write his or her own name on the blackboard. Another option is to elect a student sheriff who writes the names of misbehaving students on the blackboard and keeps a record of all classroom misbehavior (Curwin & Mendler, 1988).

When a student disturbs class, the teacher holds a class discussion about the bad behavior in an effort to evoke group pressure and force behavior changes. The teacher might also wait for a peaceful moment and then jokingly say to the student, in front of everyone, "You've been quiet for some time, wouldn't you like to say something?" (Dreikurs, Grunwald & Pepper, 1982).

The above examples are taken from scores of suggestions given by the New Discipline theorists. They appear indistinguishable from punishments and in some cases are crude and cruel. Yet in each instance there is an assurance that logical consequences have simply been applied (Kohn, 1996). It would seem wise for teachers to examine not only those logical consequences suggested by the various theorists, but also the whole process of administering both logical consequences and punishment.

CONTROVERSY REGARDING DISCIPLINE RESEARCH

Most discipline research is ill-conceived from the standpoint of having appropriate measurement criteria. Characteristically research centers on the relative incidence of student misbehavior and the faithfulness of students in doing assigned schoolwork but ignores credible school purposes such as the development of responsible autonomy, intellectual capability, democratic functioning, inquiry learning skills, and moral character. Ascertaining these important outcomes is ordinarily forfeited in favor of performances on standardized achievement tests and a low incidence of classroom disruptions.

In addition, little attention is paid to what might be termed harmful "side effects." These may consist not only of what a particular approach fails to accomplish, but also its role in promoting undesirable outcomes. For example, schooling that requires students to sit quietly and do all their learning independently usually neglects the development of social skills. Consequently students may not develop necessary social skills nor achieve a sense of being cared for and accepted. Under such conditions, students may come to hate school, and by association hate learning as well. This may lead to an increased level of social isolation along with more bullying and school violence.

With an improper focus, researchers may fail to determine the extent to which a particular discipline method helps children learn how to be autonomously responsible and function successfully in a democratic community. They may also have no idea whether desirable outcomes such as development of inquiry skills and high moral character were achieved or thwarted.

In addition, with current research efforts it is unlikely that any conclusions can be reached regarding how discipline tactics help or hinder student need fulfillment. Unfortunately the "effectiveness" of discipline methods is usually characterized in simplistic terms rather than broaching a sophisticated understanding of the many things that happen in the classroom under very complex conditions.

In reality, not only in schools but also in society at large, there are many threats to democratic living. It is common for individuals representing various organizations to take advantage of fellow citizens and impose restrictions of various kinds to suit their own purposes. In schools, the natural control inclinations of teachers and other school personnel are an ordinary constraint on students' ability to exercise their legitimate role as bona fide citizens with basic inalienable rights. Such factors as immaturity and the like are presented as justifiable reasons to deny them the rights guaranteed them by the Constitution and the Bill of Rights.

The Supreme Court has consistently supported the need for students to enjoy all rights pertaining to their citizenship in a democratic society (Goss v. Lopez, 1975; Tinker v. Des Moines Independent School District, 1969). Teachers need to more consistently promote democratic principles through the development of philosophy and theory that genuinely reflects democratic ideals. Each individual teacher must examine various discipline theories and models in an effort to determine the degree to which they embody purposes and employ practices that are completely consistent with democratic ideals.

Chapter Three

School Discipline and Societal Implications

Educators commonly attribute student unruliness to problems at home and in society generally. Of course, schools are also responsible for many of these problems, and denying their role works against finding appropriate solutions. It would be better if educators visualized student discipline problems as a complex network of interacting elements to which they make a significant contribution. It does no good to blame student discipline problems on others as if in so doing, their role can be discounted.

It should be recognized that many problems that come from homes and society become elaborated in the school, and that there are also problems for which the schools are primarily responsible. Of course there are social and family problems that teachers have very little potential influence to counter, but there are also various home and societal problems that teachers can help eliminate.

Employing learning communities in the schools can be a significant factor in helping to curtail many problems, even some of those that originate in homes and society generally. What follows is a description of some of the problems that originate outside of the school but have the potential to adversely affect classroom decorum and learning effectiveness. Some of these problems are responsible for creating difficulties for children that affect their lives generally.

THE ROLE OF THE HOME IN PROMOTING MISBEHAVIOR

Various factors at home have significant negative affects on children's be-havior in school. Children may have difficulty satisfying their needs when their parents are frequently away from home. This may lead them to seek out associations and activities with potentially devastating consequences, and that perhaps are even illegal. Gang activity is one of the outcomes of parent neglect or absence.

Even when parents are at home, conflicts may destroy meaningful family relationships and encourage gang affiliation. Factors such as divorce and poverty, as well as physical and mental abuse, can adversely affect children's ability to function properly in school. Children from dysfunctional families ordinarily face self-concept difficulties, pessimism, depression, violence, and crime.

Negative Effects of Punishment and Grades at Home and in School

Some negative situations that students encounter in their homes are actually reinforced by teachers; punishment, for example. Some children have experi-enced excessive control and considerable punishment in their homes. Their common response is to become more aggressive and disruptive. This usually encourages more abusive punishment and a corresponding increase in out-landish responses from children. These reactions have a tendency to spill over into the school, where elaborate systems of punishment are already in place and where deviant students find their unruliness subjected to further punishment. It is no wonder some students become so recalcitrant.

Human beings need considerable freedom. They want to control their own lives. At the same time they have an inclination to control others (Glasser, 1984). As children mature, they increasingly seek independence. Conscientious parents ordinarily allow and even encourage their children to gradually assert their independence. However, some children believe this gradual allowance for increased autonomy may be too slow. In this and other ways some parents tend to stifle children's desire for freedom.

Also the unwillingness of parents to actively promote their children's autonomy is the source of much rebellion and family discord. In these dys-functional homes, parents' punitive control may not only lead to extreme rebellion, but also criminal behavior, or inordinate withdrawal (Gordon, 1998). Obviously these consequences can drastically affect children's behav-ior in school.

It should be recognized that teachers can do little to neutralize some negative school elements. Grading is an example. Negative effects of grading do not come exclusively from the school. Much of the inappropriate pressure comes from the home. Interestingly some teachers modify aspects of grading in an effort to protect students from detrimental consequences. One thing that is done, as will be detailed in the next chapter, is to inflate grades. They may also give students an opportunity to earn extra credit when they fail to do their assigned work.

Also, teachers may use grades to exert greater control over student behavior. Some teachers even modify their students' grades if they turn their work in late or disrupt class. These modifications are, of course, unrelated to achievement. The courts have actually ruled against having grades represent anything but students' academic accomplishments, but many teachers continue, in desperation, to use them to regulate student behavior when other tactics prove ineffective.

Interestingly, grading is one area where parents commonly contribute to the problem. Some parents put undue pressure on their children to get high grades. Because university admissions and scholarships ordinarily depend on the grades students achieve, it is a powerful expectation that causes some students to give up and others to strive for high grades by whatever means they can acquire them, including cheating.

Parents use grades to reinforce children's academic behavior, but also as punishment if their grades are not high enough. For example, it is common for parents to give their children rewards such as money, cars, telescopes, trips, and so on for achieving high grades. But children who fail to acquire acceptable grades and complete assigned school homework may be subjected to punishments such as being denied opportunities to participate in family activities.

One handicap some children acquire in school is the belief that ability, not effort, is the main ingredient of success, and thus many sell themselves short by not trying as hard as they would if they believed their efforts would pay off (Covington & Beery, 1976). This attitude is promoted through grading and has fateful consequences for both successful and unsuccessful students. Menacingly, successful students are subject to the detrimental effects of elitism and arrogance while their less-able peers sink into learned helplessness (Weiner & Kukla, 1970; Kohn, 1998).

In response to parental control, children with learned helplessness establish a failure-expectation pattern that they perpetuate continuously. In fact, these students may blatantly sabotage their own achievements. One way they do this is to create standards they know exceed what they can accomplish and then deliberately do low-quality work. This helps them avoid setting a realistic precedent they feel unable to repeat on demand. Teachers commonly accept these elevated standards as evidence that students are willing to try, thus unwittingly reinforcing irrational goal setting that often has its beginning at home (Aronson & Carlsmith, 1962; Covington & Beery, 1976).

Other tactics children engage in to avoid the threat of possible success include coming to class late, claiming not to have heard what was assigned, feigning illness, pretending to be busy, and daydreaming. They try to arrange circumstances so their failure can be blamed on something other than their supposed lack of ability. They try to convince themselves that their failure is no indication of their potential and is, therefore, not a real measure of their worth. These children become expert in keeping their actual ability a secret. Because there are usually strong sanctions for not trying, these children often combine nonparticipation with such tactics as giving false effort (Covington & Beery, 1976).

Some children's self-concept problems are centered in their efforts to achieve at very high levels to garner adult approval. Parents and teachers usually respond by raising standards because these children have routinely demonstrated they can improve. However, they come to feel that higher standards define their worthiness. Thus, they feel acceptable only when they can achieve higher expectations. When they start to reach the upper limit of their capability, they fear they won't be able to continue to produce, thus putting their self-concepts in jeopardy.

Instead of working to achieve success, these youngsters simply try to avoid failure. When they sense they can no longer perform at a sufficiently high level to satisfy both themselves and others, suicide may be considered as their only alternative. Regrettably, after a lifetime of others setting higher standards for them, many of these children begin elevating achievement standards on their own in an effort to achieve additional accolades (Covington & Beery, 1976).

Self-Concept and Home Life

One of the common deficiencies created in both homes and schools is failure to help children develop an optimistic view of life. Without optimism, pessimism and depression usually emerge. An optimistic life orientation does not come from children being told positive things about themselves or from having images of victory, but rather from experiencing self-earned success.

A positive self-concept is dependent on being optimistic. However, the home environment may promote pessimism instead. This may be the result of abuse or failure to receive the attention and assurance necessary to become fully integrated, optimistic persons. Pessimistic children are inclined to look at themselves as helpless in comparison with more capable adults and require their parents' assistance to help bridge the gap between childhood and adulthood (Harris, 1967).

When children are overwhelmed with helpless feelings, they repeatedly seek adult approval. They seem to need perpetual assurance that they are acceptable and competent. Their self-confidence depends on how successful they are in getting required help and recognition. Also, their intrinsic motivation to learn is influenced by the degree of perceived confidence they acquire in childhood. Their academic success in school depends on having a positive image of what they are capable of doing (Goldberg & Cornell, 1998).

In addition, a good deal of children's confidence comes from having personal control over their lives. Unfortunately, dysfunctional families subvert their confidence by providing very little of the emotional support and confidence-building experiences children need to achieve a sense of personal accomplishment and capability. Extreme personal problems are the usual result (Biehler & Snowman, 1982).

Teachers should interact with administrators and counselors to alter school policies and procedures that they believe can negatively affect self-concept. There may be little that can be done to directly modify what takes place outside the school, but potential school changes can help to counteract the influence of various detrimental aspects of home life. For example, schools may implement a drug education program, promote environmental protection, organize a variety of service opportunities, institute tutoring for younger children, and support gang prevention. All these can be employed as constituents of democratic learning communities. This way, students can experience a need-satisfying atmosphere of care that may be missing at home.

The Effect on Children of Working Mothers and Divorce

The detrimental effects of family life can come about from abuse as well as neglect. Neglect can be a problem when parents are caught in work situations that limit the time they can spend with their children. Increasingly children come home to an empty house or apartment, and without adult supervision engage in detrimental activities to fill the time before parents arrive home. This is often a time when they meet and interact with peers who help think up questionable activities. At the very least, a parentless environment may be an isolated, unfriendly atmosphere for some children, with detrimental psychological implications.

Coleman (2002) indicates that due to family dysfunctions, 15 to 25 percent of American children (twelve to twenty million) suffer from severe emotional problems. This represents a drastic increase since the 1980s. Since then the rates of homicide, suicide, severe depression, and related anxiety disorders have risen anywhere from 100 to 400 percent. The cause, Coleman says, is inadequate parenting in consequence of mothers entering the workforce along with skyrocketing divorce rates. She points out that at the present time, five thousand children commit suicide each year. This represents an 800 percent increase since the 1950s and a 400 percent increase since the 1980s.

American children are alone in this increase among other Western and industrialized nations. For example, the suicide rate for youth in the United

States is ten times higher than in Canada. Serious depression for youth has increased from 2 percent in the 1960s to 25 percent in the 1990s. Serious assaults by juveniles have increased 700 percent since World War II. Youth homicide has increased 168 percent between the mid-1980s and mid-1990s.

Children are often not resilient after experiencing the divorce of their parents. Divorce puts more mothers into the workforce. In 1995, 64 percent of U.S. married mothers with preschool children were in the workforce, compared with 30 percent in 1970. Today these figures are likely much higher, because single mothers now account for approximately 50 to 65 percent of all mothers. About 50 percent of all marriages end in divorce. Thirty-one percent of all children in the United States live with only one parent or neither. In 1997 approximately 30 percent or 6.5 million American children between the ages of one and five were enrolled in day care programs. Unfortunately, it is estimated that six out of seven day care centers have abysmal programs.

Children who are home alone unsupervised are greatly influenced by the media as well as their peers. It is not only the content of television programming that can be detrimental—television fails to promote logical, sequential thinking and is tied to children's inability to form meaningful relationships. It also promotes behavioral and emotional difficulties, including violence. Television along with computers can diminish creativity, imagination, and motivation and depress attention span and a desire to persevere. Computer games tend to promote social isolation, depression, and school failure. With regard to the Internet, in 1998, seventeen million children, ages two to eighteen, were online. This was expected to grow to forty-two million by 2003 (Coleman, 2002).

Divorce is one of the more significant problems children face. It puts pressure on them in several ways. For example, some children feel personally responsible for the breakup of their parents. In addition, the parental love they would ordinarily be exposed to is reduced, simply because one or both parents find insufficient time to spend with them. Also, parents commonly engage in postdivorce battles wherein former mates may be undermined in front of the children. This is a particularly devastating experience for children, who need to see both parents in a positive light. Finally, in divorce situations, financial problems often make it necessary for both parents to work. Greatly reduced adult supervision is often the result.

Deprivation of Love and Attention

Insufficient attention at home leads many children to excessively seek it at school. But given the number of students in most classes, it is often even more difficult to satisfy attention needs in school than at home. Then, due to receiving very little attention for their positive efforts, many children discover that unruliness is a more sure way to acquire the attention they seek, even if it is negative. Because they are reactive rather than preventive in their orientation to student discipline, teachers inadvertently focus more on misbehavior than on positive student behavior. In the absence of positive attentiveness students are reinforced by negative attention and consequently become more disruptive. In this way, patterns of misbehavior are built up simply because children have not been able to acquire the positive attention they need either at home or in school (Dreikurs, Grunwald & Pepper, 1982).

Children ordinarily measure how much they are loved by the attention and approval they receive. When parents are excessively absent or become too preoccupied to provide sufficient attention, children feel unloved. Many parents have the erroneous idea that the quality of time spent with children can make up for an insufficient amount of time. But it is unlikely that children can be satisfied with very little high-quality time. Rather, it is more probable that high-quality time would promote a longing for more time because it is more desirable.

Many times it appears that children are unable to satisfy their need for attention sufficiently no matter how much time is spent in the presence of their parents. This is probably because the lack of quality time is interpreted as scarceness. Thus, parents may be present but still ignore their children. For some children attention deprivation may be so acute, even after acting out repeatedly to get their parents' attention, that they simply give up and begin to withdraw and may occasionally engage in particularly egregious behavior.

Few parents understand that seeking attention is really an effort by children to control interactions with others. It is an attempt to achieve sufficient control to perpetually ensure a sense of belonging. Ordinarily children won't abandon their efforts to be noticed just because the attention they receive is of high quality (Glasser, 1998).

It is noteworthy that children can become so preoccupied in their quest to receive desired attention that they gain very little from school, particularly if they feel deprived. In addition, parents who are withdrawn and remote, neglectful and passive, risk the likelihood of shutting their children down emotionally. Emotional stress in connection with love deprivation has been significantly associated with violence (Walsh & Beyer, 1987). Astute teachers will not wait for children to misbehave before providing the attention they crave. Instead they will create a social environment in the classroom that fosters acceptance and care. Learning communities can be particularly effective in this endeavor.

THE ROLE OF SOCIETY IN PROMOTING SCHOOL DISCIPLINE PROBLEMS

Negative family and social influences are often interrelated. In some cases the negative social influences might have been avoided had there not been substantial parental neglect or abusive child-rearing practices. Sometimes the abuse comes from parents' ignorance regarding child rearing. In other cases, parents' abusive inclinations are contributing factors. In addition, social intrusions may occur, over which parents have very little control.

Gang Activity and Illicit Drugs

When there is neglect or rejection at home, children may search elsewhere for acceptance. To some children, gangs are an attractive alternative. Gangs may satisfy children's need for attention and acceptance and provide a way to acquire a sense of identity. Unfortunately, there is an inherent trap, because gang members ordinarily demand and receive greater allegiance from associates than is commonly required by their own families. Ironically, gang members are ordinarily forced to choose between gang loyalty and family allegiance, thus solidifying gang identity.

As evidence of their worthiness to affiliate with a gang, members are often expected to participate in acts deplored by the rest of society. They may, for example, be required to participate in illicit sex, armed robbery, mugging, or drive-by shootings. They may also be required to periodically repeat such acts to confirm their commitment to the gang's value system. Thus, members are forced to choose between the gang and their family as well as society generally.

Gangs are territorial, and members are frequently involved in open conflict with rival gangs. The clashes usually involve turf, privilege, or property. Confrontations often turn violent. In addition, trafficking in illegal drugs is predictably associated with gang activity. Drug abuse and associated gang violence have become so severe in many schools that school officials must enlist the help of local law enforcement personnel to maintain order. Gangs can be very upsetting in school, and once established, are difficult to dislodge (Lal, Lal & Achilles, 1993).

Although physical and sexual maltreatment are associated with gang involvement (Thompson & Braaten-Antrim, 1998), ordinary social events and associated prejudice contribute to criminalizing some urban youth and driving them toward gang affiliation. Teacher racism as well as institutional racism stereotype many students as doomed to fail or destined to become gang members (Katz, 1997).

Peer pressure enforced by gangs and cliques in school contribute significantly to students' misbehavior. If children's peer groups consider school a joke, they may go along with the crowd and consequently put little effort into their studies. Nearly every large high school has such a group, which is commonly recognized but constitutes a problem that is rarely addressed.

Interestingly, peer pressure is the single largest influence on female gang involvement. Girls often turn to gangs for protection from neighborhood crime, abusive families, or potential harm from rival gangs. For girls, lack of parental warmth and affection along with family conflicts are linked to gang affiliation (Walker-Barnes & Mason, 2001).

The Influence of Technology

An increasing number of students carry and listen to portable iPods and MP3 players, which predictably interfere with learning. In addition, youths frequently play rap music that is confrontational and violent and has been identified as contributing to various youth crimes. Sometimes the lyrics of the music suggest that violent acts be carried out against particular segments of society, such as police officers. Rap music is available to youths from various sources. They can download a huge volume of selections on their iPods or purchase compact discs. It is also available through music video channels on television.

There is also a rapidly growing market for renting or purchasing DVDs that contain violent and/or pornographic material. There is evidence that this kind of programming has a negative impact on children's behavior and is related to various kinds of criminal activity (Paik & Comstock, 1994). Also, pornographic materials have become more readily available to children via the Internet, where children have to contend with predators who stalk them with impunity. Through "chat rooms," many have been lured into liaisons with these predators and sexually abused. In 1999 twenty-four million youths, aged ten through seventeen, were online regularly, where they encountered sexual solicitations they did not want, sexual materials they did not seek, and people who threatened and harassed them (Finkelhor, Mitchell & Wolak, 2000).

Unfortunately filtering software developed to screen objectionable materials and protect children may not be sufficiently effective (Siegel, 1998; Taylor, 1998). This problem becomes even more serious, as the number of children who regularly use the Internet has grown considerably (Coleman, 2002).

Many children have become obsessed with video games, which not only contribute to violence as it is depicted in the games themselves, but also occupy an unprecedented amount of time formerly devoted to school studies. Video games provide children with models of violence and domination over others, hatred, contempt, and callousness. This emotional stimulation has taken the place of experiences that promote caring and commitment along with joy and zest for life. Video games also encourage bullying and school violence. Excessive time spent playing video games keeps children from learning social skills and acquiring emotional adjustments necessary for cooperative learning in the classroom (Watson-Ellam, 1997).

One way to help counter the negative influences of various forms of media is for children to be involved in meaningful learning activities at home that hold their interest. Traditional homework assignments are unable to accomplish this for many students. However, involvement in learning communities provides a means to bridge the gap between school and home and help children become meaningfully involved in positive activities in place of distractions such as TV, video games, and text messaging. Not only can they be involved in what is important to them personally, but also in what is important to groups at school who are depending on them to accomplish particular learning tasks.

Racial and Class Conflicts

Racial and class conflicts have a long history in the schools. Forced integration has begun a process of change that is still unresolved. Racial inequity spawned by prejudice is a continuing problem in the schools. For example, by one means or another, Black and Hispanic children find themselves in remedial classes in disproportionate numbers, where the academic challenges given to their more fortunate White classmates are lacking (Banks, 2003; Gamoran & Berends, 1987).

Also, despite efforts to modify conditions for Blacks, Hispanics, and other minorities, they continue to fall behind economically. Children from economically challenged families seem to be unremittingly relegated to lower economic status and consequent poverty. The result is rampant unemployment and crime. Children who grow up in such environments inevitably experience far less success in school. The problems they encounter in their neighborhoods follow them to school, where they interfere with learning, emotional adjustment, and social responsibility development.

Schools in these neighborhoods consistently experience more discipline problems, lower academic achievement, and more dropouts. This unfortunately undermines students' capacity to escape from the conditions that keep them in poverty from generation to generation (Gollnick & Chinn, 1994).

Educators need to help break the stranglehold that race and social status have on various minorities. Perhaps the most potent possibility for making necessary changes lies with employing learning communities. This learning configuration helps children deal with class and racial disparities as a central focus of their educational experiences.

In learning communities, the differences between children are celebrated, because they constitute a way for them to obtain a better understanding of the world in which they live and to more fully comprehend the complexity of the human environment. Learning communities also help them become prepared to interact more successfully with many races and classes of people, and consequently become better able to live successfully within the challenging context of the real world.

Chapter Four

Student Assessment in Learning Communities

Properly conceived assessment is an essential aspect of education as well as the discipline program. The educational process and all associated components including discipline should be routinely examined to ensure quality and make improvements. When students see assessment as inappropriate, they often rebel. Because education is a very complex endeavor, it is important to create measurement instruments that are sufficiently comprehensive and valid. Every effort should be made to determine which components are appropriate to measure and which are not. Evaluation should be valid and reliable.

Measurement instruments should not only measure intended curricula, they must also help determine what is appropriate to teach. One of the central issues is whether or not what should be taught actually is being taught. Regarding this issue, there are at least seven different curricular sources: (1) curricula defined by the district and state, (2) curricula teachers would apply if they were allowed free rein, (3) curricula as dictated by federal and state agencies, (4) curricula as suggested by professional organizations, (5) curricula as suggested by scholars and professional educators, (6) curricula as defined by a careful examination of what students require for success in life, and (7) curricula as would be created with helpful input from students. These seven sources are not usually acknowledged, let alone carefully delineated, described, and compared to each other.

Obviously, there may be some overlap regarding different curricular sources, but there are some rather significant differences between them as well. When it comes to evaluation, it is critical to identify what is being measured. It does little good to make assessments based on curricula that have not been carefully differentiated from competing sources and rationally accepted as the single, defensible instructional program for a specific school district. Even then, the fact must be accepted that a particular measurement instrument is likely to have only limited validity for a specific curriculum orientation.

The professional school staff must first organize an educational program that is consistent with what children need before creating the means for determining its effectiveness. Both teacher-made tests and standardized tests can be called into question in terms of making valid assessments. Once a curriculum has been accepted, it is very unlikely that a standardized test could be found that credibly measures all that is expected. These tests will unquestionably have a different focus than that ordinarily sought by the schools. This is because they are constructed by testing agencies far removed from any particular school and its concerns.

Test makers could not possibly take all district and state curriculum considerations into account in test construction; thus, if states and school districts wish to use these tests, they must modify the curriculum they prefer so that it fits what test makers decide is important. In addition, standardized tests are usually confined to measuring only a narrow aspect of student achievement and ignore other critical educational components. Even teacher-made tests usually fail to measure intended goals of schooling, particularly when it comes to the development of higher-order thinking along with various attitudes and skills.

Often any kind of paper and pencil test is inappropriate. However, they are used because of their ease in scoring and their supposed objectivity. This presumed objectivity must also be properly characterized. These tests may have scoring objectivity, but they are not objectively created. They are subject to all kinds of influences that could compromise their validity. For example, a teacher may favor a particular part of the subject in constructing tests while students are led to believe other course content has primary importance. Or perhaps the teacher's motive is to ensure grades approximate a normal curve rather than actually ascertaining the level of student achievement, or determining the quality of instruction. Also, what is measured in this way may be much different from what is intended.

The aspiration that the curricula employed in the schools can somehow satisfy the disparate positions regarding what students should learn is a false hope. In terms of very fundamental aspects, various proposals vary to such an extent that resolving differences is inconceivable. This is true not only for the curricula themselves, but also the means used to evaluate school effectiveness. As defined by the Constitution, states are responsible for schools. In recognition that each school district in the state may have unique characteristics and needs, states have traditionally turned curriculum development over to them.

More recently states have moved to take more control of the schools by imposing particular instructional objectives, regulating textbook adoption, and giving year-end tests. The purpose is to try to ensure greater educational quality and to somehow make schooling "teacher-proof." Consequently, teacher decision making has increasingly been wrested from them. It is implicitly assumed that they are incapable of making critical decisions about schooling. The irony in this is that the curriculum is usually implemented by teachers without careful oversight by state school officials.

In their hope to better control the teaching process, state officials create common sets of objectives for all students and impose standardized tests with questionable validity. For example, tests in science almost without exception fail to determine the quality of students' inquiry research skills even though this is the central stated objective of professional science education organizations as well as many state education departments.

In addition, assessment is made exclusively regarding student achievement, leaving other aspects of teaching-learning unexamined. For example, the teaching process is never directly defined and assessed through standardized tests. Teaching quality is simply assumed to be validly measured on the basis of student test scores. Given the complexity of various elements that contribute to student academic performance, it cannot be assumed that teachers are solely responsible for either high or low scores. And, of course, these test scores do not provide any guidance to teachers about their teaching, nor do they measure such hopeful outcomes as socially acceptable values and character development, let alone children's intellectual progress.

Initiatives such as the No Child Left Behind Act of the federal government also help distort the true purposes of education. Without really trying to define what education should be, they attempt to impose standardized testing on the schools. Pressure is created by attaching monetary incentives to test results. The effect has been to hold classroom teachers exclusively responsible for the scores their students achieve.

Standardized curricula and testing not only deprive teachers of necessary decision making, they also keep students from giving essential input to the teaching-learning process. In addition, there is no absolute certainty that students should learn what is dictated by what is commonly required. Agreement is likely for some information learned, particularly as defined generally, but many specific concepts do not have mutual support. Even so, many curricular components are selected that can only be defined as the preferences and biases of individuals in power.

This is also true of the teaching-learning process. For example, testing students regarding their ability to retrieve memorized facts implies a learning process that features knowledge transmission. However, it has been conclusively shown that information is not simply absorbed as presented, but rather assimilated into personally created conceptual structures. This fact supports the idea that students should help in directing their own learning processes and determining what they learn.

This requirement is amplified by the knowledge explosion. It is difficult for anyone to definitively determine what knowledge is most essential. For example, scientific knowledge doubles about every five and a half years at the current, but ever-increasing, rate. Also, much knowledge is obsolete. By the time the average medical doctor completes his or her training, half of all the information acquired in medical school is out of date (Cross, 1985). Similar conditions exist in other areas as well.

LEARNING ASSESSMENT AND STANDARDIZED TESTING

Teachers use a variety of methods to evaluate student learning. Most commonly they administer teacher-made tests. Other methods include papers, research reports, demonstrations, and projects of various kinds that result in products such as paintings, mock-ups, and photographs. In many instances, objective tests are preferred because they are easier to use for grading purposes. Multiple choice is the most common test format. All of these so-called objective tests have their strengths and weaknesses. Objective tests are easy to score, but it can be difficult to construct items that clearly measure what is intended.

Different problems are encountered in using essay tests. For one thing, these tests usually provide students with a very narrow sample of content, leaving out many of the concepts that they may judge as important. In addition, essay tests are very difficult to score consistently. Various biases produce questionable assessments by the evaluator. For example, grammatical or punctuation errors often distort a teacher's estimate of actual quality. One positive aspect of essay tests is their ability to examine high-level cognitive processes.

Problems Associated with Standardized Testing

Standardized tests are commonly used to evaluate student achievement. Ordinarily they are given as year-end assessments and used to determine the quality of instructional programs and teacher competence. Regarding the measurement of teacher competence, negligible consideration is given to potential influences from outside the classroom even though they may have a greater impact, both positive and negative, on student achievement than teachers do. It is implied that teachers have the responsibility to overcome the impact on students of any of these factors that can produce negative results.

To properly determine the appropriateness of using standardized tests in this way, various contributing factors should be addressed and their relative impact identified. Of course, this is only in part possible, given their obscurity. It is easier to hold teachers accountable than to attempt to ascertain causative factors that may be more influential than teachers regarding the scores achieved by students. Consequently, the potent and perhaps more powerful influence of parents and the social environment of students is usually ignored.

Some detrimental experiences and dispositions that teachers are unequivocally supposed to negate include questionable peer associations and relationships, abusive home life and experiences, lack of parents' support, traumatic social events, aversive school conditions, effects of mandated curricula, students' personal problems, negative student dispositions, along with students' deleterious attitudes about these and other factors.

Students may be greatly influenced by their peers in terms of school achievement. Thus, children whose friends are positively involved with school tend to be engaged in the same way themselves. Those who associate with students who have a history of negative school experiences and consequent unfavorable attitudes also view the school in negative ways.

The dynamics of group relationships and the level of acceptance students feel also affect them in positive or negative ways. Students who are not accepted by their peers, or who are bullied by them, commonly withdraw, suffer various psychological problems, and find it difficult to concentrate their attention on schoolwork. Schools have traditionally failed miserably to curtail bullying, although a new emphasis in this area has spurred more interest and some positive developments.

Many parents hope the schools can be more successful than they have been in redirecting their deviant children. Sometimes because of teachers' training and supposed expertise, parents expect them to be more successful than they have been in curtailing the unruly behavior of their children, even though it is the result of dysfunctional family attributes. Parental neglect and poor parenting can have an enormous impact on children's success in school.

In addition, the way in which parents interact with their children regarding their school experiences can have either positive or negative influences. Excessive pressure to succeed can turn children off, as can an attitude of disinterest. Punitive parent responses to student failure can make students even less receptive to teachers' efforts to educate them.

Poverty, drugs, gangs, and other factors in society greatly affect students' school success. Some children belong to gangs and live their lives as their peers dictate. Many times they are appositional as a group and direct fellow gang members to resist their teachers. Other children live their lives in fear of gangs, which may greatly disturb their school concentration. Many children are unable to concentrate on their schoolwork because of the need to look after younger siblings while their parents work.

A good many students find various school operations aversive. For example, excessive surveillance, punishment for misbehavior, and overwhelming amounts of homework can take their toll. Students can also be turned off by the prescribed curriculum and the need to spend an excessive amount of time learning information that they believe has no present or future benefit, and consequently fails to hold their interest.

They also may find it hard to accept the adage that the work they are assigned will have future value, and that when they are older they will finally be able to understand its worth. They are expected to accept what they are told about the significance of assigned learning with little or no evidence that it is true. They will in fact forget much of it long before the time it is supposed to become useful. Much that is learned is supposed to prepare students for college. Those who don't believe they are candidates for a college education or simply don't intend to enroll in a university are not motivated by such admonitions.

Aside from their teaching skills, teachers' dispositions and personalities also influence students' classroom attitudes. In fact, teachers' personalities can lead students to have more positive views of them even when what they are teaching is of little value. In a study by Coats and Swierenga (1972) it was found that teacher charisma was more important in teacher ratings than their effectiveness. In their study, students were exposed to actors who taught bogus information and then rated these actors' effectiveness as compared with regular teachers who taught bona fide concepts. The students rated the teaching skills of the actors much higher than regular teachers. In addition, despite the fact that actors had not taught students important information, students believed they had.

It has also been found that the personality of the students significantly influences how they feel about their teachers (Younge & Sassenrath, 1968). Students are influenced by the subject being taught, age and sex of their teachers, and their own age and sex (Bledsoe, Brown & Strickland, 1971). Obviously, students' attitudes about their teachers and the classroom are influenced by a multitude of factors, most of which teachers have very little control over and for which they consequently should not be held accountable, particularly when it comes to scores on standardized achievement tests.

Problems Associated with the Construction of Standardized Tests

Additional problems are inherent in the use of standardized tests. Some relate to the nature of test construction. One of the issues is linked to the fact that standardized tests are based upon the assumption of normality. This is true even though it is claimed that current high-stakes tests are criterion referenced. This is because normative comparisons are inescapable when classifying students (Madaus, Russell & Higgins, 2009).

In creating norm-referenced tests, it is assumed that the scores students achieve in responding to test questions will form a normal curve. It is presumed that all sufficiently large populations are essentially equal in terms of the distribution of their capabilities and achievements. If the test has been appropriately constructed, scores must approximate a normal, bell-shaped curve, assuming the group being tested validly represents the entire population. Presumably the normal curve also represents the way grades should be distributed to students.

Standardized tests that do not produce a normal distribution of scores are judged invalid and in need of modification. However, teachers should realize that the normal curve is based on an "assumption," not on absolute truth. One interesting related fact is that children as they enter school are much more alike than they are by the time they leave school. Their test scores finally come closer to fitting a normal curve by the time they finish their time in public schools. It seems that school experiences help create a "normal" distribution of achievements when in fact children are much more alike in terms of intellectual abilities early on than they later appear.

When the assumption of normality is believed to be true, the task for test makers is to continually refine test items until they produce a normal distribution with the group used to "norm" the test. The question regarding the validity of the normality assumption is considered less important. Thus, the general applicability of the concept is rarely questioned and never investigated. The only issue that is entertained is whether or not test scores fit the normal curve. The possibility that particular populations might not fit the normal curve is usually not questioned. Consequently, the so-called normal distribution is more a function of the test itself and its norming group than the total population.

The questions for test makers to address include (1) whether or not a subpopulation is the same as they assume the general population to be and (2) whether or not the achievements of students have been framed by testing and grading and do not really describe an unadulterated student population. Standardized tests are always normed with subpopulations that are assumed to represent the general population.

In developing tests, subjects might be selected from a single region of the country that very well may not be equivalent to other areas along various dimensions. Consequently, tests may represent regions, not the general population. Most of these tests are used to measure student achievement both inside and outside the norming region. In evaluating the quality of their instruction, teachers can legitimately wonder if their students actually represent the general population and whether or not their learning and test responses have been inappropriately shaped by testing and grading experiences in school.

Another critical issue that must be addressed is whether or not the test being created actually measures what is emphasized by teachers and is consistent with the curriculum as defined by various entities. In reality there is no way any standardized test can be consistent with so many disparate opinions about the curriculum, or the learning experiences implemented in an enormous number of diverse classrooms. Consequently, it is highly unlikely that such tests will address many of the concepts teachers believe are important.

When standardized tests are imposed on the schools, teachers of necessity may have to abandon the curriculum to which they earlier felt committed and teach concepts and ideas for which they have little enthusiasm. In addition, when test makers do not know what teachers value, it is very difficult to create valid tests. It is far easier to base tests on test makers' personal views and ignore those espoused by teachers. Also ignored are language and cultural differences (Madaus, Russell & Higgins, 2009).

The result is teacher disenfranchisement as teacher-proof curricula are imposed on them. However, educators should understand that standardized tests don't represent the curricula prized in any particular school district or state. There is no way for test makers to incorporate all such differences into the tests they create, nor rationally address the inconsistencies inherent in various curricular advocacies. The tests simply reflect their personal biases and experiences.

Other issues regarding the construction of standardized tests are commonly overlooked. First, these tests sample a very narrow segment of any domain of knowledge because they are merely forty or fifty items long. Second, standardized tests are credited with an unwarranted degree of precision. Without properly considering this lack of precision, educators make decisions regarding student academic progress when the differences in scores obtained from year to year or between one student and another are simply due to the standard error of the test itself. To get an accurate measure, even when the test is valid, students would have to be tested several times successively. This is never done. Even if it was, accuracy could be compromised by such things as the development of student test-taking skills or the lack of reliability between the various forms of the tests used.

Unfortunately, the precision and accuracy of standardized tests may be sacrificed in an effort to sell more tests. The companies that create and sell standardized achievement tests, like all for-profit businesses, exist primarily to produce revenue for their shareholders. In an effort to sell to the largest possible market, they of necessity must disregard the enormous diversity of the population. In doing this, test makers are obliged to create one-size-fits-all assessments, even when the various states or school districts sponsor significantly different curricular emphases.

No particular test is likely to be a good fit for all areas. This state of affairs is illustrated in a study of five nationally standardized achievement tests in mathematics for grades 4 through 6. These tests were analyzed along with four widely used textbooks in the subject area. It was concluded that 50 to 80 percent of what was measured on the tests was not adequately addressed in the textbooks (Freeman et al., 1983). Add this to the fact that those who construct tests, as well as textbook publishers, tend to feature content that is emphasized in more populated areas.

Additional problems are associated with formulating test items. Standardized tests require items that only about half of the students can answer correctly, so that student scores can be spread out as required under a normal curve. Thus, if a test item is answered correctly by about 80 percent of the test takers, it must be discarded. Consequently the vast majority of items on standardized achievement tests are of "middle difficulty."

Interestingly, the items that students could easily answer are eliminated in the test construction process, even though they cover the content teachers tend to stress because they consider it important. The result is that the content teachers consider important and teach well is not included on standardized tests. It is, therefore, absurd to use these tests to measure student achievement and teacher effectiveness (Popham, 1999).

It should be pointed out again that standardized tests not only fail to validly measure course content, they also adversely affect the instructional process. There are many documented instances of teachers eliminating a good deal of the intended curriculum to devote more time to preparing students to perform well on standardized achievement tests. Also, it is common practice for some teachers to teach outside their area of preparation to focus more time on test preparation in the subjects emphasized in the tests, namely math and English (Clinchy, 2001; McNeil, 2000; Merrow, 2001).

In addition, high-stakes tests usually narrow the curriculum and encourage instruction geared toward lower-order cognitive skills. Also, when these tests are used to sanction schooling based on student scores, incentives are created for pushing children who score low into special education classes, keeping students from advancing to the next grade, and encouraging many students to drop out of school. The purpose of this is to help schools look better. Ironically, having children repeat a grade does not help them perform better the next time around. Often they become discipline problems, make poor social adjustments, lose self-esteem, and display no academic improvement despite the fact that they have spent an additional year at the same grade level (Darling-Hammond, 2007).

Standardized tests have inherent biases because students' responses to questions are heavily influenced by their native intellectual ability as well as what they have learned outside of school. Furthermore, students have vastly different learning inclinations. As Gardner (1994) indicates, children have at least eight distinct learning orientations. These vary with each individual. With these variations, children tend to respond differently to items commonly found on standardized achievement tests. Ironically, these tests are differentially biased depending on the particular intellectual skill with which students are endowed. Moreover, standardized tests include only a few of these inherent learning orientations.

It has also been discovered that children from financially advantaged families are favored by standardized tests because they have ordinarily been provided much more stimulus-rich environments, which predictably are similar to the backgrounds of the test makers (Popham, 1999). It is interesting to note that some of the standardized tests contain items that have no right answer, items that have multiple right answers, and items where the official answer is wrong (Bracey, 2001).

The validity of test results can be compromised by the selection of cut scores. Cut scores are those scores that separate test takers into achievement categories (e.g., passing or failing). Because of measurement error, a student who passes could conceivably be less than adequate and a person who fails to pass could be especially adequate. Using cut scores to categorize students ignores measurement error.

Employing tests with low reliability also distorts the achievement picture. For example, with a test having a 0.95 level of reliability, 19 percent of the students are misclassified. Misclassification increases to 29 percent when the reliability is 0.90 and is raised to 38 percent with a reliability of 0.80. These errors increase dramatically as reliability drops further (Madaus, Russell, & Higgins, 2009).

Educators should not unquestioningly accept standardized achievement and aptitude tests as valid. In some cases the test makers have an obscure agenda that in all likelihood is driven by a profit motive. The revision of the Scholastic Aptitude Test (SAT) provides a flagrant example. This test is used all across the country to screen high school students for entry into college.

The SAT is essentially an aptitude test. Yet current test developers at the Educational Testing Service (ETS) have decided to turn it into an achievement test, like its competitor the American College Test (ACT). The stated purpose for doing this was to influence public school curricula. Test developers wanted to frame the curricula of the public schools according to their own biases. They also hoped that the new SAT would serve as a tool of social change and social measurement (Cloud, 2003).

The implications are enormous. Turning curriculum development over to such entities is unconscionable. When this is done, the tests become political rather than rational and designed to benefit ETS rather than children and the schools. Also, as the SAT becomes focused on achievement, it will be less able to measure underlying intellectual skills. Instead, students will be forced to accumulate a plethora of specific facts.

It should be recognized that ETS may be responding to monetary pressures such as the one that comes from the president of the University of California, ETS's biggest client. The constraint was in the form of a threat from the University of California to no longer require applicants to submit

SAT scores. The university called for the exclusive use of standardized tests that assess mastery of specific subject areas rather than undefined scholastic aptitude.

The cost to ETS would be substantial. Seventy-six thousand students submit their SAT scores with their applications to the University of California. The tests cost $28.50 each for a total of $2,166,000 (Cloud, 2003). The same kind of pressure tends to dictate what is included in textbooks. States with lesser populations are saddled with texts that are framed by the desires of more populous regions. It is unfortunate when monetary rather than educational considerations determine school experiences as well as the means for evaluating student achievement.

In the SAT revision there are problems with the changes in both the format and the content. The new test has a writing section that is unquestionably impossible to reliably score because of the number of different people who will be employed to score it. The content problem revolves around what specific information should be tested. For example, in the literature section, specific pieces of literature have been left out that have always been considered some of the best and most accepted literature available.

Such exclusions will, of course, encourage teachers to teach the content that is in the test rather than focus on the literature they judge to be superior, assuming they become aware of what the tests contain. There is also the problem of which literature various students have read. They will obviously be differentially prepared. Their success will depend on whether or not teachers happen to select the books that show up on the test (Cloud, 2003).

The changes ETS wishes to make in school curricula are substantial. They involve explicit aspirations to make modifications in education that have always been the prerogative of states and individual school districts. The result would be for a small number of individuals with questionable credentials, and no sense of local needs in terms of curriculum development, to make changes that affect the entire country. In addition, the anticipated changes make preparations to take the test more costly. Thus, in order for students to become properly prepared, ETS recommends that they double the usual amount of time they spend writing.

As laudable as this appears, it is unlikely to occur. First, more writing time must be taken from the study of other subjects. Second, this would require a substantial increase in the number of English teachers. It is naive to think that that many teachers are currently available. In addition, most school districts are already strapped for sufficient funds to run existing programs. Current teachers could not be expected to spend more time. They are already overloaded. Obviously writing scores will plummet for those who do not get the increased amount of help. In the end it will glaringly discriminate against poorer school districts (Cloud, 2003).

Many standardized achievement tests focus primarily on knowledge acquisition. This is based on the erroneous assumption that being "educated" is essentially the accumulation of factual information. It has long been known that the retention of factual information is very limited, yet most instruction in school appears to be based on the assumption that much of what is memorized is retained. Another tenuous assumption is that the factual information presented to students in school is unquestioningly useful and can be recalled anytime in the future.

Some who acknowledge that most memorized facts are soon forgotten defend the practice of teaching facts with the adage that forgotten information will be easier to learn a second time. Though this might be true, it doesn't answer the question regarding whether or not information assimilation is really valuable in the long run. Obviously certain important facts are associated with nearly every field of endeavor, but much of what children learn is never used later on even if it is remembered. Some valuable things are commonly learned in school, such as important conceptual information, attitudes, and intellectual processing skills. There is also value in learning to appreciate art, music, and literature. These important outcomes are not acquired by memorizing facts.

Perhaps the most important contribution schools can make in the lives of students is to teach them problem solving, inquiry, and social skills, along with encouraging the development of moral character and an attitude of care. Truly educated students have acquired these skills and attitudes. Unfortunately, they are rarely included in the school curriculum and not measured on standardized achievement tests. With the pressure brought on by the No Child Left Behind Act and the imperative for students to score high on standardized tests, they often experience an education far less valuable than what they would ordinarily have received.

The desire behind the No Child Left Behind Act may be credible, but the criteria used for measuring the quality of schooling rely too heavily on assimilating factual information, and in the process create standards that don't really fit what a high-quality education should be (Clinchy, 2001; Merrow, 2001). The practice of students memorizing information can also be questioned in terms of retention as well as value. Research indicates that they are only able to remember 35 percent of meaningful information they have memorized after one month (Cronback, 1965). Also, no evidence suggests that memorized information is critical to success in life and character development.

THE INFLUENCE OF GRADES

Few practices in schooling are so blindly accepted as appropriate and yet are as deleterious as grading. Grades supposedly serve multiple purposes, some of which are rarely questioned. They are assumed necessary with no allowance for questioning their appropriateness. They may serve valuable purposes, but at the same time include attributes that are truly harmful. Grading began in the nineteenth century at Yale University (Laska & Juarez, 1992) and has since permeated educational institutions at all levels. Grades ordinarily are assumed to simply provide necessary information and to be otherwise benign. However, they have been found to have more far-reaching negative effects than usually presumed.

In defending grades, their use in sorting students for employment or university admissions is often presented. It is true that high school grade-point averages (GPA) reliably predict academic success in college (Tan, 1991; Pettijohn, 1995), and thus are commonly used as a basis for admissions. However, neither high school nor college GPAs are satisfactory predictors of occupational success (Cohen, 1984).

Parents usually want to know their children's relative academic standing in school. They are also eager for their children to gain access to college. Grades are used for this purpose. However, parents are much more concerned that their children are happy, balanced, independent, fulfilled, productive, self-reliant, responsible, functioning, kind, thoughtful, loving, inquisitive, and confident (Kohn, 1998).

Most parents are likely unaware of the problems associated with grading. If they really knew the negative consequences of grading, they would be the first to reject the practice. Research shows that grades and other rewards tend to reduce intrinsic motivation (Harackiewicz & Manderlink, 1984), diminish responsibility and produce less helpfulness and generosity (Fabes et al., 1989), decrease concern for others (Balsam & Bondy, 1983), curtail cooperation (Kanter, 1987), and kill creativity (Amabile, Hennessey & Grossman, 1986).

In defending grading, it is often supposed that the competition generated by grading is much like life generally, where everyone has to compete for jobs and advancements. Competition is often believed to be an unavoidable fact of life, helping to motivate us to do our best while building character and self-confidence. These outcomes are myths, however (Kohn, 1992). Cooperative learning is a far better format for developing these skills than is competition for grades (Johnson & Johnson, 1991). The inevitability of competition in human interactions comes from the assumption that human survival depends on it. However, cooperation generally has far more survival value (Kohn, 1992).

In addition, competition is often touted as a necessary and appropriate way to build character and self-confidence, when in fact it is the most pervasive mechanism for developing anxiety in our culture (May, 1977). It goes almost unnoticed that during competition, one's self-esteem depends on the uncertain outcome of the contest, whether it is a test or an athletic event. Losing in competition is a particularly pernicious kind of failure because it communicates to the individual a message of relative inferiority and typically exposes them to public judgment and shame (Kohn, 1992).

The toll that grading takes on children early in life is hardly noticed. But it does in fact foreclose on the hopes and aspirations of many students and consigns them to lower academic ranks, lesser social status, and reduced employment possibilities. As early as kindergarten, because of clues expressed in one way or another by their teachers, youngsters can already identify those of their classmates who are more or less successful (Covington & Beery, 1976).

Researchers have also discovered that grading undermines the motivational process. When grades are used to reinforce learning, as is often the case, children become conditioned to them. Grades then become more important than learning. Students eventually come to detest the learning that is required to achieve grades (Lepper, Greene & Nisbett, 1973). In fact, the greater the incentive offered through grading, the more negatively students tend to view the activity for which it was received (Freedman, Cunningham & Krismer, 1992).

Children who are given rewards for learning tend to choose easier tasks, make more errors, do work of lower quality, and use illogical problem-solving strategies (Condray, 1977). They also display a greater tendency toward dependence and conformity, avoid pursuing challenges, and lack innovativeness (Butler, 1992). Furthermore, they take little interest in exploring any subject in class that has no payoff in terms of grades (Kohn, 1992). Grades tend to cripple ethical and social development and have a tendency to breed intolerance, diminish trust, and interfere with communications between students who receive high grades and those who don't (Kohn, 1998).

Cheating is also a well-documented outcome of competitive grading. Many times it is done to avoid the social consequences of failure (Milton, Pollio & Eison, 1986). Grades encourage students to cut corners and engage in duplicity to achieve what they wish (Bok, 1979). They also predictably produce anxiety, hostility, resentment, disapproval, envy, distrust, contempt, and aggression (Horney, 1973).

It is obvious that grading has ethical considerations, and it is libelous that these aspects of grading are not consistently addressed so that the evaluation process is not tainted with so many detrimental effects. Grades should be understood in terms of all their implications. Parents and educators need to decide whether the benefits are really worth the potential harm.

EDUCATIONAL QUALITY AND GRADE INFLATION

Grade inflation and its effects have long been a problem not only in public education but also in universities. Substantial grade inflation has been documented for more than four decades at the college level and even longer in secondary schools (Gose, 1997). For example, it is reported that GPAs increased .432 points in universities over the period from 1960 to 1979 (Juola, 1980). In another study that documented grade inflation during the period of 1969 to 1993, it was found that the number of A's given had quadrupled while the number of C's had dropped by 66 percent. In another study, GPAs were reported to have gone from an average of 3.07 in the mid-1980s to 3.34 in the mid-1990s, even though 2.00 is supposed to be average (Kamber, 2008a).

It has been suggested that grade inflation is due to a steady increase in the quality of students over the past thirty years (Bromley, Crow & Gibson, 1978). However, the decline in SAT and the ACT scores seems to indicate that current students are less qualified than their predecessors. It is insightful to note that the drop in scores has taken place during a time when educators have given much more attention to preparing students to take these tests, and have at their disposal written materials that have been specifically designed for this purpose. This suggests that the decline in ACT and SAT scores may well be due to grade inflation.

It appears that with grade inflation, students find it unnecessary to devote as much time to their studies to satisfy their quest for acceptable grades. With GPAs steadily increasing during a time when standardized test scores have substantially dropped, this seems to be the logical conclusion. In connection with this, Kamber (2008a) reports that even though college students are told that they should spend two hours outside of class for each hour in class (roughly thirty hours per week), only 8 percent of first-year students and 11 percent of seniors did so.

Causes suggested for grade inflation include recruitment competition and retention of students as well as internal policies that allow students to avoid being penalized by low grades, such as pass/fail options and lenient course withdrawal and retake policies (Biggs, 2008b). In addition, at the college level there is an increased reliance on adjunct and part-time faculty and an expanded use of student evaluations of teaching for hiring, tenure, promotion, and salary decisions (Kamber, 2008a). Student evaluations of faculty and efforts to promote self-concept development appear to be the most persuasive causes.

Faculty evaluations are more prominent in universities, while self-concept concerns are more likely in the public schools. University faculty members realize that giving poor grades is not in their economic best interest.

They justly conclude that low grades lead to low faculty ratings by students, with a corresponding reduction in class sizes (Beaver, 1997), and perhaps the eventual loss of their jobs.

The result is lower academic standards (Basinger, 1997), leaving students with a distorted view of their academic achievements and abilities (Baummeister, 1996). Consequently students come to believe that they are better prepared for the world of work than they actually are. Employers are thus less able to identify qualified candidates, and many must provide additional training for new employees (Gose, 1997). In the process, the credibility of universities is undermined, requiring other agencies to act as gatekeepers between school and certification.

Goldman (1985) claims that the consequences of grade inflation at the university are absolutely predictable. Eventually, undergraduate degrees will be viewed about the same as high school diplomas are today. As a result, some colleges will institute exit examinations to uphold the sagging value of their degrees. Predictably, business and industry will increasingly disregard college degrees in matters of placement and promotion, relying instead on their own in-house evaluations because it has become impossible to distinguish graduates who are excellent from those who are barely adequate (Biggs, 2008a).

Regarding the practice of students evaluating teaching, research has shown that they are unable to judge the validity of the content in instruction. Instead they attend to the expressiveness and seductiveness of the teacher's lecture (Johnson, 2003). Thus, they represent a defective source of information for ensuring the quality of instruction. Grade inflation due to the threat of negative teaching evaluations appears to be instrumental in lowering standards.

Sometimes it is suggested that grade inflation problems can be solved by shifting the task of evaluating and grading from the teacher to someone else (Hunt, 2008). This, of course, ignores the issue of whether or not a normal curve should serve as the basis for grading or that the grading process itself should be called into question. It is also suggested that the practice of students rating their teachers should be abandoned, given its lack of validity.

While grades appear to have less impact on students' futures than standardized test scores and other factors in the public schools, student ratings of professors continue to have an enormous effect on their income, tenure, and rank advancement. Students' ratings are almost the only source of information about teaching effectiveness that is routinely relied upon by those who make decisions about faculty teaching competency and rewards at the university level (Hunt, 2008).

The effect of grade inflation on students is even more devastating. They need learning experiences that they believe are of high quality. They cannot be expected to work hard at becoming educated unless they know what they are asked to do leads to important, fulfilling work in the future. However, with inflated grades, many students realize that what they are doing is not substantial and of high quality. But they are deceived into thinking that what schools expect is all that is needed. Consequently, students routinely perform far below their capability, and they know it (Glasser, 1998). They persist in low performance because that is all that is expected. They are without clear incentives to do better (Glasser, 1992).

It is noteworthy that in the public schools grade inflation has come about primarily in an effort to protect students from presumed self-concept problems that are believed to inevitably develop when high expectations are in place. Supposedly, grade inflation helps promote a more pleasant classroom atmosphere, protecting students from self-concept problems while at the same time enhancing achievement (Sykes, 1995). Actually, self-esteem plays only a minor role in academic performance.

Instead, what is referred to as earned self-esteem is needed; this comes about when students have to work hard to achieve learning goals. However, efforts to bolster self-concept actually interfere with its development (Baummeister, 1996). It has been concluded that most efforts to improve students' self-esteem have actually eroded it. This happens because of an emphasis on how students feel rather than on the quality of their work. If persistence and the need to meet challenges had been emphasized, fewer children would have suffered self-concept problems and resultant depression (Seligman, 1995).

Interestingly, during the period in which self-concept has been excessively promoted by reducing expectations and trying to provide students with artificially contrived success experiences, depression has grown in epidemic proportions, particularly among young adults and youth. People born in the early 1900s experienced depression at only a 1 percent rate by the time they were in old age. By 1925 the rate had risen to 4 percent, while in 1955 it had grown to 7 percent among people in their early twenties (Robins et al., 1984). It has also been found that 60 percent of women born in the early 1950s had experienced depression by the time they were thirty years old. By comparison, women born around 1910 experienced only a 7 percent rate of severe depression by the time they were in old age (Klerman et al., 1985).

It is insightful to observe that victims of depression are much younger than in earlier years. Individuals born in the 1930s typically experienced their first depression between ages thirty and thirty-five. In contrast, those born in 1956 were first depressed between the ages of twenty and twenty-five (Klerman et al., 1985).

There has also been a substantial increase in depression among adolescents and children. Thus, by age fourteen, 7.2 percent of adolescents born between 1972 and 1974 had suffered severe depression, as compared to 4.5 percent of those born between 1968 and 1971. The rate of extreme depressive disorders among twelve- to fourteen-year-olds in the southeastern United

States was reported to be 9 percent (Reich et al., 1987). Seligman (1995) has concluded that the increase is due to society's fear of damaging children's self-concepts if they experience stress; consequently they are shielded by teachers and parents from difficult experiences that ironically would have strengthened them and helped them avoid pessimism and depression.

Educators and others have feared that unless students' feelings of anger, sadness, and anxiety were cushioned, there would be dire consequences. However, these emotions motivate people to change themselves so they can achieve their goals. In the process they eliminate negative emotions. Depression occurs when people fail to achieve their goals, not in consequence of experiencing difficulties while working toward them (Seligman, 1995).

Intriguingly, local efforts to rectify the problems created by grade inflation seem always to be constrained by imperatives announced by the federal government. Also, grade inflation is supported by the fact that it is self-sustaining and addictive. The more a teacher, department, or an institution indulges in inflating grades, the more difficult it becomes to rigorously grade student achievement. Students come to depend on high grades, while teachers find some satisfaction in increased popularity for their role in issuing them. In addition, administrators and trustees at the college level, who have made student recruitment and retention key measures of institutional success, are reluctant to push for policies that may work against these goals (Kamber, 2008b).

It should be noted that in the process of increasing academic standards for universities, the Council of Higher Education Accreditation never included grade inflation as part of its agenda. The council indicated that it believed various institutions would find it intrusive and inappropriate for them to make prescriptive statements regarding grade distribution despite the fact that the council took a very active role in making prescriptive statements about assessment of student learning and other faculty responsibilities (Kamber, 2008b).

ALTERNATIVE ASSESSMENT

For years some educators have recognized the potential problems associated with grading their students, particularly grading on the curve. However, it has only been in recent years that this practice has come under careful scrutiny and recognized for its impropriety. Some teachers have reacted to this recognition by making modifications they hoped would lessen grades' negative impact. However, sufficient and necessary changes are usually beyond the reach of most classroom teachers.

Many teachers unwittingly inflate grades in an effort to soften negative impact on students without realizing they are simply creating a different problem. Others try to make grading more humane by involving students in the evaluation process. Some even allow their students to grade themselves. But after all is said and done, grades, with their accompanying negative baggage, are still generally administered. In most cases, grading responsibilities are part of teachers' contractual responsibility.

Though it may appear to be more humane to allow students to grade themselves, this practice can create unanticipated problems. For example, when students grade themselves, some overestimate their accomplishments while others underestimate them. This is perhaps no more a problem than that of teachers using invalid tests. However, it encourages students who are inclined to overestimate their accomplishments to distort the reality of which they are very much aware. They are tempted to create a lie in an effort to improve their comparative image among their peers.

Those who underestimate their success may worry about what others may say about them if they grade themselves as they honestly think. If students evaluated themselves without making comparisons to their peers, this would be less of a problem. Children have to see that making valid evaluations of their progress and achievements is in their own best interest. Distorting their assessments should be seen as personally detrimental.

Because of the problems with traditional testing and grading, some school districts have initiated what is referred to as authentic assessment. Rather than graded on the normal curve, students' academic accomplishments are evaluated according to especially high performance expectations. Their work is compared to the performances of writers, businesspeople, scientists, community leaders, designers, or historians. Rather than tests, their work consists of written essays, research proposals and reports, mock-ups, models, and the like (Wiggins, 1989). Some believe such expectations are too high. However, authentic assessments are more consistent with acceptable life expectations than traditional testing.

Obviously children don't need to be as capable as experts in the field, but they benefit from comparing their work to that of high quality. In this way, they can understand the kinds of standards that will eventually be applied to their work. This allows them to see the actual products from the world of work rather than trying to assess their capability from a test with limited validity. Most of the time the expectations they face are entirely different from the content of tests, but are more consistent with what they will eventually have to know and do in the adult world. Generally, authentic assessments cannot be made with tests.

One way to track student achievement is by using portfolios. This practice is becoming more widespread (Calfee & Perfumo, 1993). Portfolios contain such items as papers, research reports, artwork, and pictures of models, furniture, and houses students help build. Students decide for themselves which examples of their work to include. This makes it necessary that they learn how to validly assess their work. Their decisions regarding what to include are part of the evaluation process.

Because each student decides what to include in his or her portfolio, it is evident that what is collected will be significantly different from the work of their peers. It is, therefore, inappropriate for student portfolios to be compared and graded. Ironically, in some locations, teachers are asked to assign grades to portfolios even though these two assessment processes are fundamentally inconsistent with each other.

Portfolios can be assessed in different ways. Students may (1) assess their current work as compared to earlier efforts, (2) try to make comparisons with similar work by other individuals at the same age and experience level, (3) compare their efforts to those of professionals, and/or (4) compare the history of their progress to that of others. It seems appropriate to use all of these strategies to get a more comprehensive estimate of achievement. In this process, students can more fully take responsible ownership for documenting their learning.

In addition, with students making personal assessments, they can become more reflective about their own learning and achievement rather than depending on the opinions of others. They gain a better sense of themselves as learners and more fully understand what it takes to achieve excellence through self-regulation. Also, they learn how to validly assess their own learning. This is a benefit to them both in school and later in life (Athanases, 1997).

Some children who are evaluated exclusively by teachers develop an attitude of helplessness regarding what can happen to them in school. Thus, when they fail, they assume they can do nothing about it. Consequently they believe that making greater effort along with organizing themselves more carefully has very little effect on what they can accomplish (Smith & Price, 1996). Ironically, these children not only deny success once it occurs, they frequently act counterproductively to keep success from occurring. As mentioned in chapter 1, they sabotage their own success in order to avoid future expectations that exceed what they believe they can accomplish (Aronson & Carlsmith, 1962).

Rather that performing adequately, these students try to make their teachers believe they are doing their best. That is because teachers tend to punish students for noneffort. This leads children to engage in deceptive endeavors. They thread their way between the threatening extremes of high effort and no exertion at all. They believe they must at least appear to be working to avoid teacher punishment, but not exert themselves enough to risk public shame if they should try their best and fail. A plethora of excuses are commonly invented to maintain this precarious balance (Covington & Beery, 1976).

Modifying this perspective is very difficult, particularly in the schools where this frame of reference likely developed. This perspective comes from the practice of only teachers assessing student work. When this happens, students are inadvertently taught that their own assessments are inherently invalid.

In practice, evaluations vary from teacher to teacher, and for a single teacher from one assignment to the next. Because of this inconsistency, students eventually come to believe that their grades are a matter of luck or fate. This is illustrated in the experiences of most students—sometimes they work very hard and get low grades, while at other times they receive high grades with little effort. Once this view is established, no amount of praise for their efforts or success experiences will likely alter it. Rather, students with this mind-set must learn to make their own assessments and come to realize that their judgments are valid.

STUDENT SELF-EVALUATION

Self-evaluation is an essential element in learning communities. Of course, the issues are whether or not students can make valid assessments of their accomplishments and if it is to their benefit to do so. It is impossible for students to grade themselves on the traditional ABCDF system. That is because grades by definition represent comparative assessments. To do this, each student would have to know how their achievements compare to their fellow classmates'. But they don't have this information, either in traditional classrooms or in learning communities. Also, in learning communities, student achievements may be so different from other students', such comparisons are inconceivable. Even in traditional schools, if teachers individualized instruction as has been recommended for many years, neither they nor their students could make valid comparative assessments. The same is true in learning communities.

When comparative grading is not the issue, students can put together an assessment of their work with the purpose of making improvements by examining their present work as compared to previous efforts, analyzing similar work accomplished by others at their age level, scrutinizing the work of people with advanced training and experience as compared to their own, and looking at the history of their rate of progress as compared to others. Students need to be taught how to use criteria in making these judgments.

Students who have been exposed to traditional grading likely will need help making assessments that are not biased by ego-salving estimates of their performances. Students must learn to make honest appraisals without being influenced by the specters of grading that once held them bound. In learning communities, there is no useful purpose for children to even consider how their achievements fit into traditional grading. Excellence is unlikely when such comparisons are made. Without grading, students' self-concepts are less at risk, and consequently valid self-assessment is more certain.

What is the teachers' role in helping students learn to make valid self-assessments? Ongoing instruction is a necessity. Students will not quickly overcome the negative effects of being graded, nor their inclination to bias their appraisals of themselves. Teachers will need to repeatedly assure them that their judgments regarding their accomplishments should not be inflated as their inclinations might dictate.

They also need to learn that their work doesn't really lend itself to comparisons with the accomplishments of classmates. They can thus be encouraged to advance their own idiosyncratic learning agenda within their learning group without fearing they might make inappropriate choices. It is also improper for them to look at others' work in their learning group and judge its quality as compared to their own. Because students are encouraged to take on different roles in learning communities, no comparisons should even be attempted. Everyone's contribution should simply be valued and its virtue extolled.

There is no question that teachers need to examine students' portfolios and the personal evaluations they make of their work. The purpose of this is to satisfy themselves that students' assessments are reasonably accurate. They also need to teach them what is needed to improve their assessments. In doing this, it should be recognized that judgments about students' achievement satisfy different purposes. Some students may justifiably aspire to higher levels of accomplishment than others.

Students have various aspirations regarding their studies. Some want to reach a maximum achievement level in a particular class, while others may wish to emphasize other subjects. It is unrealistic to assume that all students have similar ambitions. Some intend to attend college, while others wish to use their learning experiences to prepare for other things. In learning communities these variations are acceptable. It is also possible that some students may change their minds about their goals. This is appropriate too. Part of a teacher's role is to have students periodically address any changes in what they plan to do after graduation.

All students have certain commonalities regarding what can be gained from school. For example, social competence, healthy family life, the ability to understand sophisticated information about political happenings, the nature of the physical and biological worlds, historical implications of current happenings, psychological phenomena, and the like are essential for all. Experience with the arts is also very important. The inquiry-oriented curricula of learning communities provides the proper orientation toward achieving

Chapter Five

The Need for Change

It is the opinion of many educators, parents, employers, politicians, and students that our current education system is failing not only in terms of the instructional program, but also in terms of school discipline. In many respects, this is due to schools' rigid, bureaucratic structure. It is judged ineffective in teaching all children. It was never envisioned to teach learners in all their diversity, discern each student's particular blend of needs and capabilities, and effectively defeat various obstacles to learning while avoiding student disruptiveness (Darling-Hammond, 1997).

Some may point to various improvements over the years, but there are also many problems. Though standardized test scores don't necessarily validly indicate problems, they at least register the fact that student scores in the United States are falling behind those in many other countries. Actually standardized tests are likely part of the problem. These tests are designed to promote higher standards, but they do not. In addition, standardized testing is accompanied by a plethora of abuses, including cheating on the part of teachers and administrators that lead to less effectiveness (Popham, 1999; Merrow, 2001; McNeil, 2000; Clinchy, 2001).

In reality many proposed school improvements fail to make fundamental changes to a system that year after year supports learning processes that are unnatural for children and that result in considerable dissatisfaction and outright failure. Take for example the large number of school dropouts. It is a stark reminder that something is not working. This, of course, is a symptom of underlying problems that have not been corrected, even though it has been known for many years where many of the issues lie.

One of the symptoms of this problem is the very high proportion of American high school students who do not take school or their studies seriously. Over one-third say they get through the day by goofing off with friends and disrupting learning in their classrooms. Two-thirds indicate that they have cheated on a school test during the past school year. Interestingly, the high school peer culture demeans academic accomplishment and scorns students who try to be successful in school.

It is alarming to note that parents are just as disengaged from their children's schools as are their children. More than half of the students indicate that their parents have no idea how they are doing in school. One-sixth of the parents report not caring whether or not their children get good grades (Steinberg, 1996). In the face of such information, it is commonly concluded that standards should be raised, or that students should spend more time in school. It is ironic that educators and others would recommend students do more of what they obviously find disengaging. It is no wonder that discipline problems significantly disrupt learning in many classrooms.

With the implementation of the No Child Left Behind Act (NCLB), a phenomenon referred to as "push-out" has been introduced. This describes the increased school dropout rates due to high test score accountability, which has inadvertently created incentives for school administrators to encourage low-scoring students to drop out, thus helping average test scores to rise (Losen, 2004). This increasingly takes place between the ninth and tenth grades (Abrams & Haney, 2004).

In addition, the number of students held back in the eighth grade has increased dramatically. About 70 to 80 percent of these students won't graduate. This is primarily due to high-stakes testing, which actually was promoted by the government publication of *A Nation at Risk* in 1983 and reemphasized by NCLB (Rodereck, 1994). The NCLB act required that states standardize their curricula and mandate standardized tests (Haerr, 2006). School districts responded by forcing teachers to teach to the test and in the process create standards that dictate shallow, facts-based content with no depth and no creative teaching (Poetter, 2006).

It is intriguing to note that in one school district with 25,000 students, 4,700 were eligible to transfer out of a failing school into a high-performing one as dictated by NCLB. Also, roughly 1,800 students had a right, due to low test scores, to title funds to obtain supplemental academic services. Only one child in each category opted for a change or additional help. This was because administrators discouraged these adjustments in various ways, using the rationale that they were protecting public financial resources. In connection with this, parents were told that they might not be able to transfer all their children to a new school and that transportation might not be available. Also, parents were required to meet with a school administrator and others to defend their desire for a change while at the same time being given reasons why the transfer was not desirable.

School officials in the above-mentioned district felt that with NCLB, they had been set up to fail and thus needed to take action to protect themselves.

They generally abhorred an accountability scheme that they believed disrupted their school assignment procedures, drained money from their coffers, and threatened their administrative autonomy (Howell, 2006).

It should be noted that standardized testing associated with NCLB is likely the reason for an increase in the popularity of homeschooling in recent years (Hammons, 2006). Students who decided to remain in school found disengaging conditions that tended to promote disinterest and misbehavior. Their lethargic detachment from learning as it existed in post-NCLB schools further derailed them from the potential for exciting learning.

As I think back on my own schooling experiences as compared with observations and experiences of thirty-six years as a public school teacher and teacher educator in the university, very little has changed regarding fundamental problems. It may not be nearly as common to see a bunch of keys whiz by your head because you were not paying attention as routinely occurred in my junior high school shop class, or for a disinterested student to be thumped on the head with the blunted middle finger of my math teacher for fooling around when he or she should have been working on assigned problems, but most of the problems that existed in the 1940s and 1950s are essentially the same as those children experience today. That is because most innovations involve superficial changes rather than addressing long-standing fundamental issues.

It is also the case that changes have not been based on educational research and democratic principles. Also, many teachers apparently still believe that students should learn primarily by simply absorbing information transmitted to them in the form of lectures, textbooks, and worksheets. In addition, though greater emphasis has been placed on democratic processes in the literature regarding classroom instruction, discipline still focuses primarily on teacher control through punitive measures or reward systems. Most teachers do not promote intellectual skills, moral development, or self-regulation.

Linda Darling-Hammond explains that forward-looking individuals have long envisioned entirely different kinds of schools, but their ideas have generally been ignored. They conceived of schools that were thoughtful, reflective, and engaging. Their basic learning orientation was one of shared inquiry. Students in these schools would feel sufficient support for their independent thinking and thus would be willing to take risks. In directing their own learning, students would be engaged in assessing their own ideas as well as the results of their own learning, and in the process would be able to develop a valid sense of the quality of their own work and that of their peers.

In such enlightened conditions, teachers would function more like coaches, mentors, wise advisors, and guides than information transmitters or gatekeepers. Students' uniqueness would be so personally valued that they would autonomously seek high standards, because in the process they would be able to satisfy their idiosyncratic needs as well as accentuate their own talents in a learning format that fit their own style.

Schools would be places where children would want to be because they not only found intellectual growth there, but also very caring teachers and peers. Such schools never become widely available in most communities because they exist in a policy environment that does little to support them and much to obliterate them. Furthermore, very little has been done to prepare teachers to teach in the complex ways required by learner-centered education.

In addition to this, most recommended changes have not been publicly supported. The public seems content with schools that perpetuate the same old problems (Darling-Hammond, 1997). It is as though to admit that the basic structure of schooling has serious problems somehow contaminates teachers and administrators personally as products of and perpetrators of a failing system. We are left with schools that are poorly understood by both policy makers and teachers and that graduate students who are ill-prepared for life in a complex, pluralistic democracy.

One example of the perpetuation of poor educational practice is the increase in the amount of homework assigned to children to get them better prepared for standardized tests. Even elementary school children are given homework assignments, though research shows this practice not only fails to promote achievement, it alienates children and makes them dislike school (Cooper, 1989).

At the secondary level, homework consists primarily of drill and practice for passing standardized tests. It is alarming to note that a direct relationship exists between the amount of homework and levels of anxiety, depression, anger, and other mood disturbances children suffer (Kouzma & Kennedy, 2002). Some suggest that homework helps students learn to take responsibility, build study skills, develop perseverance, follow directions, improve neatness and completeness, and increase self-discipline and initiative along with independence. This is not supported by research (Kohn, 2006).

OBSTACLES TO INTELLECTUAL DEVELOPMENT

The single most important objective of public school education is preparation for life in democratic communities. Yet doing what is necessary to prepare children to live effectively in a democratic society seems to be a subversive activity from some perspectives. It appears reasonable that schools should prepare students to think and perform at high levels and that their behavior would have moral uprightness. However, in practice many in authority think that educating a group of independent-minded young people is a threat to the rules that they erroneously assert govern life generally.

Others fear that independent-thinking children may upset the social order from which they personally benefit. In reality, they fear they may lose control, and that empowering students may make them less pliable and more rebellious and thus harder to manage. They fail to realize that it is excessive control that generates disruptiveness. The result is that true preparation in schools for democratic living is extremely rare. These bureaucratically organized educational institutions disenfranchise teachers who wish they were allowed to work more effectively with children rather than just covering the prescribed curriculum. They also cause students to feel alienated from their teachers (Poplin & Weres, 1992).

It should be noted that higher-achieving students come from states that do not regulate education regularly and do not have statewide testing systems. Moreover, these states have boards for regulating professional standards to promote quality teaching. These boards have enacted rigorous requirements for teacher education and licensing (National Commission on Teaching and America's Future, 1996).

In many states, teachers are expected to implement teacher-proof curricula. They are thus left with little or no decision-making responsibilities in the classroom. Stripped of the role of making valid pedagogical decisions based on what transpires in complex classrooms, many teachers tend to almost mindlessly institute the low-level learning expectations encompassed by the accompanying imposed standards. Consequently, students experience teaching that does not cater to their personal needs and learning dispositions, nor help them to develop morally and acquire the levels of thinking needed to live successfully in a democratic society (McNeil, 1988a). It appears to be more important to create minimum standards with which to sort students.

When students only have to memorize information and parrot it back on standardized tests, little capacity is developed to use the information in novel ways or to connect what they are learning with other concepts and principles. Learning consists of isolated events with few connections and no relevant applications. Essentially their knowledge is inert. It cannot be called upon, transformed, or meaningfully applied to problems and situations commonly faced by students presently and in the future (Brown, 1994; Gardner, 1991; Good & Brophy, 1986; Schoenfeld, 1988).

Information that is easily transmitted by teachers tends to be disconnected from experience. But when children engage in self-directed, hands-on learning, which is aimed at higher-order thinking, they are better able to remember and apply what they have learned. They become more skilled in making appropriate connections between current and previous understandings and drawing on personal experiences to enhance meaning and understand how to apply what they learn to concrete problems (Shulman, 1987; Darling-Hammond, 1993).

It is ironic that the bureaucratic effort to improve school accountability through standardized testing often impedes student learning. The fact remains that children have different needs and personalized ways of learning, and tend to learn at different rates depending on the circumstances. Standardized tests are not designed to deal with such indisputable differences.

Effective teaching must be consistent with how children actually learn. However, bureaucratic decisions force teachers to ignore natural learning in favor of implementing the standard curriculum in a prescribed way, not because it is appropriate, but because it can be readily measured. Interestingly, teachers' knowledge about learning can actually be a liability when it conflicts with these imposed expectations (Darling-Hammond, Wise & Pease, 1983).

Increasingly, prescriptive educational policies that are created through the political process in the name of public accountability effectively reduce the schools' responsiveness to the needs of students and their learning inclinations. Not only do students get frustrated, their parents do as well. These frustrations are in part responsible for the current discontent with public education and encourage many to break loose from the system through home schools, vouchers, charter schools, and other arrangements.

Bureaucratically based decisions about schools are unable to provide help with something as complex as teaching and learning. Dictating school practices leaves the schools unprepared to deal with the complicated issues confronted by teachers each day in the classroom. Bureaucratic management is incapable of directing an appropriate education for students who do not fit the mold upon which prescriptive practices are based. These supposed solutions to problems in school will predictably fail because effective teaching is not routine, students are not passive recipients of direction and instruction, and the daily classroom operations are not simple and predictable and consequently cannot be standardized (Darling-Hammond, 1997).

Rather, teaching is very complex work, perhaps the most complicated work we do, and is characterized by simultaneity, multidimensionality, and unpredictability (Jackson, 1968; Lortie, 1975). When students don't fit the structure, they often become frustrated and rebel. It should be reiterated that discipline problems are more a problem of school failure than inherent student disruptiveness.

EFFECTS OF ADMINISTRATIVE STRUCTURES ON LEARNING

There is little question that excessive structure adversely affects learning and classroom propriety. Flexibility, adaptability, and creativity are among the most important traits for teacher effectiveness (Schalock, 1979; Darling-Hammond, Wise & Pease, 1983). This kind of teaching stimulates higher-order thinking far more than teaching that focuses on extensive preplanning and rigid adherence to lesson objectives and coverage of facts (Zahorick, 1970).

Much higher achievement levels on complex performance tasks have been found among students who experience active learning in real-world contexts that call for higher-order thinking, consideration of alternatives, use of core ideas, and various modes of inquiry (Newman, Marks & Gamoran, 1995). Students so occupied are far less likely to disrupt instruction.

McNeil (1988a) indicates that when bureaucratic controls dictate the nature of teaching, the curricula are usually trivialized by teachers, thus undermining valid educational practices. In response to administrative directives, teachers tend to increase structure in their classrooms, thereby controlling their students just as administrators control them.

Then when students consider their school experiences trivial and not sufficiently realistic and credible, they comply with teacher expectations in minimal ways and fail to achieve the excellence of which they are capable. When this happens, principals conclude that student apathy is brought about by boring, uninspired teaching and fail to see that in reality it is the result of their controlling administrative practices. Ironically, they commonly react by imposing even more restraints, thereby trying to solve the problem with its cause.

In addition, when schools exercise bureaucratic constraints, tension develops because of the contradictory goals of educating students and controlling them. When teachers are over-controlled, they feel disenfranchised because their suggestions regarding how to improve teaching are ignored. While administrators may claim that their focus is on student excellence, they tend to emphasize minimum standards instead. Teachers respond to this by expecting less of students academically and accepting minimal student compliance with rules and regulations. Rather than expecting students to gather and interpret critical conceptual information, teachers instead require them to simply memorize prescribed lists of unrelated facts.

McNeil's (1988a) research reveals the fact that when teachers encounter excessive administrative control and fail to find support for their personal autonomy as school professionals, they tend to create their own aberrant domain of authority. Their reaction is to tightly control course content through dictatorial classroom routines along with teaching strategies that emphasize carefully organized lectures and objective tests. This, of course, provokes student resistance. The result is more classroom discipline problems and more consequent irrational control tactics.

McNeil (1988b) discovered that teachers were less controlling when they were less controlled themselves. They promoted more and better student learning and continued to learn and improve themselves. The relative autonomy provided to teachers and students constitutes one of the most necessary changes to really improve education.

The conditions described by McNeil (1988b) usually occur when efforts are made by administrators to help schools become smooth-running organizations and to meet minimum standards. The effect is for teachers to gradually eliminate meaningful learning experiences and parcel out course content in the form of manageable facts contained on simple worksheets and handouts. Thus, a vicious cycle of lowering expectations is set in motion, and the school begins to lose its legitimacy in the eyes of students as a justifiable place for serious study and learning.

These consequences come from the compromising of authentic learning as a result of school administrators yielding to pressures imposed on them from education departments, boards of education, and various special interest groups. They are also influenced by school codes and regulations prescribed by state legislatures as well as national imperatives designed to manipulate schools through funding inducements. These influences are often contradictory, coercive, and counterproductive. To promote better schooling, administrators have to resolutely resist such pressures.

HIGH-STAKES TESTS AND LEARNING

The usual way outside entities try to manipulate schooling is through high-stakes testing. As indicated in chapter 4, the purpose of these tests is to force greater adherence to national standards that are assumed to be good and appropriate. Not only have the standards been seriously questioned, the means for determining compliance has as well. Even if it is assumed that the standards are appropriate, these tests themselves appear to be a threat to the standards (Merrow, 2001). More importantly, they are a threat to the quality of education. It is essential for educators to carefully assess the use of high-stakes tests and their inherent harm to education. For instance, they should avoid undermining the quality of the curriculum through "teaching to the test." They should also shun the common practice of discriminating against various groups of students because of the pressure associated with high-stakes testing (Clinchy, 2001; McNeil, 2000).

In addition to promoting unprofessional excesses by administrators and teachers, high-stakes testing has undesirable effects on students. First, it greatly diminishes the breadth and fullness of the curriculum and often limits teaching and learning to less-important information. Second, students are restricted from involvement in curriculum decision making. Third, high-stakes tests condition students to follow teacher directions and learn in pre-scribed ways, thus eliminating opportunities to become engaged in inquiry investigations. Fourth, students become oriented toward meeting minimum standards instead of striving for excellence. Fifth, high-stakes tests are not valid measures of high-level intellectual capacities and life-preparation skills. Sixth, high-stakes tests fail to measure many of the valid interests and accomplishments of students. Seventh, standardized tests fail to measure problem-solving skills, work habits, and such virtuous dispositions as hones-ty, dependability, and loyalty (Goodlad, 2002).

Armstrong (1998) indicates that high-stakes testing is probably the single most inhibiting influence on the functioning of children's genius. He says that genius involves curiosity, playfulness, imagination, creativity, wonder, wisdom, inventiveness, vitality, sensitivity, flexibility, humor, and joy. Obvi-ously worksheets and tests can never capture the spirit or essence of these qualities.

In the process of preparing for high-stakes tests, an excessive amount of time is consumed that could more profitably be spent learning what is really important (Meier, 2002). In addition, critical knowledge and skills usually cannot be measured by multiple-choice test items, the preferred testing for-mat of high-stakes tests. Consequently, learning activities focus almost ex-clusively on what can be simply measured rather than concepts and princi-ples that knowledgeable teachers have traditionally considered important.

Some of the skills that fail to be considered in high-stakes testing are critical life skills such as problem solving and decision making. Many of the problems children face require more sophisticated decision-making prowess than they currently possess. This is shown by the poor decisions they make both in and out of school. Many times the complexity of life situations requires the ability to examine various components that are in conflict with each other. For example, many young people are involved with gangs, sexual promiscuity, and drug abuse. Without appropriate intellectual development they cannot see the big picture and understand the consequences of such activity. Many also do not apply themselves to their schoolwork.

It is clear that some youths do not understand the implications and conse-quences of much of their behavior. They seem to consider only such ele-ments as peer acceptance, not realizing that certain potentially devastating outcomes also exist that can permanently affect their lives. They find it hard to weigh all the potential effects in the balance. Sometimes these kinds of activities are simply chalked up to rebellion. However, they are just as likely to be the result of poor decision-making skills.

Another part of the problem is the failure of schools to help children make plans toward critical life goals. Without such objectives in mind, children have nothing to guide them in their decision making. Add to this the fact that they have no training in problem solving, and the outcome is a recipe for making regrettable decisions.

Good decision-making skills include a life plan that has been carefully organized around viable long-term goals that have personal meaning for the individual and predictably provide for a lifetime of satisfying, carefully thought out experiences and consequences. In the schools, such goals can have the benefit of appropriate teacher guidance and the use of sophisticated problem-solving skills. Decisions that are made with such goals in mind effectively lead to a fuller, more satisfying existence.

Problems can't always be avoided, so when they appear, they need to be dealt with effectively. In many cases good decision making helps the individual avoid problems that unwittingly occur. It also helps provide students with the sensitivity needed to avoid creating their own problems. The development of personal problem-solving skills also has a social benefit, because personal problems almost always have social components that impact society at large. In effectively dealing with personal problems, students simultaneously help society avoid many problems with which it might otherwise be plagued.

It seems almost ludicrous that such a recommendation needs to be made. Yet the widespread use of high-stakes tests makes this necessary. Validating the means for assessing student achievement must wait upon a thoughtful analysis of the capabilities needed in a complex democratic society. The usual task of simply memorizing information is inconsistent with these modern-day requirements. Children need many capabilities that simply cannot be validly measured through commonly used testing formats. These must be acquired within real-life contexts so that students can more adequately make valid applications (Glasser, 1986).

It should also be pointed out that the range of students' interests is much broader than those represented in high-stakes tests. However, the legitimacy of any particular interest or skill is constrained by whether or not it is included on the tests. Those not covered by the tests are by definition considered unimportant. Not only does this limit what is considered valid, but it will likely limit the students' success in taking the exam, particularly if students' interests have successfully drawn their attention away from the subjects covered by the exams. The result is for students to be penalized for having interests different from those covered by these exams. Instead of enlarging personal capacity, test-taking purposes are emphasized. These purposes should be compared with what is forfeited when personal interests are so constrained.

THE NEED FOR MORAL TEACHERS

Another critical change needed in the schools is for teachers to become more explicit examples of moral living and to provide students an environment in which to become more caring, moral people themselves, along with learning how to successfully participate in democratic communities (Fenstermacher, 1990; Meier, 2002; Noddings, 2002). Moral people exhibit such virtues as tolerance, open-mindedness, honesty, fairness, justice, and even-handedness.

Students involved in this kind of preparation are much less likely to disrupt school or engage in extremely violent behavior, as has become increasingly common in modern schools. Often these problems are gang related or reactions to bullying. Obviously it is imperative that the neglect and alienation that promote a proliferation of gang activity and bullying along with drug and alcohol consumption be eliminated (Hyman & Perone, 1998).

It has been pointed out that predominating characteristics of American society may be responsible for many of the difficulties encountered in public schools (Goodlad, 1994). One of these attributes is increased mobility. Loss of a sense of community is often the result, in addition to diminishing friendships. Because humans are social by nature, the lack of a strong supporting community tends to erode one's sense of well-being and connectedness along with interpersonal commitments normally associated with community membership. Moreover, the moral imperatives associated with community living become less well-defined and much less important.

Historically it has been discovered that in their later stages of development, teaching in the world's major civilizations became less morally focused, with more emphasis given to forms, rituals, and technical knowledge. This result has been associated with the decadence throughout these societies. In earlier years, each of these societies stressed intimate tutor/learner relationships in education. Person-to-person interactions were promoted, and the primary goal of education was for teachers to encourage moral development and to practice moral principles themselves. It is well recognized that failure to promote moral development had grave ramifications for students in these societies (Meyers, 1968).

The Nature of Moral Education

Moral education emphasizes such themes as proper social conduct and character development along with diligence, respect for elders, community responsibility, personal integrity, and similar virtues. Today the role of teachers in providing a moral education for their students has been subdued in deference to the prevailing secular—and even antireligious—intellectual climate. Rather than viewed as essential to moral education, teachers are seen as highly skilled technicians who provide students with technical information. However, teachers' moral role in instruction is critical in helping to create an ethical, properly functioning society.

Because children lack experience, they are usually incapable of defending themselves from negligent or selfish teachers. Simply put, they need moral nurturing if they are to become committed, fully functioning adults. Irresponsible or careless teaching is likely to have profound negative effects on children's moral growth and development (Wynne, 1995). Such conditions are inherent in the NCLB act, given the many corrupting activities of school administrators and teachers who try to avoid the punitive consequences associated with students' failure to meet test standards.

Teaching must be seen by educators as a moral endeavor because of its significant impact on the young. Moral considerations regarding what is fair, right, just, and virtuous must be integrated into all that transpires in the schools. It is because students are young and immature and limited in sensitivity and judgment that it is necessary for teachers themselves to be imbued with moral attitudes and behavior (Fenstermacher, 1990). Unfortunately this is not ordinarily the case.

Considerable emphasis has been given to restructuring education, but little attention has been devoted to the moral enlightenment of youth, the encouragement of effective thinking skills, the promotion of judgment, and the development of indispensable human virtues. Rather, the emphasis is on the status and prestige of teachers, testing for teacher competence and student achievement, and on career advancement (Fenstermacher, 1990). It seems self-evident that the induction of students into moral living requires teachers themselves to be examples of moral living. Both in teaching and in their personal lives they need to be the epitome of moral thinking and living (McHenry, 2000; Noddings, 2002).

One of the ways that teachers can help cultivate the moral development of children is through reciprocity. This involves shared accountability for student learning. Unfortunately, teachers are ordinarily held accountable when students in their classes fail to learn. This has been especially so since the enactment of NCLB. It is explicitly assumed that teachers can somehow ensure that even the most recalcitrant students learn effectively regardless of their uncooperative attitudes or the existence of outside negative influences. Thus, even though parents may be uncooperative, or students may come from homes or community situations that subvert education, teachers are still expected to counter all of these influences.

However, without shared responsibility, students cannot be counted on to do their best to learn effectively. This is particularly difficult when teachers are held accountable for student learning even though decisions about the curriculum and the learning process are increasingly made far away from the school by individuals who may not have any idea about the learning issues in particular classrooms. When even teachers are not empowered to make decisions about school curricula, it is not possible for this important task to be shared with students.

Many times those who make decisions that significantly affect the learning process are not sufficiently schooled in the particulars regarding teaching and learning. Yet it is naively assumed that their decisions are valid and should be binding on teachers. The result is for teachers to increasingly be held accountable for employing tactics they may not professionally support. Outside policy makers expect teachers to teach as directed without an opportunity to provide input regarding curricular decisions (Darling-Hammond, 1997; Meier, 2002).

Teachers as Moral Examples

If teachers are expected to be moral examples, they must be empowered with appropriate decision making in the classroom. By the same token, students must share in the decision process. Appropriate reciprocity demands that there should be an appropriate balance regarding student and teacher input in the learning process. When students are not involved, the learning process is subverted and their accountability role undermined.

It is morally fallacious to expect teachers to teach as directed and simultaneously have bureaucrats and administrators at various levels transfer all responsibility for student learning to them. If teachers are to be held accountable, they must be allowed to make appropriate decisions. If students are to be held responsible for their own learning, and it is necessary that they must if they are to learn effectively, then it is necessary that reciprocity be the guiding principle.

Without shared involvement, students cannot be counted on to do their part. And disenfranchised students not only fail to effectively learn, they are inclined to sabotage the learning of their peers. Teachers need sufficient autonomy to make important decisions regarding their classes, particularly those that help empower their students through shared responsibility for learning. This generally requires less interference from school administrators and fewer restrictions from state boards and other control-oriented entities.

Research shows that instead of protecting students from risk, some of these common school policies put them further at risk, intensifying the problems of children and youth who are already in desperate circumstances. Many of the difficulties students suffer are within the power of classroom teachers to solve, such as problems associated with grouping and tracking practices, inappropriate expectations, and poor curricular and instructional decisions (Goodlad, 1994).

Decisions that come from outside the classroom make it difficult for teachers to promote moral student behavior. Moral decision making must always incorporate personal autonomy; otherwise, the decisions that are made are not moral ones. That is the reason that both teachers and students must be empowered in the decision-making process. As long as regulatory decisions come from outside the classroom, there is little hope that students will be able to develop moral, self-regulating capacities, and as long as they fail to do so, they will be unprepared for life in democratic communities.

When children are empowered in moral learning communities, they become valued group members and become involved in caring relationships and meaningful learning experiences for which they increasingly take responsibility. The result is for them to assume greater ownership and achieve at higher levels of excellence.

Student moral development is essentially an inquiry process with teachers taking on a role as facilitator in which they sometimes act as the devil's advocate to promote reflective thinking, move students toward greater autonomy, and empower them to think for themselves. Students can thus learn to draw appropriate inferences, clarify their thoughts, define concepts, and make value judgments. They can consider the thinking of others and in the process create more elaborate schemata of knowledge (Russell, 2007).

Again, a learning community is the most useful instructional format for developing critical thinking and for creating a society in which excellence and behavioral responsibility flourish. The goal of the community is to have children transcend exclusively thinking on their own and through interactions with others create more complex, realistic conceptions of the world and thus learn the credible implications for their goals and behavior. Children are thus able to engage in forms of reasoning not available to them individually (Lipman, 1991).

Within a community students learn how to integrate personal desires with community values and expectations. In this process it is critical for students to express personal views even if they appear divergent from the group. These expressions should never be sacrificed for the sake of peace and harmony. When harmony is overemphasized, a caring community may evolve, but it would not be a moral one (Power & Higgins-D'Alessandro, 2008). The goal is to educate children for democratic living and through their ethical inquiry and discussions acquire virtuous habits (Russell, 2007). Students so educated are more likely to reach out into the larger society and become connected with accomplished adults, who can help initiate students into the broader communities they represent.

Unfortunately, the culture currently being created in schools has a tenuous moral base, one that is dominated by test-based accountability rather than preparation for democratic living, and thus more likely to be counterproductive so far as moral education is concerned (Strike, 2008). If schools in a democratic society do not validly support the principles of democratic living, they are either socially useless or socially dangerous. They are likely to educate students who tend to go their way and become indifferent to the obligations of citizenship. Alarmingly, these schools are likely to educate people to become enemies of democracy—people who fall prey to demagogues and who back movements and rally around leaders who are hostile to a democratic way of life. According to Apple and Beane (1995), such schools are either futile or subversive and have no legitimate reason for existence.

In the social arena decisions are strongly influenced by norms. When people make choices, they commonly take others' beliefs into account, thus gaining insights regarding how they are likely to react to decisions. Emotions, preferences, values, and beliefs along with social bonds and obligations are critical in decision making that involves other people. Shared values and beliefs ordinarily shape our expectations and interactions with others. Without the ability to satisfy common expectations, trust and continued involvement are not possible.

Various communities in which the individual holds membership shape thinking and regulate successful interactions, and consequently need satisfaction. Because group norms influence choice, self-interest has to be moderated for people to interact successfully. Thus, selflessness is one of the critical attitudes encouraged in learning communities so that social connections can be maintained and important needs addressed.

In developing moral behavior, serious reservations should be addressed regarding extrinsic rewards. These rewards are given in an effort to shape student behavior. However, as already mentioned, the development of moral behavior depends on free choice. Extrinsic rewards are given to control student behavior rather than having them govern themselves. Consequently, rewards are at odds with moral development. It is better that intrinsic motivation is employed. This is motivation from within, where activities are perceived as meaningful and are sustained independently of extraneous external factors.

Motivation can also be shaped by moral ties that emerge from the individual's acceptance of duties and obligations toward others as well as efforts to learn that are derived from commitments regarding shared values and beliefs. Moral ties tend to be grounded more in cultural norms and expectations than in personal gratification, and consequently are usually stronger motivators than either extrinsic or intrinsic rewards. For example, students are usually more highly motivated while undertaking group projects such as pollution cleanup efforts or zero tolerance for illegal drugs than while preparing for tests. Keep in mind that it is commitment to the group and their shared beliefs that drives such undertakings (Sergiovanni, 1994).

Learning communities depend on teachers who have internalized principles consistent with society at large to provide the moral guidance and instruction needed in the classroom (Noddings, 2002). Research by Johnson (1990) indicates that public school teachers ordinarily enter the teaching profession with purposes consistent with principles that support the development of learning communities. Interestingly, private school teachers maintain this value orientation while their public school counterparts move away from attitudes that support learning communities and promote moral development.

Private school teachers maintain an identity that emphasizes bonding with others and sharing a common habitat, thereby developing a sense of neighborliness and kinship. While the relationship between private school teachers and their students is characterized by collegiality and understanding about what is shared and the obligations associated with these connections, public school teachers tend to develop a contractual value orientation. Their connections with students are contrived instead of authentic and result in students feeling disconnected and isolated (Johnson, 1990).

In his research, Johnson (1990) also discovered that private school teachers were more likely than public school teachers to have cultural bonds with others in the school. They expressed less ambiguous descriptions of their school's goals and purposes and were able to articulate shared values with precision. In addition, they were able to describe in detail how their own values were consistent with the school's traditions and aspirations.

In contrast, public school teachers rarely expressed the defining nature of cultural bonds. They described the schools in which they worked as having diverse purposes, vague histories, spurious traditions, and an uncommitted stance toward values. It appears that over time public schools successfully move teachers toward an isolationist orientation regarding their students and the school generally. The issue is whether or not public schools have any interest in helping students acquire authentic values to ensure their success in democratic communities. If so, drastic changes will be required. It will necessitate the formation of democratic learning communities that are staffed by caring teachers who are given sufficient autonomy to truly incorporate moral education in the classroom.

Moral Development and Communities

Human beings need to participate in communities. Schools need to change so as not to subvert this need as they commonly do when they dictate excessive structure and alienate students and teachers. Humans have a basic need to belong, to be connected to others, and to identify with a common set of values that give direction and meaning to life. Without common mores, values, goals, and norms, people are alienated from others and themselves. Ultimately they feel disassociated from society and become socially and personally disillusioned. Learning communities provide an antidote to such possibilities. This learning configuration encourages the development of a collective conscience along with moral awareness and the emergence of mutual obligation (Durkheim, 1964).

Community brings about duty and attachment along with self-determination. Duty helps the individual achieve a sense of self-constraint in consequence of feeling obligated to the community. Attachment denotes the sense of membership, commitment to group norms, and the development of a unique community identity. Self-determination is achieved when personal agency becomes integrated within a strong sense of awareness regarding the importance of duty and the fulfillment associated with attachment to the community (Durkheim, 1964).

Educators must deal with the fact that students cannot fulfill their needs outside community involvement. When their needs go unmet, they commonly disengage from learning and stoke classroom disruptions. Most children are unaware that fulfilling their needs depends on a role that helps other group members satisfy their needs as well. They need proper instruction to achieve this understanding. They must come to realize that they can fulfill their needs only when a reciprocal need-satisfaction scenario is adhered to by everyone.

Within a learning community, children can be taught that failures to help others achieve need satisfaction will unquestioningly undermine fulfillment of their own needs. For learning communities to successfully operate, members must be able to achieve an appropriate level of need satisfaction while realizing that this requires a degree of sacrifice on their part. They must become committed to looking after the interests of others. The community itself must be valued for what it can offer its members.

Because the community is so essential, all members must help maintain it. To be successful group members should not coerce, punish, manipulate, boss, criticize, blame, nag, or badger each other. Instead they must choose to care for others, listen carefully to what they say, support their learning and research, as well as befriend and trust them (Glasser, 1984).

NEEDED CHANGES

To prepare children for a valid life in a democratic society, substantial changes are needed in the way schools operate. Currently they represent an antithesis of what is required. However, making necessary changes will not be easy. School practices have a long tradition in consequence of resisting change over the years. Unfortunately, much about how they operate has become an accepted, valued routine. This is in part due the ease of employing such tactics rather than teaching approaches that require individualization.

Also, in traditional schools a greater priority is given to measuring student achievement on standardized tests than to properly conceptualizing education. It is erroneously assumed that both teaching and learning can be improved when test results are used as a stimulus rather than employing changes that articulate with reasoned decisions about teaching and learning and have the benefit of a long research history.

Commonly, educators find it hard to imagine changes beyond minor adjustments. Often it doesn't occur to them that change is needed. In addition, making substantive changes is very difficult and time-consuming. Also, to admit that changes are needed labels one as having been ineffective. To most teachers this is an attack on their sense of well-being if not their character. They are more likely to become defensive than to enthusiastically make necessary adjustments. Rather than entertaining possible improvements, they are inclined to recklessly attack them.

Most of the changes teachers find acceptable are of the superficial kind. These modifications don't really require them to alter much of what they currently do. Unfortunately, because of this attitude, educators rarely examine what is really ailing schools, preferring instead to focus on shallow, easily applied modifications, even though it can't be verified that these proposed changes can successfully solve the problems. Suggestions that are usually implemented don't really change anything. They are akin to a physician who treats symptoms instead of addressing the causes of disease.

One of the common scenarios for reform is a plea to return to "the basics." Somehow it is thought that this will cure everything. It is interesting that no one usually asks whether or not the basics that are so highly treasured in traditional education ever were the best education for anyone (Noddings, 2002). Unfortunately, a return to basics ordinarily emphasizes the need for schools to meet prescribed standards that are enforced through high-stakes testing without first verifying that the standards relate to meaningful, valid learning. Ironically, even if all concerned agreed on the standards and even managed to create valid tests, we are still left with little evidence that what schools teach matters in the real world (Merrow, 2001).

If time and effort were taken to validate the appropriateness of prescribed curricula, and this was done within the context of its value to students along with incorporating a learning environment consistent with the way children actually learn, greater assurance could possibly be obtained regarding their inherent usefulness. But, of course, this has never been done.

Schooling has not only changed very little in the past one hundred years, it has not been seriously examined in terms of becoming more relevant in our modern, complex society. This suggests that it is not deemed necessary to change school practices even though there is a well-understood need to replace the traditional fact-based, rote-dominated structures with those that help develop intellect, necessary decision-making skills, social sensitivities, and moral values.

In recent years there have been calls for change of a more substantive nature. However, they are commonly viewed as being too liberal and expecting too much from children regarding how effectively they can manage their own affairs in preparation for entry into democratic communities. Likewise little confidence is expressed regarding the ability of teachers to appropriately manage such educational experiences.

Changes that support information processing and inquiry are seriously questioned because it is falsely assumed that students benefit more from accumulating facts than from thinking effectively and solving problems, or that memorizing facts can without appropriate problem-solving experiences somehow promote higher-level intellectual development. Anyone who carefully examines what happens in schools must admit that their fact-accumulating purposes are a reality and that intellectual development and problem-solving skills have taken a backseat to knowledge assimilation.

In addition, current schooling is essentially unconcerned with values and development of the skills essential for life in democratic communities. Schools are still administered as they always have been, with hierarchical decision making. Policies are created at the top by individuals and groups far removed from the daily operation of classrooms and oblivious to what is really required to prepare children for life in complex democratic societies. These decisions are filtered down through various levels where they tend to be translated into rigid rules and procedures with less credence given to teacher decision making in individual classrooms. Students are also denied any role in deciding how and what they learn (Darling-Hammond, 1997).

Various changes have been recommended to help alleviate problems in schools and help them adjust to current economic, social, and cultural realities (McHenry, 2000). Interestingly the changes recommended are substantially different from those made in earlier times (Smith, 2001). In the past, changes such as flexible schedules, site-based management, teacher-proof materials, team teaching, and tracking were proposed. More fundamental changes are now recommended that deal with underlying elements of natural learning processes.

The conception of the teacher's role is also being greatly modified. Thus, it is recommended that instruction focus on higher-order cognitive functioning, which goes beyond simple recall, recognition, and reproduction of transmitted information to an approach that promotes intellectual experiences such as evaluation, analysis, and synthesis along with formulating arguments, ideas, and intellectually based performances (Darling-Hammond, 1997). Teachers are encouraged to have their students engage in extensive, in-depth inquiry experiences that have current meaning in their lives, rather than limiting instruction to the assimilation of huge amounts of factual information (McHenry, 2000; Smith, 2001).

With these kinds of changes, the evaluation system will also have to be revised. Instruments that measure simple recall will have to be replaced by those that address higher cognitive processes. Greater importance will need to be given to self-evaluation and portfolios. More sophisticated measures will be needed to determine depth of understanding and allow students to apply their skill and understanding to personally meaningful activities (Glickman, 1993).

Assessments should help determine students' intellectual progress rather than simply making comparisons between students regarding information recall. Evaluation will need to take into account considerable student input and choice regarding their learning activities. Measurement instruments cannot be standardized and still assess the fundamental aspect of the learning process that involves student choice and group decision making. They must be able to determine the value of teachers and students working together around personally meaningful, authentic problems (Darling-Hammond, 1997).

Researchers also recommend that schools foster experiences for students that are truly democratic, that emphasize caring to promote a greater sense of community among students, teachers, and administrators. In current schools, it has been found that relationships between students and their teachers are characterized by mistrust manifested in authoritarian treatment, demeaning statements, and petty rules that many students will break sooner or later (Darling-Hammond, 1997; Noddings, 2002; McNeil, 1988b).

Schools must also include students' families and the community at large to offer learning experiences that provide a genuine understanding of how democratic communities actually work (Meier, 2002). Students need to be authentically involved in helping to solve community problems that can affect them. For example, they may address problems such as pollution, care of the elderly, drug dealing, gang activity, and public violence. They must be involved in making decisions regarding real community problems (Glickman, 1993).

In learning communities, teaching is much different than in the traditional classrooms. To be effective, teachers must be empowered with far more decision-making opportunities than most currently enjoy (Bohn & Sleeter, 2000). It is generally conceded that current teacher training programs are deficient in preparing teachers for the enhanced role they must occupy. As already pointed out, at the present time they are trained as information transmitters with little moral responsibility.

Because of the role they must employ, morality should be a central feature of teacher training. They must be able to help their students choose and hold visions of what is good, and thus prepare them to responsibly participate in and benefit from autonomous living in society as it presently exists (Bull, 1990).

To reiterate, moral behavior is impossible without the requisite level of autonomy both for teachers and their students. Also, teachers must have acquired appropriate moral attributes to be able to help their students become moral people. Thus, they must be honest if they are to teach their students to be honest, generous if they expect generosity, and diligent if they hope their students will demonstrate diligence. Students must observe their teachers thinking critically while in their presence, providing a template for their own development of critical thinking (Fenstermacher, 1990).

Moral instruction must be intentional rather than a hoped-for incidental outcome of instruction. Otherwise its development will be seriously thwarted (Noddings, 2002). Learning communities provide an excellent format for moral education so long as the environment they create is authentic and appropriately connected to real community living (Meier, 2002).

Chapter Six

Instruction and Discipline in Learning Communities

Over the years greater emphasis has been placed on promoting democratic principles in school instruction and discipline. However, in many respects, schools have remained very much the same, particularly in terms of rigid control exercised over children in terms of what they learn and how they should behave. As explained in earlier chapters, this has been the result of many factors, including initiatives by the federal and state governments, management procedures, and the failure of educators to employ teaching-learning practices consistent with student learning inclinations, needs, and behavior.

The mismatch between schooling approaches and the reality of student learning inclinations and motivation as well as need satisfaction has resulted in teaching-learning situations that turn many students off and provoke others to rebel. The curriculum offered to students essentially consists of elements students find neither useful nor motivating because schooling bypasses what they would find interesting and beneficial in favor of exhaustive memorization of information that only serves to prepare them for high-stakes tests and college admission examinations.

Such curricula predictably prepare them for college classes, but not for vocations or life generally. And because college courses do not correlate well with success on the job, there is reason to examine schooling at both levels. In the public schools, students would be much better served by experiences that help them learn to think and solve real-life problems and properly adjust to life in democratic communities. What they need is learning that articulates with the way humans inherently learn and that satisfies important needs. They also need to deeply explore important knowledge by using a learning format that focuses on issues, contradictions, and complex conceptions.

Children also require learning activities in association with their peers so that they can satisfy their needs within a social context. To do otherwise robs them of the ability to really fulfill their needs. They fail to learn that their needs can only be gratified in a social environment. They do not learn that we all depend on each other, in a reciprocal way, to really live successfully. This is what democratic living is all about. Unfortunately, society is replete with examples of people who fail socially in consequence of not knowing how to appropriately interact with others because they habitually take advantage of them in failed attempts to satisfy their needs in antisocial ways. When this happens, their needs go unmet.

The need for successful social relationships is important in its own right. Not only do all humans require human interaction to satisfy certain basic needs, they also desire social associations, because in them they can experience a sense of care for others and feel cared for themselves. Fulfillment in life goes begging unless we feel others care for us and accept us as significant. This never can occur unless members of a society genuinely care for and look after each other. Schools need to promote a caring environment rather than the aversive, competitive one that is commonly present.

A caring environment in school will not develop so long as children are not helped to understand the nature of appropriate communications. Many youngsters fail to communicate properly because they are unaware of certain basic impediments to human expression. Most of these problems are associated with the nature of life growing up. Because of these childhood experiences, many youngsters fail to make a proper transition from the control-oriented interactions they experience as children to those that promote healthy relationships with others.

Children need to achieve a sense of empowerment concerning their lives so that their inherent need to be self-directed can be fulfilled. Excessive control thwarts this need and the desire they have to be free and set their own course in life. However, they are routinely denied opportunities to become responsibly self-directed because they are considered too immature and likely to make devastating mistakes if they are permitted to help govern their own school activities. It is implicitly assumed that schoolchildren can never learn how to manage their own behavior and make wise choices regarding what they learn. However, this has never been successfully proven.

Educators also erroneously conclude that students are not motivated to learn, when in fact they are never unmotivated. However, what they wish to learn may not be the same as what their teachers desire at a particular time. Teachers usually try to get students to learn the same things at the same time and use extrinsic reinforcers or punishment to enforce their desires. Students would be better off if teachers employed intrinsic motivation techniques. This could be accomplished if teachers coached them instead of coercing them.

Constructivism is the learning theory that most closely approximates the way humans naturally learn. However, when children enter school, their natural learning inclinations are thwarted by the structures imposed there. By nature, humans direct their own learning and engage in thought processes that do not correspond with school learning expectations. In addition, schools impose an unfamiliar learning context on children. This greatly handicaps student learning not only in terms of the learning process, but also in the value of the knowledge and skills they acquire.

A learning-community orientation to education can supply an environment in which the above-listed learning necessities can be provided. It engages students in learning that is consistent with their natural inclinations and that helps them prepare to live successfully in a democracy. Learning communities empower students to live a responsible, autonomous life that at the same time helps them satisfy their needs appropriately and develop a true sense of care for those with whom they effectively associate.

THE NATURE OF LEARNING COMMUNITIES

Fundamentally, learning communities are a symbiotic blend of personal independence, social responsibility, and group action. Together these components better approximate authentic life functions and more fully provide the critical necessities of life than does the exclusive focus on individualism that is often encouraged and embraced. In reality, society depends more on thoughtful group actions than on independent accomplishments. Independently oriented living likely leads to isolationism and even anarchy. Far less is accomplished when independence is valued more than meaningful group interaction and achievement. However, when individual concerns are melded with social responsibility, more sophisticated, meaningful learning as well as the enhancement of many necessary skills and attitudes is possible.

The longer group members belong to a learning community, the more they feel compelled by the group attitudes and dispositions and the more their actions reflect group norms and standards. Their within-group actions tend to be self-sustaining, with participants feeling compelled within themselves to synthesize personal and group orientations and using this integrated demeanor in all their actions.

Eventually they become ardent participants in group learning in addition to more responsible partners, bound to each other and their teachers by reciprocal networks of moral obligation. They become more able to connect personal rights and freedom to group commitments, obligations, and duties. A sense of duty regarding the welfare of others evolves that strengthens the connecting bonds and solidifies relationships and promotes caring (Sergio-vanni, 1999).

Over time students and their teachers acquire insights regarding themselves as learners and use these to improve group function and learning. They become more accommodating to members of the group who have different interests and ideas and who develop at different rates. They eventually come to value these differences as the means by which they acquire greater insights regarding conceptual knowledge as well as social functioning. They learn to revel in the insights and talents of others and allow these diverse perspectives to help frame classroom learning activities.

Group interaction is highly valued in learning communities. Active discourse provides the means through which group members can make in-depth explorations of various values and interests and acquire greater intellectual growth and social sophistication. In this way, group members can develop a sense of care and become more interested in helping and supporting each other. Members become committed to the learning and development of other participants and through this, acquire a sense of responsibility for each other. Moral obligations become amplified, not only in terms of present behavior, but also in terms of one's future role as a citizen in a democratic society (Sergiovanni, 1999).

Establishing a covenant is a critical aspect of properly functioning learning communities because it represents the commitment of the group in favor of principles of operation about which they refuse to be dislodged. These principles, along with associated goals and instructional plans, are considered too important to abandon for other purposes (Glickman, 1993).

In a covenant community, not only students and teachers but also administrators and parents share certain purposes, values, and beliefs and feel a strong sense of commitment to the group. They come to believe that the welfare of the group is more essential than that of any one individual. This is true even though the group is very committed to satisfying the personal desires of each member, because the welfare of the group articulates well with that of each individual. Everyone comes to see that their most cherished objectives are inextricably connected to group values and ideals.

An important part of the agenda of a learning community is for those who assume leadership to not only work toward achieving a consensus of ideas and commitments, but also to model these considerations in their own lives so that all participants are better able to envision ways to use these responsibility-oriented applications themselves. When this is done effectively, group members can acquire a greater sense of satisfaction than is possible among those who focus exclusively on themselves.

The covenant in a learning community provides the value orientation needed for extraordinary student accomplishments along with a vision that reflects their hopes and dreams. It provides an incentive for extraordinary achievement among all who have a stake in the school. Ultimately, this vision provides a conception of what the school stands and lives for. This is what drives students toward community purposes (Brandt, 1992).

The covenant is a binding, solemn agreement regarding what the learning community is as well as the commitments members made to each other. It is created out of a consensus about the purposes and beliefs that bind participants together around common values and purposes and embraces a sense of mission and group ownership (Sergiovanni, 1990). Interestingly, an examination of present-day schooling reveals a near vacuum with respect to mission. Furthermore, it has been found that as students go through school, their role as decision makers decreases regarding the curriculum (Goodlad, 2000).

In a covenant-based learning community a number of questions are routinely asked about how it is to function. They include but are not limited to the following: What kinds of learning experiences are likely to help students to become persons of character in a properly functioning democratic society? How can teachers help students to think deeply about themselves and others? How can teachers help their students make responsible decisions about what they learn? What is the nature of the learning process?

Additionally, the following questions are asked: What kinds of learning experiences are consistent with the way children learn? How can teachers help students to engage in learning that is personally satisfying and meaningful as well as significant from the viewpoint of society? What is it that members of society believe students should learn, and how consistent is this with what will properly prepare students for the present world and the world of the future? What role should teachers assume to help their students learn to work successfully with adults? What should teachers do to get parents and the community at large involved in learning communities?

Additional questions include, What can be done to help students truly care about each other and about school? What can teachers do to help students focus on common purposes? How can teachers help students develop commitment and a sense of obligation toward each other? How can students be helped to be responsibly autonomous within a community environment? What is the best way to help students become good leaders as well as good followers? In a learning community it is imperative that these and similar questions are addressed. Because they frame the essence of the curriculum, they cannot be ignored as they usually are in traditional schools.

Each learning community is responsible for creating its own questions along with finding out the answers. It is certain that disagreements will occur. Yet it is necessary that consensus eventually is achieved, particularly regarding those issues that are central to the purposes and operations of the community. When experiencing difficulty reaching agreement, teachers must be wary of giving up before the group achieves closure regarding these very important questions. They should not consider these deliberations a waste of time, but rather a process that actually enhances the work of the group as well as an understanding of group dynamics. Teachers should also recognize that the process itself has critical growth propensities and consequently is worth their students' time.

One of the essential characteristics of learning communities is their focus on morality and ethics. Students receive instruction on this important consideration and have their teachers as examples. Emphasis on ethics is an essential component of all relationships. Students learn what moral principles apply to life in a community and how to assume responsibility for their own behavior. Teachers also help students understand what traits or dispositions are morally good or bad and what they can expect as desirable and undesirable reactions to their behavior.

It is critical to note that moral considerations and ethical standards are to be drawn from the entire community and not coercively or arbitrarily imposed. Students should eventually see these paradigms as central to their own sense of well-being and way of living. They should become a part of their character. Students should consider these criteria as flexible guidelines that incorporate sufficient autonomy for all community members to participate in making decisions each feels good about (Coombe, 1999).

For students to acquire a sense of acceptance, teachers much teach them to respect each other. This involves valuing each participant because of his or her uniqueness. In learning communities student differences usually become more noticeable than in traditional classrooms. However, rather than these differences promoting exclusiveness and possible abuse, they are celebrated. There is no stereotyping with regard to race, class, or student abilities and capacities. Personal idiosyncrasies are used by the group to advance a more complete and comprehensive understanding of the world and help students acquire greater insights regarding how it operates.

Learning communities promote inclusiveness. Members do all they can to ensure all members are drawn into the whole range of interactions during learning. Students are taught to integrate all individuals to provide the greatest possible diversity. This makes a significant impact on their conceptual understanding as well as social astuteness. Students and their teachers eventually share a common culture, with the attendant values and guidelines regarding conduct and expectations. Students and teachers are thus united in their learning endeavors rather than pitted against each other, as is often the case in traditional schools.

Members of a learning community learn to truly care for each other. While respect involves passive acceptance, caring is characterized by individuals actively looking after other group members. It is proactive and involves individuals reaching out and initiating positive interactions. Thus, a caring person will not only initiate acts of kindness, they will actively try to relieve the discomfort of others as well as happily provide additional comfort. This involves attitudes that are deeply felt. The individuals experience considerable satisfaction from helping others learn at higher levels and are willing to make personal sacrifices to render useful assistance.

Over time considerable trust develops in learning communities. Otherwise, there could be no significant interactions between community members. When genuine trust evolves, an atmosphere is created in which participants are willing to make authentic disclosures, work energetically with associates, and engage in more meaningful relationships. In addition, more significant and successful learning takes place. Students become willing participants because they are assured that no one will ever inappropriately use the information they disclose to group members.

Students acquire a sense of empowerment as a result of being listened to carefully and taken seriously by group members, including teachers. They have confidence that no one would intentionally hurt them. Moreover, they have considerable decision-making power and are routinely consulted for their opinions regarding matters that concern them. Because of decision-making empowerment, students' interests are taken into account, thus stimulating greater vigor and commitment to learning along with acquiring a sense of ownership. This has a very significant impact on the quality of learning.

Because greater commitment is achieved by students, they begin to form strong interpersonal attachments with their peers, which helps to energize the work they do. In the process they tend to internalize the goals and values of the group and try to achieve at the highest level possible (Raywid, 1993).

The various attributes outlined above are interrelated. Thus, commitment would not emerge without empowerment, and empowerment would be unlikely without trust. Also, until community members are respected and sense that they are valued unconditionally, and cared for, trust will never arise. These conditions do not exist in bureaucratically run schools. Teachers and students both have to be empowered decision makers for a learning community to exist (Hiatt & Diana, 2001).

MORAL TEACHING IN LEARNING COMMUNITIES

In a moral democratic society, the decisions citizens make are influenced by norms. These involve emotions, preferences, values, and beliefs held in connection with social bonds and obligations that relate to decision making. The community to which individuals belong helps shape thinking and constrains the ways in which members can justifiably fulfill their needs. Thus, group norms affect choices each person makes. The result is for self-interest to be moderated and selfless behavior to emerge.

It is commonly thought that rewards are necessary to extrinsically moti-vate human actions. However, in community organizations it is more accu-rate to say that what is rewarding is a more powerful influence. Of course most individuals can be motivated by promised rewards. But when an indi-vidual does something that is enjoyed and perceived as intrinsically meaning-ful, it is even more motivating. An even greater motivating factor is connect-ing behavior to moral ties. In this case, the individual acquires a sense of duty and obligation and functions in connection with shared values and beliefs. Because moral ties are grounded in cultural norms and expectations, they are usually much stronger than either extrinsic or intrinsic motivation (Sergio-vanni, 1994).

Moral education includes such themes as moral conduct, character forma-tion, diligence, respect for others, responsibility, and personal integrity. As previously mentioned, teachers themselves must be examples of these impor-tant dispositions. The teachers' role in this respect is critical in a harmonious, properly functioning democratic society and in particular the operation of a moral learning community. Because of their immaturity and inexperience, children may have difficulty properly conceptualizing the constituents of moral behavior. In addition, they are likely to be incapable of defending themselves from negligent or selfish adults, particularly their teachers. Such conditions can obviously have profound negative effects on children (Wynne, 1995).

Teaching itself is a moral endeavor because it represents human activities undertaken with regard to other human beings. Consequently, moral matters are always present. Because of students' lack of maturity and the potential to be misguided, it is all the more imperative for teachers to have the highest moral integrity. Unfortunately, at present little attention is given to the moral development of youth nor the moral status of teachers. In the place of moral teaching the emphasis is on the status and prestige of teachers, on testing for teacher competence and student achievement, and on career advancement (Fenstermacher, 1990).

In summary, to induct students into moral living, teachers are required to be examples of moral living themselves. In their teaching and personal lives they need to model moral attributes (McHenry, 2000; Noddings, 2002). If the school curriculum doesn't contain a sufficient emphasis on instructing youth regarding moral principles, teachers are unlikely to focus on being moral examples. Because of the role they occupy in the lives of children, these conditions can undoubtedly have very negative repercussions.

LEARNING AND CONSTRUCTIVISM

The constructivist view of learning is consistent with instruction in learning communities and importantly has, during the past three or four decades, had a most notable influence on the way teaching is characterized (Fensham, 1992). Instead of focusing on behavior and reinforcement principles, as has been true in the past, there has been a move to characterize learning as cognitive processing. The result has been to abandon the idea that learning is simply assimilating information and instead define it as a personally directed conceptualization process.

Constructivists believe that teaching should fit the way children naturally learn (Matthews, 2000). Researchers have discovered that each student has a unique conception of the world that has been personally organized in connection with his or her life experiences. Thus, students' conceptualization depends on previous experiences and the way they have come to view and process information (Confrey, 1990). Consequently, each student's conceptual organization is unique.

The brain does not passively absorb information. Rather, it actively constructs its own interpretation of new information and draws inferences based on already-held conceptions. In this process, some information is selectively ignored, particularly when it appears inconsistent with current conceptions. Accordingly, for students to learn with understanding, they must actively construct meaning by comparing previous learning with new considerations (Phillips, 2000). In doing this, the individual must create a model or explanation that fits personal logic and real-world experiences.

Because students don't simply absorb information in the way teachers present it, some might advocate that students simply be set free to learn what they want. This, however, would greatly restrict the value of what was learned. On their own, children are very unlikely to come to understand complex conceptual schemes that have taken the best minds hundreds of years to build up. For example, children are not likely to pursue an understanding of concepts such as velocity, acceleration, force, genes, social structure, and democracy on their own.

An associated issue is children's learning context. Not only would it not occur to them to study important topics, they may be neither intellectually nor experientially prepared to engage in such study. The task for teachers is to determine how to teach a body of knowledge that is in large part abstract and has no connection to children's prior experience, nor their inherent learning inclinations (Matthews, 2000).

At the same time it must be remembered that children do not simply absorb information when it is presented. The challenge for teachers is to help students construct personal meanings for themselves that are essentially consistent with conceptual knowledge on the subject (Solomon, 1994). Thus, effective learning cannot be limited to student-directed inquiry. But skillful teachers can help their students integrate scholarly knowledge with their own group and personal inquiries. This is a necessity because inquiry-based investigations represent the natural way we learn and construct knowledge (Schwartz & Lin, 2001).

In studying the classroom learning process, it has been found that (1) students tend to maintain the same understanding of conceptual knowledge they had in younger years despite having subsequently been provided with more accurate conceptualizations. Thus, children's ideas are very tenacious and resistant to change; (2) when children's views of the world are changed through instruction, they are often quite different from those intended by their teachers; (3) children tend to modify the information they are taught so that it is not in conflict with their earlier ideas (Osborne & Wittrock, 1983).

These findings indicate that teachers should provide instruction consistent with the way children naturally learn; otherwise, hoped-for results may not be obtained. It is not clear at present whether children's inclination to retain earlier concepts is a function of willful rejection of what is being taught or if they are unable to articulate natural brain function with the way classroom instruction is commonly implemented. Either way, the solution is to provide learning experiences that correspond with their learning proclivities.

LEARNING THROUGH INQUIRY

Inquiry is the best fit for the constructivist conception of learning. When properly employed, inquiry learning maintains student interests, satisfies important needs, and helps students experience intellectual as well as social development. During the inquiry process, caring teachers help their students confront interesting, relevant problems that provide the means to promote thinking and acquisition of a valid conception of important information.

When this technique is applied as it is in learning communities, students acquire the benefit of interacting with their peers. In doing this, they obtain a fuller knowledge of the inquiry process along with more complex understandings of conceptual information. During the inquiry process, students can take what they learn from their own thinking and experience, as well as that of their classmates, and interpret the world from as many vantage points as possible and gain increased insights (Green, 1988).

As students become involved with their peers in inquiry learning, they acquire cooperative learning skills along with a greater sense of care for others. This helps them achieve a higher degree of commitment for shared purposes as well as securing greater interest regarding what they are learning.

These attributes of learning communities help to drive the learning process. Experiences there help them acquire a greater elucidation of meanings and a variety of life interpretations as they adjust to life in the real world (Green, 1988).

True inquiry involves student-generated questions. Teachers have to be wary of giving input that robs students of this imperative. Their role is to help students ask sophisticated questions that have significant value, but without creating the questions themselves. This is sometimes a difficult task, because in traditional classrooms teachers ask nearly all the questions; this, of course, is likely to have become habituated in the way teachers conduct most classroom instruction. By encouraging students to do high-level inquiry investigations rather than asking questions that frame instruction, teachers help their students think of the implications of the questions they ask and help them make sure that related research is of high quality.

Teachers should help students differentiate between substantive questions and those of little consequence. At the same time their investigations should be intrinsically interesting to them. They also need to understand what may confound their understanding and nullify the validity of their findings. In addition, students should be discouraged from pursuing questions to which they already know the answers. Many times the members of the learning group can give needed assistance to others in addressing these issues. Consequently, teachers should not too quickly draw attention to problems.

Learning communities provide an enhanced ambience for promoting high-level student questioning. With the help of peers, students can create questions at a much higher intellectual level as well as devise more thoughtful means for addressing them (Scardamalia & Bereiter, 1992). In this research configuration, students become more passionately involved, use evidence in scholarly ways, and create arguments of high quality. Their research tends to become more sophisticated over time (Engle & Conant, 2002). They also become more motivated to help associates and learn from them, along with demonstrating increased productivity, student ownership, and cognitive engagement (Crawford, Krajcik & Marx, 1999; Ebers & Streefland, 2000).

It has also been found that students who participate in inquiry learning have better content retention, participate more flexibly in dealing with hypothetical situations and counterexamples of research, produce more novel ideas, engage in more complex forms of argumentation and explanation, are better able to transfer information to other knowledge domains, are more adept at summarizing complex explanations, and are more skilled in determining what constitutes valid evidence to support their research findings (Brown & Campione, 1994).

Teachers should occupy a coaching role in helping their students determine topics for study and strategies for carrying through with their investigations. They must satisfy themselves that student inquiry activities are bona fide efforts to acquire useful knowledge and develop inquiry skills. They should also provide a way for students to share their knowledge with classmates and to individuals beyond the classroom.

RESPONSIBLE AUTONOMY THROUGH STUDENT EMPOWERMENT

The desire for free choice appears early in life, even among toddlers, who for the sake of being self-directed commonly insist on performing certain tasks they are entirely unprepared to accomplish. They may, for example, insist on running the vacuum cleaner or tying their own shoes long before they are capable of doing so. This desire for freedom accompanies each individual throughout life.

When children's freedom is restricted, they commonly rebel. When they are young, this may be in the form of temper tantrums. Later they may be more calculating in their resistance and simply engage in behavior that adults don't accept and even abhor. This is particularly so during adolescence, a time when children sense greater capability but continue to be limited by adults who fear they may injure themselves in various ways. The result is for children to grow up without the necessary freedom to acquire a sense of responsibility.

It appears to youths that adults don't really understand their capabilities, nor do they trust them. Trust may be the issue young people are inclined to use to challenge adults in an effort to acquire more personal freedom. The irony lies in the fact that youths do in fact have more capabilities than adults seem to believe, along with a greater potential for assuming responsibility for their actions. In addition, when they are excessively controlled, they are denied the very ingredient required for responsibility development. Adults appear to believe that the passage of time is all that is required for children to mature and consequently deny them the proper constituents for learning this critical capacity.

Teachers often defend their coercive actions by claiming that young students will certainly act irresponsibly if they are given even a limited amount of freedom. This conclusion appears confirmed by the behavior of children when they are controlled. When they misbehave, as they are inclined to do under such circumstances, it is assumed that they are naturally rebellious. The teacher's reaction is to control more intensely, thus creating an increasing level of misconduct.

When students do comply with teacher demands, it is often concluded that they are learning to be responsible, but responsibility always contains a freedom component. Without freedom, true responsibility doesn't exist.

What many teachers fail to understand is that students who comply with their instructions often do so reluctantly when they see no other alternative. After all, teachers hold access to grades, college entrance, and attractive employment. Even so, some students rebel anyway, sometimes forfeiting college degrees and associated life opportunities. This itself is evidence of the need children have to achieve sufficient autonomy.

It should not be concluded from this that children should just be turned loose with the hope that they will automatically develop responsible autonomy. Rather there is a necessary interaction between autonomy, responsibility, and maturity that teachers must orchestrate. Rather than withholding opportunities for self-determination until students are mature in some abstract sense, teachers should include greater freedom within the strategies for increasing responsibility. As children become more able to act responsibly upon the freedom they have been given, they should be provided greater autonomy. The strategy is proactive rather than waiting for responsibility to suddenly appear.

It is probably better to err on the side of offering more autonomy to youths who are aching to be free. And it should not be considered catastrophic if children are not always wise in their judgments and decision making. Teachers should recognize that they are in a learning process. These issues can be addressed in classroom meetings, with students assessing their actions and the natural consequences that are likely to follow. Within a discussion format involving input from peers and expert questioning by teachers, youths can properly assess their behavior and create necessary adjustments.

It is often confusing to include agency as a significant constituent of learning communities. On the surface this appears to be a contradiction, because autonomy is commonly considered to be independence from the input and influence of associates. However, most individuals wish to be involved with others while at the same time having a requisite amount of freedom. Thus, there must be a blending of the two. Successful communities require a degree of freedom for all members. Otherwise, they stagnate. Thus, the group must be committed to individual desires while at the same time catering to the fact that each individual can satisfy his or her needs only within a community. In ongoing operations input from all community members should be sought regarding all matters with which the community is concerned.

Students who have been schooled in the absence of meaningful, social interconnections because of a near-exclusive focus on autonomy are characterless and without defined purposes. Freedom should never be considered as absolute autonomy devoid of responsibility (Taylor, 1985). Thus, for proper student empowerment in a democratic society, students must learn to choose for themselves and create an identity within a social context. This involves making commitments to others and freely fulfilling them.

In learning communities members make self-generated contributions that each individual believes are important to others. Their actions do not depend on being assigned specific tasks, but rather come from their own initiative. Because they are self-initiated, they are personally invigorating and meaningful, and carry the strength of personal commitment. Consequently, what they accomplish is likely to be of high quality. Each person has the responsibility to specifically determine how to serve other members of the learning community, while at the same time satisfying personal learning needs.

Teachers may express concern that promoting agency will lead to lower achievement. Actually the opposite is true. Higher achievement is an outgrowth of more self-regulated learning. This has been proven in a number of different educational settings (Watkins, 2005). It should be noted that people work with greater commitment toward collective goals than individual ones (Csikszentmihalyi, 1990). Thus, through proper employment of agency in learning communities, there can be higher achievement along with increased need satisfaction and commitment.

FULFILLING STUDENT NEEDS IN LEARNING COMMUNITIES

While student needs are unlikely to be met in traditional classrooms, learning communities provide an environment for most needs to be satisfied. This is not only due to the nature of children's learning experiences there, but also because one of the central tasks of participants is to ensure that their associates' needs are satisfied. When students' needs fail to be met, discipline problems can become rampant, violence more vicious, and achievement levels substantially decreased for many students. Learning communities faithfully avoid such complications.

The purpose of most human behavior is to satisfy personal needs (Glasser, 1998). But when conditions make it difficult to accomplish this quest, some students rebel while others may simply give up. In any case, their learning will be adversely affected. A good share of the misbehavior exhibited by children in school involves an aberrant attempt to satisfy their needs. These aberrations are usually viewed by teachers as rebellious inclinations that students bring with them to class, when in fact they are precipitated by conditions in the classroom that keep them from adequately satisfying essential needs (Glasser, 1990).

Much of the routine of schooling frustrates students' ability to satisfy their needs. For example, very few opportunities for students to interact with each other are a genuine part of traditional classroom learning. This is because the bulk of the learning involves listening to lectures and engaging in independent seat work (Goodlad, 1984). Yet one of children's most critical needs is for social interaction.

As already mentioned, students need sufficient autonomy to direct much of what they do. Most classrooms have insufficient freedom for students to satisfy this need. And because much of the prescribed school learning is commonly characterized by students as unrelenting drudgery rather than meaningful involvement, they fail to satisfy their need for fun. In addition, the learning tasks routinely assigned by teachers are unlikely to generate full effort by students and thus fail to help them achieve a true sense of accomplishment (Glasser, 1990).

Most theorists agree regarding human needs and concur that need satisfaction is an essential element of school success. They agree that students (1) need to experience positive relationships with classmates and teachers that involve achieving a sense of significance, belonging, collaboration, love, and acceptance; (2) desire academic success that involves a true sense of competence regarding meaningful knowledge and skills; (3) want to have considerable control over what happens to them, thus desiring to make many personal choices and becoming involved in directing their own learning; and (4) wish to contribute significantly to the well-being of others (Glasser, 1998; Kohn, 1993). All of these needs can be more completely fulfilled in learning communities than in traditional classrooms.

LEARNING AND MOTIVATION IN LEARNING COMMUNITIES

Satisfying personal needs is perhaps the most potent source of student motivation. The process of learning itself is motivating, so long as students can be sufficiently self-directed. Children find it very motivating when through their learning they discover knowledge that helps them better understand the world and brings critical elements under their personal control. However, because of the poor fit between the way they naturally learn and the methods they are exposed to in school, many students are not motivated. The result is that many of them perform well below their capabilities. This, of course, reduces their interest in school.

When children enter school, they commonly expect learning to be like the classroom activities they have previously experienced. When they discover it is not, their interest in school declines. For many, the longer they are in school, the less desire they have to learn. There are also negative effects on self-concept and success expectations. Furthermore, motivation shifts from an intrinsic orientation to an extrinsic one (Brophy, 1998).

During their school experiences, children develop either an internal locus of control or an external locus of control in consequence of the success they experience there. Those with an internal locus of control attribute their success to ability and effort, while those with an external locus of control believe success comes as a result of luck or fate and their failures from low ability. The limited success they experience is usually attributed to external factors such as the momentary generosity of teachers, lucky guessing, or an unusually easy task (Weiner & Kukla, 1970). Students who believe that success or failure is within their control routinely assume that they can be successful, even when they have initially failed at some task. Those with an external locus of control, on the other hand, believe failure is a permanent condition.

Interestingly, an external locus of control is created primarily from the school practice of teachers exclusively assessing student achievement. Students experiencing this have usually received low grades after working hard and high grades after low effort. They are consequently led to conclude that their success is essentially unpredictable. This can be countered, but rarely is, through attribution retraining. Properly employed, attribution retraining helps students attribute failure to insufficient effort and poor learning strategies rather than lack of ability (Craske, 1985).

The key to successful attribution retraining is controlled exposure to failure. Students need to cope with failure by recognizing that it comes from remediable causes and is within their power to overcome. Thus, failure has no finality but rather can and should be corrected. Students learn to do this by spending more time on task and creating different strategies for problems they try to solve. Teachers help students acquire tolerance for frustration, persistence in the face of difficulties, and a belief that continued effort will eventually lead to success (Clifford, 1984; Rohrkemper & Corno, 1988).

Most contemporary views of motivation focus on its cognitive and goal-oriented features. Thus, most human motivation is considered to be a personal phenomenon. This is a significant departure from behavioristic theory, which has long dominated behavioral science. From a behaviorist point of view humans are considered relatively passive except in response to reinforcers designed to satisfy basic needs. Cognitive psychologists, however, accept the contrary view that behavior can be influenced by rewards, but individuals routinely make choices contrary to extrinsic reward systems.

Personal, goal-directed theories emphasize intrinsic motivation. Behavior is thus seen as an outgrowth of free choice, curiosity, spontaneity, and personal interests. Consequently, no extrinsic motivating force is needed to drive learning. From this perspective, motivation depends on the satisfaction of three innate psychological needs: competence (developing and exercising skills that help adjust to and control the environment); autonomy (self-determination in deciding what to do and how to do it); and relatedness (affiliation with others through pro-social relationships). Thus, children are inherently motivated to make social connections with others, to function effectively without constraint, and to feel a sense of personal control and initiative while doing so (Deci & Ryan, 1985, 1991).

In learning communities intrinsic motivation is employed, while in conventional schools extrinsic motivation prevails. In traditional schooling the task teachers face is getting students to learn what they would otherwise choose not to learn. However, in learning communities, students are empowered with free choice under the expert guidance of their teachers. This way, students can become more fully involved with their intrinsic interests and also exercise the enthusiasm created by personal autonomy. The threats, deadlines, directives, rewards, and competitive pressure administered in most traditional school settings diminish intrinsic motivation because students interpret them as efforts to control their behavior (Deci, Koestner & Ryan, 1999; Ryan & Deci, 2000).

During the 1970s, 1980s, and 1990s it was generally accepted that extrinsic reinforcement undermined intrinsic motivation. During this time it was learned that extrinsic rewards reduced students' inclinations to continue behavior they found intrinsically motivating. They apparently became conditioned to the rewards they received and learned to value these more than the learning behavior for which they were given (Deci & Ryan, 1985; Heckhausen, 1991; Lepper & Greene, 1978).

Initially it was assumed that the effect of extrinsic rewards on behavior was inherent in the use of rewards. However, subsequent studies indicated that the undermining effect only occurred when students were given rewards they knew were designed to pressure them to behave as directed. Thus, perceived control was the cause of reduced learning. The effect occurred when students realized that their behavior was being carefully monitored for the purpose of controlling them (Kohn, 1993).

What appears to undermine intrinsic motivation is not the use of extrinsic rewards, but instead, offering them as incentives after telling students the purpose of the rewards. This process teaches students that the reason for learning is to obtain rewards, not because learning itself is valuable. Thus, intrinsic motivation can be adversely affected when rewards (1) are very attractive or presented in ways that call attention to them, (2) are given for participation rather than achievement, and (3) are connected to particular behavior as control devices rather than a natural outcome of learning (Brophy, 1998). Of course this is what characterizes extrinsic reinforcers as they are usually applied in the classroom.

Teachers often try to motivate students through competitive activities and grades. It is assumed that all students are motivated by grades. However, only those students who receive the highest grades appear to be motivated. The academic performances of low achievers are adversely affected by grades. The purpose of these students is simply to serve as contrasts to the achievements of more successful students. They justifiably feel like chaff on the threshing floor. They are not motivated. Rather, they usually suffer a loss of confidence and find little to encourage full effort in school (Epstein & Harackiewicz, 1992; Moriarty, Douglas, Punch & Hattie, 1995; Reeve & Deci, 1996).

Children are intrinsically rewarded when they recognize that their learning has made them more competent and when it enhances self-understanding and self-actualization. Students generally find school unsatisfying if they fail to experience autonomy and competence along with satisfying relationships. These are enhanced in learning communities where they explore significant personal interests in connection with meaningful group learning activities.

RELATIONSHIPS IN LEARNING COMMUNITIES

Relationships in learning communities must accommodate the needs and desires of their members and employ an atmosphere of care. This environment promotes collaboration and sharing along with a commitment to community purposes (Sergiovanni, 1994). The common good of a learning community represents the collective good of each of its members. Consequently members' interests are pursued by the group in connection with the community achieving its purposes (Glickman, 1993). The focus of the group on the interests and desires of each individual helps bind them together due to the personal and group well-being this engenders.

Relationships are strengthened when community members' behavior is not strictly predefined. Each individual has considerable latitude in decisions and actions. Stereotyping each other creates narrow expectations, which interfere with personal flexibility and stifle intellectual growth and development. Relationships are strengthened and learning enhanced when students can determine the roles they wish to occupy in the group.

Students report that the teacher relationships they value the most are those that make them feel worthwhile, promote their independence, motivate them to learn, and help them to cope with life inside and outside school (Pinata, 1999). Students appreciate teachers who protect them from harm and promote their success. Relationships are improved when teachers properly respond to students' likes, dislikes, and prior experiences. Thus, it behooves teachers to learn as much personal information about their students as possible.

Teachers' relationships with their students can be greatly improved by avoiding control episodes (Greenburg, Kusche & Spelz, 1991). In addition, teachers must make themselves available to their students for one-on-one help. Although this is nearly impossible in traditional schools, it is a critical constituent of learning communities. In private sessions, teachers need to communicate information that shows they are genuinely interested in students and have a desire to help and protect them from harm. This kind of attitude must be engendered so students are likely to open up and honestly communicate their concerns.

Teachers need to help their students genuinely care for each other. Unfortunately, many young people not only fail to develop a capacity to care, but they appear not to know what it means to be cared for. In addition, some also confuse control for care. This attitude is commonly fed by the adult declaration that abusive control exercised over children is done out of love and concern.

Ironically, some children believe they are being cared for when they are simply being exploited, while others have given up hope that anyone will ever care for them. They rarely experience authentic caring interactions with others and consequently see no hope this will ever occur. What is needed is for members of learning communities to become engrossed in caring for each other with a special form of attentiveness. This involves a motivational shift by the person offering care toward an unadulterated focus on the needs of those for whom they care. This kind of care is rarely experienced by students in traditional schools (Noddings, 2002).

Properly provided care requires periods of undivided attention from teachers, with sufficient intimacy for children to feel they are special. Also, teachers should regularly share with their students what it means to care and have lengthy conversations with individuals and groups about practical applications. Students should be asked to focus on the nature of care as a component of classroom discussions. Their expressions regarding personal feelings about the importance of caring relationships should be encouraged.

In trying to promote a caring environment, teachers should be wary of offering praise. The result of this tactic is to invite dependency, evoke defensiveness, and create anxiety. Students who are praised commonly feel compelled to satisfy the explicit or implied expectations of others, rather than pursuing their own interests. That is how they usually interpret the meaning of the praise. Students then try to meet presumed expectations so that they neither disappoint the one who praises them nor incur his or her wrath. Eventually their sense of well-being can become connected to receiving praise as they routinely try to acquire love and acceptance.

Unfortunately, when children focus extensively on receiving praise from adults, they can eventually become overstrivers. These youngsters are driven by the devastating belief that the sole measure of one's worth is school accomplishments because of their common attachment to praise. They become excessively oriented toward high achievement because it has become the recompense required for the approval they so vigorously seek. Almost always overstrivers connect academic excellence with personal worthiness. To them love and acceptance is dependent on their achievements.

Ordinarily overstrivers have a history of academic success. However, with each achievement, teachers and parents commonly elevate expectations. These children have proven in the past that they are capable of achieving. Eventually, however, they experience the fear that they have reached their zenith and are in danger of losing the status and acceptance they have achieved and so intensely crave—a craving that is actually accentuated by the fear it may be lost.

The difficulty overstrivers experience usually goes unrecognized by adults. It is difficult to see that students who are so successful may suffer trauma brought on by the very fact they have been successful. Parents and teachers are unlikely to connect such conditions to the praise that they mindlessly offer. Nor are they likely to understand the terror these children feel as they receive the praise that serves as a signal to increase academic output they are afraid they will not be able to deliver (Covington & Beery, 1976).

COMMUNICATION IN LEARNING COMMUNITIES

Appropriate operation of learning communities depends on quality communications. Because of the nature of social interactions, participants are particularly sensitive to the nature of the communication process. Relationships depend on thoughtful, kind, and intellectually provocative interactions. Learning communities find it hard to function unless discussions convey information that can be interpreted as caring and insightful. For transactions to go smoothly and learning to advance, community members need to thoroughly understand the nature of their own statements along with those of their associates.

Many teachers and students may be unaware of the source from which some of their statements emanate. It is disarming to realize that many verbal responses are based on prior experiences and are called forth automatically without conscious awareness of their origin. They are often stated like a recorded message and are expressed before the individual has made any attempt to think about their implications (Penfield, 1952).

These experience-based messages are held within the brain in the form of three ego-states: the Parent, the Child, and the Adult. The Parent ego-state is a collection of expressions acquired during the first five years of life. They include pronouncements made by parents and other adults. Because they are formulated in childhood when there is no capacity to modify them, they are unedited. Consequently, if parents are malicious or hostile toward their children or toward each other, what children hear is internalized without benefit of mature interpretation. These messages tend to be expressed in later years as they were recorded.

The Parent ego-state is the repository of parental admonitions, rules, and other kinds of controlling statements. They involve not only words, but also tone of voice, facial expressions, and physical contact. Also included are the many restraints with which children are bombarded as they attempt to express their natural curiosity and investigate the world around them. Additionally, there are recordings of parental hostility and anger that children may believe were directed at them, and in reality may not have been. Determining the purpose of parents' hostility is difficult for them. These experiences are permanently recorded in the individual's brain, and as mentioned, are commonly called forth without conscious effort.

The Parent ego-state also consists of smiles, hugs, pride, and delight from parents and other important adults, along with the context in which these expressions were made. These positive experiences are a critical part of children's growing-up years. Their sense of well-being depends on receiving an abundance of affectionate statements. These expressions are particularly potent when they are accompanied by hugs and pats on the back.

As they grow up, children are exposed to well-intentioned platitudes and precepts, regarding which they have only a vague understanding. "Never associate with people of another race," "you can never trust a cop," "never lie," "haste makes waste," and "the idle mind is the devil's workshop" are common examples. Young children accept these as true, and they become the source of attitudes and accompanying statements. Obviously, some of what students have learned as youngsters can adversely affect relationships in learning communities if they don't learn to moderate their speech appropriately.

The Child ego-state is simultaneously recorded with the Parent and consists of verbal and emotional responses made by children regarding what they see and hear. Then later, when the individual has similar experiences, the same emotions and feelings are likely to be evoked. Again, as young children, they have no way of rationally modifying these. Consequently, they may lose control and allow anger to dominate their responses to others later in life. Also, because some individuals were made to feel guilty as children, their initial emotional response to many situations is to feel guilty, even when not being criticized. The emotions are permanently recorded in the brain but can be subdued in the same way as the Parent ego-state.

The part of the individual's personality responsible for toning down Child and Parent expressions is the Adult ego-state. The daily task of the Adult is to monitor both Parent and Child and ensure that verbal expressions are valid and useful in terms of the present circumstances. This requires considerable vigilance because of the tendency for the Parent and Child to be expressed spontaneously. More useful and constructive communications are possible when students learn to speak from the Adult ego-state rather than letting the Parent and Child prevail (Berne, 1966).

Unfortunately, the Adult ego-state is fragile during early childhood and subject to difficulties incurred when too many commands and reprimands come from parents and other adults. The Adult is strengthened through "stroking," which consists of positive experiences with others. In the schools, teachers should engage in interactions that emanate from the Adult ego-state and limit Parent or Child reactions to positive ones.

Berne also indicates that children assume one of four different life positions in consequence of their experiences. These life positions focus on the degree to which feelings about oneself are positive and the degree to which the same is true regarding feelings about others. Typically there are maladjustments when individuals believe they are not okay, or if they believe they are okay but others are not. These personality types can be very destructive socially as well as psychologically pernicious. They will typically disrupt classroom communications. Moreover, they are very likely to harm themselves and others (Berne, 1964; Harris, 1967).

Evidence that the Parent ego-state is operative includes hands placed on hips, arms folded across the chest, tongue chuckling, sighing, pointing the index finger, head wagging, a furrowed brow, pursed lips, a tapping foot, or a look of disgust. Expressions from the Child include tears, temper tantrums, complaining, pouting, a quivering lip, shrugging shoulders, giggling, squirming, laughter, or downcast eyes. The Adult ego-state is manifested in smiles of approval and requests for more clarifying information. Both teachers and their students should recognize these indicators and learn to respond to them with communications that emanate from the Adult ego-state.

CREATIVITY DEVELOPMENT IN LEARNING COMMUNITIES

One of the most important outgrowths of properly organized learning communities is the development of creativity. It is also an attribute commonly subverted by traditional schooling, in particular educational experiences driven by testing and grading and devoid of intrinsic motivation. Intrinsic motivation is the driving force behind creative processes (Hennessey, 2000). Unfortunately, teachers and school administrators appear to have considerable ambivalence and in some cases outright aversion regarding support for creativity development.

Children appear to be inherently creative, some far more than others. However, all children innately investigate their world to understand it and put it to their use and pleasure. Yet such activities often interfere with the orderly-run affairs of the classroom. Interestingly, in education there is currently more concern regarding standards than creativity. Standards, in fact, undermine the development of creativity.

Much of traditional schooling involves such restrictive strategies as the employment of behavioral objectives. In this case, educators have been told that anything that is not measurable in behavioral terms and amenable to making comparisons between students is not legitimate in the schools. Yet the convergent thinkers commonly produced by such restrictive educational experiences are unlikely to help solve future problems confronted by society. Instead of narrow-thinking people, it will be creative individuals who are prepared to help ensure the survival of civilization (Torrance, 1962). Advances in science and other fields depend on creative men and women (Combs, 1962).

Creative individuals are more concerned with meanings and implications than factual information. They are also more willing to test the limits and take calculated risks. Furthermore, they can work effectively with disharmony, dichotomies, and unsolved problems without despair (Torrance, 1962). They exhibit independence, intuitiveness, and have extraordinary drive and energy (Rubin, 1963). The creative are dissatisfied with things as they are and have faith that they can improve them. Unfortunately, they are usually regarded by their peers as crazy, wild, irresponsible, speculative, uncritical, and emotional (Hoffa, 1963).

Many times, creative students are the ones who break classroom rules and consequently are considered unruly. It should be noted, however, that this is not their basic inclination, but rather a reaction to excessive structure and control. They dislike completing day-to-day assignments and often balk at accepting teacher opinions, especially if they are given authoritatively (Drews, 1963).

Creative students often have vastly different personalities inside and outside of school. They may daydream, be bored and lazy, and be withdrawn in school, but outside school they may have boundless energy, working on little projects and experiments of their own design (Torrance, 1962). It is no wonder that teachers have a hard time ascribing the term "creative" to these unruly individuals. This term ordinarily has a positive connotation that teachers refuse to use to describe rowdy students who are in fact the most creative ones in class.

All teachers should be reminded that it is the controlling environment established by them that causes these students to rebel. Interestingly, many children who are diagnosed with attention deficit hyperactivity disorder (ADHD) are highly creative individuals. Their hyperactivity and attention deficit are the product of the system, not something they inherit or that comes about because of experiences outside the school (Sax, 2005).

Creative people are fully functioning, self-actualized human beings. They have excellent mental health. They tend not to become frustrated with life as it is, but rather find joy in it. Life means discovery and adventure along with a great sense of satisfaction. They are not disturbed by challenging life phenomena but work to make sense of the world and solve problems, which can bring further satisfaction. They see value in mistakes and accept them as a means to sharpen perception and problem-solving ability. They do not suffer from the need to always be right.

Creative individuals have a strong set of values that are applied consistently to living. To them the world is an interesting, beautiful, and fascinating place (Kelly, 1962). Given this, it seems ironic that those who make decisions about education would choose a system of schooling that stifles creativity and contributes to poor life adjustment for many students, particularly the most creative and potentially contributory to the well-being of society. Traditional schooling discourages the development of creativity, while in learning communities it is valued and promoted.

In recent years interest has increased for determining a way to make creative activities in school more accepted. This involves incorporating wisdom in creative activities and expressions. It is believed that creativity developed without wisdom may not serve children, their families, their communities, or the wider social and cultural groups to which they belong. Wisdom involves the synthesis of knowledge, creative mental capacities, and virtue. It is an expert knowledge system about fundamental problems related to the meaning and conduct of life, enabling appropriate action that takes into account multiple perspectives. Thus, wisdom requires creative expression to be circumscribed by appropriate values and virtue (Bates & Kunzmann, 2004; Bates & Saudinger, 2000).

Wisdom involves appropriate actions that consider not only multiple forms of understanding and knowledge but also multiple needs and perspectives. It also involves balancing self-interest with the interests of other individuals in addition to appropriately dealing with the complex environment in which one lives. This kind of activity encompasses creativity because the wise solution to a problem may be far from obvious (Craft, 2008).

Wise actions seem to have an essential moral quality that distinguishes them from other behaviors that might be called cunning, smart, expedient, or merely intelligent. Wisdom takes into account the greater good and one's own higher, deeper, or more lasting values (Claxton, 2008; Gardner, 2008). Properly exercised, creativity is associated with the production of something novel and valued, or the innovative solution to a tricky problem, but wisdom dictates that such actions must include moral dimensions (Claxton, Craft & Gardner, 2008).

To live successfully in the twenty-first century, students need the capacity for creative transformation. They must be prepared to manage ambiguity and diversity as well as embrace agency and responsibility in an ethical way. This they must do through reasoned judgment while sustaining the communities to which they belong and living successfully in an increasingly complex technological world.

Creativity is an essential part of children's preparation as they come to understand multiple perspectives and positions and to manage parallel and dissonant points of view without seeking single-minded, simple solutions (Haste, 2008). They must come to realize that creative activities are not just fun and easy. Real-life creativity usually requires disciplined hard work, which is fraught with times of frustration and indecision (Claxton, Craft & Gardner, 2008).

DEMOCRATIC DISCIPLINE IN LEARNING COMMUNITIES

In learning communities, discipline practices are dramatically different than they are in traditional classrooms. Various discipline models were described in chapter 2 along with a number of issues related to their use. The models vary from extreme control through rewards and punishment to those considered more democratic. The drawbacks of rewards and punishment were presented along with the difficulties encountered through employing logical consequences. As it turns out, punishment consists of a very complex set of procedures that most teachers are unable to consistently apply; even when they are implemented appropriately they are ineffective, even increasing disruptiveness in many students, with some experiencing personal harm.

The negative aspects of rewards should also give educators pause. Ordinarily they are utilized in ways that are detrimental to students. As explained earlier, the most common detriment is to undermine intrinsic motivation and create expectations that lead to very onerous self-concept problems. Students ordinarily become conditioned to rewards offered as incentives to enhance achievement. The outcome is a negative view of the learning for which rewards are given. Students also connect rewards to adult approval. Failure to acquire them becomes a threat to desired acceptance.

Some educators have recommended that punishment be replaced with what is termed logical consequences. As previously explained, students often interpret these as punishments, particularly when they are imposed on them. Even when students help determine consequences for misbehavior, they find it hard to accept them. To students they are no different than punishment.

Many of the so-called democratic discipline models utilize logical consequences as a basic procedure. Most of the time teachers implement them rather than having students help decide when they are appropriate. In fact, in applying these models, teachers commonly regulate misbehavior in one way or another, thus denying students full enjoyment of the democratic process in their schooling. Many of the models have a democratic orientation regarding much of what happens in the classroom. But teachers usually occupy a control-oriented role anytime there are classroom disruptions.

To be truly democratic, discipline must preserve self-governing principles in teaching and learning. Students must be helped to use democratic procedures not only with respect to learning, but also regarding classroom behavior. They must learn how to effectively regulate their own conduct so that optimum learning takes place without unnecessary disruptions. This can be accomplished when the same principles and procedures that define student learning in democratic communities are used to deal with discipline issues. There should be no differences in how learning and discipline are handled in the classroom.

In democratic learning communities, rather than traditional rules controlling student behavior, learning principles are used as a guide. Usually conventional rules imposed on students direct them to raise their hands if they want to speak, not to talk during quiet study time, follow all teacher directions, turn in all assignments at the designated time, keep their hands to themselves, always bring notebook and textbooks to class, do their own work, and so on. Usually these are given under threat of punishment.

However, in learning communities principles are created to guide instruction in ways that help prevent most discipline problems. The class discusses the particulars of making sure that student interactions do not disrupt others. Thus, students not only help to direct their own learning, they determine the means for ensuring that learning is not disrupted. In this learning configuration, students attempt to determine all potential problems and agree regarding how they might be avoided.

Another way learning disruptions are precluded is by having students help to plan and direct their own classroom activities. When students are satisfied with school because of their involvement in meaningful learning, they are much less inclined to engage in distracting behavior. This is perhaps the most effective way to prevent the frivolous and pernicious actions that occur when students become bored or distracted during learning episodes in which they have no role to define or direct, or when they see classroom activities as a threat to their personal wishes. When students are not allowed to participate responsibly in decisions about classroom learning, most of their needs go unmet, and they tend to react disruptively.

In learning communities students learn that interacting with their peers is central to their activities in the classroom. Learning extensively with classmates is not judged inappropriate, but rather as an integral component of the education process. They soon recognize that working with peers helps them gain new insights and enlarge their understanding of important conceptual information. It also helps them to satisfy their need for association and acceptance. When this happens, they acquire greater commitment for group learning that runs smoothly without disruptions. It helps them make sure that their desire for community learning is not threatened. Consequently, this becomes one of the important issues confronted by the class in regular group meetings.

In class discussions, students examine the potential benefit of more caring and meaningful relationships. Through their teacher's instruction, as well as interpersonal interactions, they come to understand the way relationships are enhanced, how this enrichment greatly contributes to their sense of social well-being, and how their personal support for this important constituent of learning communities is critical. Thus, they delve deeply into ways to communicate effectively so as not to injure associates. They also acquire a commitment to protect each other from any intrusion that carries potential harm. In this process they learn to value the friendship of associates and acquire an enormous sense of care for them. In support of their peers, they eventually acquire a desire to contribute to a constructive, disruption-free environment for learning.

Students also routinely discuss ways to accentuate learning by eliminating or avoiding any potential obstacles. The process of learning in a community environment can easily be threatened by individuals committed to imposing traditional approaches to education. Students may feel threatened by such overtures and require help in examining the threats and solidifying the value of their own learning agenda. Eventually students will not only become more committed to the community but also more fully enabled to effectively communicate the merit of learning communities to others. When this issue is addressed in group meetings, students can share their experiences and help each other learn to respond to others in appropriate ways.

Far fewer discipline problems emerge when students are engaged in pursuing their own interests. But simply following student interests is very shortsighted and often leads to questionable learning outcomes. Current student interests can and should constitute part of the conceptual knowledge upon which they focus their attention, but these constitute just a fraction of what they might pursue had they known of other possibilities. Student interests should be enlarged by having them consider other potential topics for study. They should be invited to explore other options of which they are unaware. When this is done, students are more likely to study subjects of greater significance with added intensity and commitment. More responsible classroom behavior can be expected.

Because the process of inquiry is the natural way humans learn, being occupied with this learning approach stimulates more concentrated efforts and fewer distractions. When students are so engaged, they can spend long periods in intense concentration. Because inquiry learning is both need satisfying and consistent with learning proclivities, students can be depended on to pursue learning without the usual interferences found in most traditional classrooms. With students so occupied, there are few if any disruptions.

Sometimes students involved in learning communities may not fulfill their commitments as initially proclaimed, or as they may be defined by associates. Though this may not be a class disruption in the usual sense, it can become a problem if students become negatively confrontational. It can also disrupt the learning of the entire group when the contribution that should have been made hampers the success of the group learning project. Issues of this kind must be routinely addressed by the group to maintain clarity of purposes and fulfillment of commitments. In learning communities students learn to process these kinds of problems in constructive ways.

There are times, of course, when a community participant may decide that a different course of learning would be to his or her advantage as well as in the best interest of the group. Even so, community members may want to hold the individual accountable for pursuing the learning tasks originally agreed upon. Much of the potential conflict possibly can be avoided when the group collectively decides to always entertain possible changes in the learning responsibilities pursued by its members. Then when changes are believed to be useful and appropriate, they can be brought up and discussed by the group to determine whether they are consistent with group goals or a hindrance.

Part of the agenda of learning communities is to create a viable means of constructively interacting with each other. Many discipline problems can be avoided when members clearly understand the kind of social discourse that can potentially ignite discord and the kind that invites smooth group processing. Communications should embrace an ambience of care and concern for the welfare of others. When this occurs, many discordant episodes can be circumvented. Usually community members realize that potential conflicts are just misunderstandings rather than intentional attacks.

Even though most discipline problems can be prevented in learning communities, occasionally they do occur. When this happens, it is not the teacher's role to immediately intervene and try to correct the problem. It is still the responsibility of students to deal with the issue. This doesn't mean that they should immediately draw attention to the misbehavior and force the negligent student to comply with previously made commitments. Rather, they should wait until later, when that particular category of misbehavior can be examined more indirectly in a classroom meeting with the idea in mind of preventing future difficulties. Future problems thus become the issue rather than the need to punish someone as payment for misbehavior.

In the follow-up session, student names are not brought up. Problems are discussed categorically with no reference to a particular incident. In this atmosphere, the problem can be carefully delineated and ways to prevent further disruptions determined. Students can also reiterate the commitments they have made to each other regarding proper classroom decorum and learning responsibilities.

It is particularly wise for the learning communities to periodically discuss potential classroom learning and discipline problems. Again, no particular event is considered. When this is properly done, students can reckon with potential difficulties without attributing problems to an individual student. This is a simple, unobtrusive way for students to remind themselves of previous decisions they have helped to make and reaffirm their commitments to each other.

ASSESSMENT IN LEARNING COMMUNITIES

In learning communities, assessment is much more broadly based and comprehensive than in traditional student achievement evaluations. Ordinarily appraisals in schools consist exclusively of student achievement assessments. In contrast, evaluation in learning communities also includes the extent to which student needs are met and examines many of the intricacies of the teaching-learning process and various factors associated with it, including moral development.

While in traditional schooling comparisons between students in terms of achievement is a central focus of evaluation, in learning communities these comparisons are deliberately avoided because of the negative impact they can have on some children. Instead of comparing students, the level of excellence achieved by each student is examined along with contributing factors. Student progress and the personal fit of the curriculum for all students are more critical factors than comparative achievement scores.

The purpose of schooling in learning communities is much more extensive than the memorized information ordinarily measured by various tests. Simply sorting students for college by making comparisons of their academic performances misses out on many items that are a concern to parents and to society generally. For example, there are living skills, need fulfillment, and for some students employment preparation. In addition, students may visualize different purposes for specific courses. For instance, some students may look upon an art class as preparation for an occupation, while others may see art as a field to teach, a hobby, or simply experiences to learn art appreciation.

Because students may have various purposes for what they learn in school, evaluation must make allowance for differences. These should be tied to student aspirations. Assessments are thus focused on the progress students are making regarding the achievement of their goals. In this way students can see where they stand in terms of the degree of excellence they have set for themselves and what might yet be required.

Teachers should honor the level of excellence students set for themselves. Consequently, making comparisons is a futile, even harmful endeavor. Various abilities and interests frame the goals for which students strive and the degree of excellence deemed appropriate. They simply need to know where they stand in terms of their own aspirations. Students should also be taught not to compare themselves to their classmates and should neither denigrate nor aggrandize themselves or their peers in terms of either goals or accomplishments. To avoid these problems, students will need to detach themselves from previous mind-sets brought on by grading practices.

Teachers should also be on the lookout for any indication that students wish to modify their learning goals and levels of excellence determined earlier. These should be flexible. However, changes should not be made thoughtlessly and without input from group members. As indicated earlier, changes can sometimes impact the work of the group, and consequently they need an opportunity to react to such proposals.

Leadership skills and cooperative learning abilities need to be evaluated. All group members should have an opportunity for growth in these areas. These assessments should be made far enough in advance that individuals have an opportunity to make the modifications that the evaluations suggest. Leadership would primarily be examined in terms of how well student leaders were able to employ the same principles that their teachers were exemplifying. Cooperative learning abilities might include attributes such as an inclination to share, helpfulness, shouldering an appropriate share of work responsibilities, following through on commitments, and refraining from annoying others.

Because inquiry learning is central to learning communities, it should also be evaluated. This can be done by observing students' research and questioning them about their strategies. In particular, teachers should focus on the degree to which students control for confounding variables and make astute conclusions regarding their findings. They should also assess the significance of the research conducted and the extent to which what was learned contributes important knowledge and understanding.

Students' communication skills should also be examined, along with the sense of care they acquire as they interact with their peers. Social skills are an important aspect of schooling and critical to the process of group learning. Students should eventually develop such attributes as sensitivity, thoughtfulness, sincerity, helpfulness, and conscientiousness. They should increasingly become good communicators and interact with clarity devoid of negative innuendos and criticism.

Appropriate schooling as well as personal and social development depends on student needs being fulfilled. Need fulfillment is central to an adequate education. Schooling that fails in this respect lacks critical motivation considerations as well as instigating a plethora of personal and social problems. Need satisfaction should be closely followed by teachers and formal assessments made to ensure better learning and development.

The unfolding of children's value systems also needs continuous examination. Educational goals regarding value development have long been part of expressed educational goals, but rarely are they pursued or evaluated. In learning communities, value development receives considerable emphasis. The values embraced by the group should have a democratic orientation and consist of such particulars as courtesy, honesty, and integrity. Values can be assessed through teacher observations as well as student writing. Students should be encouraged to discuss value issues periodically. This way they can make comparisons between various values and determine their group and personal significance. Group functioning depends on common values having an impact on all student actions.

The most acclaimed goal of schooling is intellectual development. However, as repeatedly pointed out, the usual tests administered do not validly assess this outcome. Therefore other means must be sought to determine the degree to which students become accomplished intellectually. Much of this can be determined by examining their research as well as the reports they make of their efforts. Insights can also be gained by teachers as they observe the interactions of students in their learning groups. Teachers need to evaluate students' skills in analyzing complex ideas, creating unique products and proposals, and assessing the value of comparable but conflicting opinions and concepts.

Teachers should also determine how well students can evaluate their own work. They should provide their students with instruction on self-assessment and follow up by ascertaining the validity of their evaluations. Learning how to make valid self-assessments is critical to personality development as well as preparation for life in democratic communities both in school and out. One of the common outcomes of exclusive teacher evaluation is very pernicious self-concept problems. These problems can be avoided when students participate in the evaluation process. Learning to evaluate personal accomplishments validly is also a great benefit in life generally.

The following are questions that need to be addressed in evaluating learning communities:

1. To what degree do learning community members acquire social skills?
2. Do community members openly and effectively express themselves?
3. How effective is the inquiry process in the research and reports presented?
4. What is the quality of leadership development?
5. What level of cooperative skill development is achieved by students?
6. Does the learning community adequately promote intellectual development?
7. What level of intellectual excellence do students achieve?
8. To what degree are student needs being met in the learning community?
9. Are students able to validly assess their own work?
10. How effective is the process of community building?

11. Do community members develop a cohesive set of values that they share with the group and knowledgeably articulate?

12. How well does the learning community integrate personal goals with group goals?

13. How well does the learning community help harmonize personal autonomy and group commitment?

14. Are student portfolios an accurate representation of their accomplishments?

15. Are the materials acquired for student research and learning adequate?

16. Does the teacher occupy a role that accentuates the purposes of the learning community?

17. Does the school administration provide necessary assistance for the smooth functioning of the learning community?

Chapter Seven

Instructional Leadership and Teacher Development

In recent years the role of teachers in the public schools has been redefined. Increasingly, teachers are being compelled to focus their attention on improving student scores on standardized achievement tests. As explained earlier, many find it necessary to forsake their conceptions of good teaching and classroom discipline along with what they consider appropriate curricula. Some have been required to abandon the usual classroom learning activities in favor of preparing students to take tests.

Often the "new curricula" are outside their field of expertise. Yet many are pressured to implement these curricula and ensure higher test scores under threat of lesser financial benefits or even losing their jobs. Ironically, because of pressure to ensure that students pass standardized tests, some teachers and administrators have cheated (Clinchy, 2001; McNeil, 2000; Merrow, 2001). Teachers tend to take these threats seriously.

As explained in chapter 4, teachers are often judged to be exclusively at fault for student failure, despite other considerations that have an even greater impact on student achievement than they do. In addition to what was outlined earlier, significant causes such as the following might be added. Student performance in class can be substantially affected by attitudes children develop at home and in the community at large. They can also be impacted by local, state, and national directives over which teachers have no control. Students' peer groups can also have an enormous influence on school performance as can the history of experiences that children bring to class, including those involving previous schooling. By the time students get into a particular teacher's class, they may already suffer from various learning impediments and knowledge deficits along with patterns of classroom misbehavior.

In addition to the foregoing constraints, the curriculum and instructional program may be alien to student interests and learning inclinations. Even so, teachers are required to assume full responsibility for what students learn. Clearly this is double jeopardy. Teachers' supposed expertise is tied to students' performance in connection with a plethora of impingements over which they have no control or influence, while at the same time the teachers are required to structure their teaching to accommodate the views of various officials rather than teaching in a way they consider essential.

Ironically, many decisions about the instructional program are made in places far removed from the classroom and by individuals who may lack the necessary expertise (Darling-Hammond, 1997). Students ordinarily become the losers in this arrangement. When reciprocity is missing and they consequently are unable to assume some accountability for what is taught and learned, students refuse to claim ownership of what they do in the classroom. The result is not only a lower academic output, but diminished moral development.

It has become more common to give teachers fewer decision-making responsibilities regarding their teaching (Meier, 2002). Frequently teachers are required to teach using so-called "teacher-proof materials." Supposedly this makes it unnecessary for them to do much thinking about their teaching. As far back as the 1960s, teacher-proof curricula in the form of mastery learning were strongly promoted. These, however, turned out to be a dead end. Such curricular orientations downplayed the role of teachers too much, making them little more than instructional managers (Prawat, 1992).

These conditions have been challenged by educators. Cognitive psychologists have helped educators create more appropriate learning contexts and employ such methods as learning communities, which help to capitalize on children's inherent learning proclivities more fully. Children have been shown to be much like adults in how they think and solve problems. As they approach various puzzling life situations, they form their own theories regarding the world and use these theories to interpret new information. Furthermore, because learning is commonly a social act, teacher effectiveness is beginning to shift from capability of delivering information to the building of classroom learning communities (Resnick, 1990).

As indicated repeatedly, to be more effective, teachers need more decision-making responsibilities, not less. They need to be exempt from interferences that compromise their teaching and force a focus on standardized performance requirements. Directives that dictate standards and employ tests to determine how well they have been met actually are a threat to genuine standards (Merrow, 2001).

Teachers need to be properly trained and then allowed to use their judgment and skills in their particular classroom so that they can provide legitimate help to students in pursuit of valid learning goals. This doesn't mean that teachers are fully prepared at the time they are certified. Rather, it is the point at which they embark on a growth process. This developmental process is frustrated unless they have sufficient decision-making responsibilities in their classes.

Decisions made by people who are far removed from the classroom do not have sufficient power to promote teacher improvement. Almost without exception they fail to address student behavior problems that may be promoted as part of the curricula they advocate. Capable leadership needs to emerge within the school itself so that what is done there helps to qualify all participants and encourages students to engage in worthwhile, increasingly self-directed learning.

STRATEGIES FOR MANAGING TEACHING AND LEARNING

There are substantially different strategies for managing teaching. These strategies are based on radically different assumptions about human behavior and how individuals react to various treatments. Based on the personal views of policy makers, teachers may be seen as in need of much direct supervision within a context of specified standards and instructional outcomes. From this perspective, principals and supervisors are expected to provide teachers with clear directions regarding how and what to teach. Close supervision is required to ensure that teachers do in fact follow explicit instructions.

This supports a system of "one best way" to teach and is expedited in the form of an explicitly detailed curriculum and instruction program. These kinds of curricula come with lesson plans, time frames, and tests that teachers are required to use. Teachers are managed to ensure that their work is properly aligned with expectations. Thankfully, this heavy-handed approach is not as popular as it once was. Yet there remains the strategy of providing specified standards as a means to control what teachers do.

Structured supervision is designed to ensure that all students achieve the same objectives at specified achievement levels within a particular time frame. Supposedly this approach provides teachers limited control over the means by which their students meet the designated standards. However, it tends to script what teachers do and thus provides far less self-determination than advocates may proclaim. This is because common standards require uniform assessments. These assessments become curriculum determinants, which in turn dictate the nature of teaching.

In this system, teachers are provided with very little useful input regarding their teaching. In addition, there is a distrust of teachers and lack of faith in their capacity to make valid judgments. It is assumed that they are unlikely to do what is best for their students without external intervention (Sergiovanni, 2000). While this environment of mistrust is in operation, it is unlikely that policy makers' aspirations regarding student achievement or those of teachers will be reached.

When teachers are directed to adhere to designated curricula and students are required to follow the rules and procedures that evolve from these, the teachers' reactions to micromanagement can effectively subvert a proper consideration for what is best for students. Of course administrators believe that control is necessary to create smooth-running schools. However, when bureaucratic controls shape school operations, the curricula are trivialized and the potential for worthwhile educational experiences undermined.

Teachers respond to administrative mandates by reducing educational quality. At the same time they tend to control their students with the same intensity with which administrators control them. When students realize that their learning experiences are trivial and lacking in credibility, they don't apply themselves fully and consequently fail to achieve their educational potential.

Under these conditions, tension develops between the contradictory goals of providing students with a valid education and simply controlling and processing them. When teachers come to feel that their educational purposes and judgments are not taken seriously, they tend to elicit minimal compliance from their students. Rather than promoting student involvement in meaningful learning, teachers tend to merely require them to memorize lists of terms and unrelated facts (McNeil, 1988a).

When teachers are confronted with excessive control and find no support for their authority as professionals within the school, they create their own domain of authority by tightly controlling course content, which is characterized by dull routines. Students are inclined to resist this kind of teaching and consequently do a minimum of work. Under these conditions, teachers tend to overreact to student misbehavior rather than pursue a consistent set of principles for promoting positive student actions.

Under these conditions, students rebel in such petty ways as littering the halls and cafeteria (McNeil, 1988a). Teachers and school administrators then fall into the trap of making rules more strict and punishments more severe (Glasser, 1990). When teachers experience less control from administrators, they exercise much less control over students (McNeil, 1988b). The result is fewer discipline problems.

The critical error made by many school administrators and other policy makers is to assume that teaching is easy. They believe that teaching involves certain basic skills that can readily be acquired and employed and that teachers can be easily monitored, assessed, and controlled. Because this is assumed, they are inclined to invest very little in promoting teaching excellence and professionalism as well as teacher interaction and collegiality and other well-known improvement strategies. It is far cheaper to avoid the necessary expense of promoting teacher excellence (Sergiovanni, 2000).

People involved in any aspect of educational decision making should realize that teaching is one of the most complex of all human activities and doesn't lend itself to simple, mindless applications. Dozens of student actions occur simultaneously in typical classrooms, requiring constant monitoring and proper reactions from teachers. The number of these happenings vastly increases in classrooms with more students.

In addition, students have a multiplicity of learning inclinations and various behaviors that they have learned will help to satisfy their needs. Because of this complexity, properly applied educational theories are far more effective than the commonly used "bag of tricks" approaches to teaching. Bag-of-tricks procedures are the usual outcome of excessive supervisory direction. Educational theory helps to simplify the process of diagnosing student needs and behavior and applying proper teaching strategies and tactics. Theory is best applied by individual teachers in connection with what they observe on a day-to-day basis in their own classrooms.

To be effective, teachers must be provided with an environment that helps to build professionalism. This requires the establishment of shared purposes, values, and norms that provide a framework for teaching excellence and creates opportunities for increased collegiality with their peers. These conditions provide a means for greater teacher interdependence and the development of communities of practice.

The views of policy makers must be changed to accommodate the development of a profession worthy of faith and trust. To become a profession, teaching must go beyond the view that skills alone are needed for teaching excellence. Professional expertise requires the application of theory-based principles to a variety of situations. To effectively apply these principles, teachers must be able to determine what is actually going on in their individual classrooms. In this way they gain a better perspective regarding the ways in which students satisfy their needs.

Teachers must also know how children naturally learn along with their various learning inclinations, and be able to provide an environment in which all students can reach their full potential despite their individual differences and learning proclivities. They must be able to identify problems, find solutions, and make decisions about what to do in ambiguous, complex situations (Kennedy, 1987).

Teaching must be acknowledged as a deliberate action taken in a context involving a complex of different resources, student characteristics and needs, time constraints, and curricular frameworks. Within this context, different purposes and interpersonal interactions shape what teachers do. Teachers must be able to analyze classroom complexities and determine the way dynamic situations modify contexts as practice unfolds. While doing this, teachers must craft strategies that attend to student actions and thinking.

Teachers must be able to appropriately deal with ideas as they evolve in the complicated dynamics of classroom operations. They cannot simply restrict instruction to a set lesson plan, but rather must be able to sense promising new directions for instruction as they are indicated by student responses and questions. In the teaching-learning process, one idea will eventually lead to another until a pattern emerges that promotes understanding and provides direction to more advanced learning (Mintzberg, 1987).

Once a pattern does emerge, teachers will be able to use their knowledge of theory along with their own teaching experiences to help make appropriate strategy decisions. It is critical to realize that this analysis and decision making occurs within the context of the individual's unique teaching practice. It is a melding of personal experience with theory. Teaching professionals can generate knowledge as they engage in the particulars of their practice, spontaneously forming intuitions and discovering new paths they could not anticipate in advance. They create their practice in the application process (Schon, 1983).

Successful deliberation by teachers about their practice requires a body of experience on which to draw, the ability to mentally experiment with various options and critically evaluate possible outcomes, and the inclination to revise ongoing teaching as the situation demands. Along with this, teachers must have a highly developed sense of purpose, for purposes frame the criteria against which both instructional ideas and teaching actions are judged (Kennedy, 1987).

Good teachers can construct bridges between their students and the subject matter and address a myriad of questions. Questions such as the following must be seriously considered: How can I help students identify interesting aspects of the subject? What concepts and ideas will students find it difficult to understand? What strategies might I employ to help students understand difficult concepts? How does current student knowledge articulate with intended instruction? What resources might help in the instructional process? What is the process of concept formation?

They might also ask: What kind of experiences and explanations will help students conceptualize correctly? How can I capitalize on students' needs during instruction? How is student behavior in the classroom related to the kind of instructional program employed? What is the cause of misbehavior? Not only must teachers address questions like these, they must also become good listeners and researchers regarding their students' thinking and search for ways to teach for understanding (Wilson & Peterson, 1997).

To function as professionals, teachers must come to recognize their own effectiveness. When they fail to acknowledge their own effectiveness, their students suffer. Teachers with a low sense of self-efficacy come to believe that many students cannot learn and will not learn. The result is that students do not learn. When teachers have an appropriate sense of efficacy, they exhibit warmth, are more accepting of student responses and initiatives, and are more attentive to student needs. Students respond with more enthusiasm and more interaction with their teachers. Their achievement is positively affected (Ashton & Webb, 1986).

Teachers with a sense of efficacy are more highly motivated and committed. Efficacy is developed in a supportive school climate, where teaching and learning are characterized by collegial values and shared decision making and school culture embraces a sense of purpose along with a shared covenant. These factors help create cooperative relationships, more thoughtful interactions, greater personal responsibility for learning outcomes, fewer discipline problems, and higher personal expectations in addition to a feeling that teaching is meaningful and significant (Ashton & Webb, 1986).

TEACHING AND COMMITMENT

For teachers to become committed they must find their work meaningful, purposeful, and important. They must also have reasonable control over what they do and become personally responsible for outcomes. They must perceive that what they do is a matter of their own choosing (Sergiovanni, 1995). Teachers must become committed to teaching in an exemplary way, engage in their practice toward valued social ends, value not only their own practice but also the practice of teaching itself, and thoughtfully accept an ethic of care. These considerations are necessary components of a system that gives direction and meaning to schooling as well as a source of authority.

Exemplary teaching requires teachers to stay abreast of new developments, engage in thoughtful research of their own practice, and experiment with new ideas. It involves not only accepting responsibility for current quality teaching performances, but also includes a commitment to enhance future practice through professional development. A commitment to exemplary teaching requires teachers to be fully involved participants in an inquiry-based learning community (Barth, 1990).

Teachers who are bona fide members of a professional learning community engage in continuous inquiry. Unfortunately educators often rely too much on the opinions and suggestions of outside experts, professional staff developers, and consultants as if they didn't have the necessary expertise to solve their own problems. Typically, the suggestions of experts outside the school have a "one-size-fits-all" orientation, when in fact different schools and classroom situations ordinarily have problems that require unique solutions. Regrettably, principals and teachers often believe they lack the necessary insights and the means to solve their own problems.

School personnel will never have the capacity to solve their problems appropriately unless they abandon this perception and become confident members of learning communities. This can happen if schools give priority to school-based inquiry, where time is given for teachers and administrators to work together with the express purpose of transforming their schools into the kind of institutions they believe they should be.

In performing this important task the efforts of both teachers and administrators should be characterized by open communication, reflection, experimentation, risk taking, and trust among all members of the professional school community. The locus of change is thus found in individual schools with an assurance that modifications are within the reality of a particular school and not simply applications from individuals who are unfamiliar with the school's peculiarities (Oakes, 1992).

Excellent teachers incorporate valued social ends in instruction. In placing themselves in a position to serve students and parents, and to pursue well-defined moral purposes, teachers occupy positions as stewards. While taking on this role, teachers must respond appropriately to parental trust that all teaching and learning will accomplish the greatest moral good. Students are like members of their teachers' own families. Stewardship also involves the teachers' responsibility to prepare the next generation of morally attuned adults. It becomes a sacred obligation from which teachers should not be deterred. Moral students are far less inclined to create discipline problems in the classroom. These important constituents should also be reflected in teachers' professional learning communities.

Teachers must become committed to doing everything possible to enhance learning, promote student development, and satisfy the social needs of students. They should employ a framework through which students can become moral persons. This involves an authentic sense of care in which the relationships with others (teachers, parents, and students) are characterized by nurturance, altruistic love, and kinship-like connections.

The capacity to care involves receiving and understanding the perspectives of others, responding appropriately to them given that awareness, and maintaining caring relationships regardless of possible interferences (Beck, 1992). Educators must be wary of the idea that caring for their students may somehow compromise their objectivity.

Some fear that an atmosphere of care may reduce academic standards and promote less effective learning. Actually the opposite of this is true. Interpersonal fidelity does not imply that academic excellence, the acquisition of skills, or the needs of contemporary society should be of no concern. However, these concerns are best accommodated in an atmosphere of care, not one of shameless objectivity (Noddings, 1986).

TEACHERS FINDING A VOICE

Finding your voice as a teacher involves the unfolding of a teaching identity infused with knowledge and personal experience. It obviously requires the application of sufficient autonomy in the examination of various constituents of teaching from many sources, followed by bringing to bear personal experience and inclinations born of one's own personality, interest, and capacity. It blossoms when teachers come to recognize their own idiosyncratic teaching skills and begin to hone them in a personal way. Teaching strategies should be born of teachers' careful consideration of their own skills and goals and those of their students. A more astute recognition of personal skills can be acquired by conscientious participation with colleagues in professional learning communities.

Both teachers' objectives and those of their students should eventually achieve a state of coexistence. Then strategies should be sought that capitalize on the teachers' proclivities, the learning inclinations of students, and their common goals. Teaching and learning excellence not only involves appropriate planning, but also reflection during instruction and the application of tactical adjustments that seem indicated. After a learning episode has been completed, teachers and their students should engage in careful analysis of the experience for proper modifications to be made in planning subsequent learning activities.

Evidence that teachers are making progress occurs when they try to find the reasons students behave as they do. For example, if students fail to apply themselves to a learning task or engage in disruptive behavior, teachers should ask themselves "why" rather than simply reacting, as is often the case among teachers who employ traditional techniques. In addition, teachers achieve greater maturity as they become more willing to take risks. Creativity tends to be inhibited in the absence of risk taking. Nothing so restricts creativity as does fear of failure (Sullivan, 1963).

Mature teachers understand the process of self-directed growth, or self-actualization. Teachers become self-actualized when they (1) accept reality with all its complexities and ambiguities, (2) accept others and do not feel threatened by them, (3) feel secure enough to be spontaneous, original, and inventive, (4) focus on problems without personal biases, (5) are comfortable with themselves and enjoy both solitude and social interaction, (6) appreciate perspectives different from their own without mindlessly accepting them, (7) are genuinely happy with life, (8) have a sense of spiritual unanimity with others that is embodied in rich, deep personal relationships, (9) enjoy the process of seeking the fulfillment of their goals as much as achieving them, and (10) have a spontaneous sense of humor that never puts others down

(Maslow, 1968). Teachers with these characteristics will experience much greater success.

Teachers need to be free of the fear of censure from colleagues and supervisors. This involves other teachers and administrators' tolerating what takes place in their colleagues' classrooms along with teacher freedom from fears they may have when they teach in an atmosphere of excessive surveillance and criticism. It is paradoxical that as a profession, teaching is characterized by its isolation as well as its public disclosure whenever there is a hint of incompetence or teaching practices that others consider mistakes.

These conditions tend to keep teachers from pursuing innovations that hold promise to improve instruction. When teachers and administrators stop taking risks and instead focus on their fears, they feel threatened and tend to become aggressive, defensive, or withdrawn rather than attempting to solve problems and promoting excellence. They fear a loss of control along with associated predictable negative consequences. They tend to lash out at students or anyone else within their jurisdiction (Jalongo, 1991).

Teaching is a deeply intellectual activity. It does not consist of a set of inviolate steps or a set of unchangeable strategies. Rather, teaching is changeable and propositional and always open to thoughtful revisions, modifications, and adaptations built upon a thoughtfully determined knowledge base, personal experiences, and day-to-day interpretation of changing circumstances in the classroom. Teaching is always subject to question by individual teachers as well as by their colleagues to bring reason to a very complex process. This requires self-reflection, regular observation by colleagues, and in-depth discussions with other educators in professional learning communities regarding critical aspects of the teaching process.

Teachers need to encounter various conceptions about teaching with which they are unfamiliar. These can be provided from the research and theoretical knowledge as well as from the experiences of other educators. These ideas should be reflected upon subsequent to teaching episodes so they might provide a context for discussion and application. Such examinations of the teaching process are more likely to lead to thoughtful consideration and experimentation than passive acceptance of questionable teaching practices.

Questions regarding the nature of excellent teaching should help frame the context for a career-long quest. Teachers must be wary of the assumption that teaching can be defined by a single, simple formula, as is often the case when policy makers try to dictate the teaching process. Often this is done in the absence of relevant examples of teaching excellence, and it almost never takes into account the body of educational research or the practical problems and challenges in the classroom.

It is particularly critical that teachers accurately define and understand the process students use to construct their own meanings. For this to happen, teachers must be empowered to use what they have learned about the teaching process while sharing ideas during thoughtful discussions with peers, along with inventions and experiments they have personally undertaken.

In excellent schools, teachers and students are encouraged to inquire, invent, and experiment—even to risk failure. These practices are likely to flourish only where teachers and their students function as a community of learners. This is apt to occur exclusively where teachers and students understand the values of learning communities and have the personal determination and approval to apply them (Griffin, 1991).

For learning communities to be successful, teachers must believe that the learning process is much more important than the results achieved. This is based on the premise that students learn best from teachers who have insatiable appetites for learning. The process of learning is made to matter when teachers find new ways to teach, try them out, share their experiences with colleagues, make refinements, and try them out again. It is important that administrators participate with teachers in this process as colleagues rather than as directors. Only in this way do teachers acquire ownership for what they do along with the accompanying commitment (Dodd & Rosenbaum, 1986).

The process of becoming a teacher involves creating an individual identity in connection with the role of pursuing professional excellence. Even when institutions support the professional growth of teachers, it is still up to teachers to identify their need for growth and make plans for personal and professional fulfillment. Smart teachers are architects of their own professional growth. They recognize that they are the ones primarily responsible for planning their own development. They should keep in mind, however, that greater insight can be acquired by interacting with other teachers.

Unfortunately, when teachers dispute coercive administrative policies and procedures, they are labeled as uncooperative and unprofessional. In questioning teachers' professionalism, observers greatly underestimate the complexity of their work and supply simplistic solutions for the enormously perplexing issues teachers face in their classrooms each day, as if these naive inputs could validly address the difficulties of attempting to understand classes of thirty or more divergently oriented students and apply appropriate teaching strategies.

Think for a moment of a doctor, lawyer, or dentist who is inundated in their office by thirty people at once, all with different needs and expectations and with a variety of ideas regarding how these needs can best be satisfied. Because the individual professional is unable to adequately address all these needs at once, a lot of conflict and trouble would likely evolve. No doubt, wholesale pandemonium would ensue. Assume that all this rumpus would continue on all day every day for nine months (Jalongo, 1991).

This helps put the teacher's role as a professional into perspective. Teaching must be seen as a unique profession that enjoys very few of the characteristics of some of the other professions, but that nonetheless requires a high level of professional skill and expertise. Its complexity should never be underestimated and the solution to its problems never thought to be extraordinarily simple. This is the reason teachers need to spend their careers trying to learn how best to promote the well-being of their students within the context of a specific, real environment, and why one-size-fits-all approaches are not relevant to teaching and learning excellence even while applying a single set of teaching-learning principles.

Teachers not only make a plethora of decisions while teaching, they must also apply proper ethics and values. At the same time, they must consider decisions made by administrators and outside agencies. In the end, they must ask questions about their actions such as (1) Who benefits from the decisions I make during classroom instruction? (2) Whose interests are being served? (3) What are the effects on children? (4) What is the significance of these effects on children's lives in the short and long term? (5) To what extent do my decisions have a limiting or distorting effect on the opportunities open to children? (6) How can the best learning atmosphere be promoted in the classroom? (Tennyson & Strom, 1986).

Teaching is essentially a moral activity where appropriate questions must be addressed. Expedience should not be allowed to reign supreme. Whether or not teachers carefully consider all appropriate information about their teaching, they still have to make many moral decisions each day and experience the consequences of those decisions. Even though their actions may not directly affect them, sensitive teachers need to understand the implications of their decisions because of the repercussions they may have on students, both good and bad (Jalongo, 1991).

Because teachers are usually isolated from each other, most do not receive genuine support and input from fellow teachers. It is, therefore, critical to create structures that facilitate collegial relationships. As colleagues, teachers have equivalent goals and a collective, vested interest in their fulfillment. They enjoy some degree of personal responsibility but share common commitments (Kraus, 1984).

True colleagues lend support to each other but also encourage candid interactions when agreed-upon principles are violated. At the same time they must be supportive, acknowledge other's efforts, cooperate to solve problems, build self-esteem, listen with a nonjudgmental ear, and unconditionally welcome others into membership (Applegate, Flora, & Lasely, 1980). In learning communities, collegial relationships are essential.

Teachers should not support the status quo in education. Instead they should explore possible alternatives that promise improvement. Keep in mind that there is always conflict between the possibility of teachers supporting educational practices consistent with current research or maintaining schools as they are. Rarely has the latest research information filtered into the schools (Jalongo, 1991). Depending on their training and previous experiences, teachers may feel "out of sync" with their associates and thus not inclined to thoughtfully interact with them about teaching. It appears safer to simply carry on with traditional teaching practices. This needs to be resisted.

It is difficult to counter the influence of the status quo until collegial relationships are formed and teachers begin to cooperatively examine the research as well as conduct their own research. Even then, before teaching practices are established that are satisfactory to all, considerable interaction is required between teachers to compare their philosophies and teaching approaches in connection with research. Hopefully such associations will encourage the establishment of forward-looking techniques that have the benefit of supporting research.

CREATING A COMMUNITY OF LEADERS

It is far easier to accept the idea that schools should become communities of learners than communities of leaders. Well-established leadership schemes usually fail to deal with the implications of shared leadership. Ordinarily leadership focuses on how to get others to do what they do not prefer because it is believed they are likely to resist what is supposedly better for them, at least as determined by higher authority. From this perspective, it is the responsibility of the leader to help influence what others think and do (Kellerman, 1984; Yukel, 1989).

Essentially the goal of traditional leadership is to control events and people in ways that provide assurance that the leaders' desires will be met. This kind of leadership is contrary to the purposes of learning communities where leadership responsibilities are shared. In communities, what matters most is what is shared, what the community believes in, and what it wants to accomplish. This community of mind becomes the primary source of authority for what members do (Sergiovanni, 1994).

In schools that apply learning community principles, both principals and teachers are committed to making visions of educational excellence come to fruition. To accomplish this, they have equal responsibility. It doesn't fall to the principal to ensure the accomplishment of institutional objectives. In responsible professional learning communities, rather than leadership being defined as exercising power over others, it evolves out of group focus regarding the accomplishment of shared goals. Thus, various members of the school faculty may lead out in areas in which they are particularly interested and qualified to pursue.

Even parents can provide leadership in the schools depending on schedules, expertise, and personal inclination. Leadership within a community of educators should operate much like it does in a community of learners in the classroom. Responsibility should be deliberately shifted among members so that all participants have an opportunity to hone their leadership skills and acquire the commitment that comes with directing shared endeavors.

In reality, leadership is the ability to bring out the best in others and to motivate them to share leadership roles in the school. Leaders must be able to give up power and the desire to control and instead take on an attitude of serving others along with pursuing agreed-upon school purposes (Sergiovanni, 1994). School leaders must put students at the center of decisions they make. Decisions made on the basis of expedience should be shunned.

While in a leadership role, teachers should always ask what effect various actions will have on students and what the students' responsibility should be. Students should be involved in reviewing curricular programs for relevancy and be given responsibility to help govern the operation of these programs (Cristofoli, 1992). In teacher interactions, strategies should be evolved that will be successful in this quest. In this kind of leadership, less emphasis is given to people-handling skills and more to the power of shared, compelling ideas and meanings held by all involved.

During the growth of community, the nature of leadership itself can be expected to evolve. In the beginning, principals may need to think of ways to help teachers satisfy their individual psychological needs, while later their focus is more likely to be on creating relationship ties that bring teachers together in reciprocal bonds of care and shared expectations. Eventually teachers and principals should establish shared values and create ties that produce true collegial associations, with all bound together by reciprocal caring and acknowledged interdependence that comes from mutually held obligations and commitments (Sergiovanni, 1990).

Collegial cultures develop bonds of trust among members that transcend congeniality. They provide a forum for reflection and honest feedback, for challenge and disagreement, and for accepting responsibility without assuming blame. In collegial cultures, group members move beyond consensus, resist giving one another premature reassurance or quick fixes, and interact deeply so as to uncover and analyze problems and find solutions (Lieberman & Miller, 2008).

Leadership requires redefinition as the sources of authority regarding leaders' responsibilities are modified and as attention is given to shared ideas rather than points of disagreement. This is because bureaucratic leadership relies on institutional authority within a context of bartering and directing. Moral authority, on the other hand, depends on bonds of care and agreed-upon agendas. This is in contrast to bureaucratic organizations where participants have different goals and orientations that inherently promote distrust and lack of cooperation.

Because most people are familiar with traditional, bureaucratic leadership and unacquainted with the moral leadership found in learning communities, a transition process can be expected in any move to incorporate new leadership strategies. As already mentioned, the initial effort will be to meet participants' needs. Later more attention can be devoted to building relationships and shared purposes. Once a community of mind begins to develop, it becomes a substitute for traditional leadership. The school becomes a place where people care for each other, help each other, and devote themselves to the work of the community while committing themselves to a life of inquiry and learning (Sergiovanni, 1994).

As collegiality becomes established, leadership increasingly functions apart from outside direction. It becomes a part of the everyday expression of teachers and principals at work. Teachers tend to depend more on their own judgment in connection with interactions with their colleagues. In the process, the pressure often felt by administrators is eased. They are less worried about providing direct control and instead spend their time creating conditions that encourage others to emerge as leaders (Sergiovanni, 1992).

A professional learning community consists of a group of educators who are engaged in a common struggle to achieve an understanding of the nature of their students' needs and learning proclivities so they can offer them a better education (Lieberman, 1996). The learning process must be carefully studied and discussed until teachers achieve a state of unanimity about it along with the best way to implement consistent instructional strategies. Children's idiosyncrasies and needs must be a part of this discussion so that all critical considerations are melded into an agreed-upon approach to teaching to which all are committed.

A shared vision must be developed through distributed leadership with clear goals that focus on new, more powerful views of student achievement. Leadership must help provide direction and guidance for implementing the vision and keeping it constantly in view while helping the entire school community remain faithful to the vision in daily practice. Initially this may involve helping all participants refrain from controlling actions along with celebrating diversity.

Unless diversity of expertise is valued among members, simple-minded, one-sided decisions are likely to be made that fail to address the complexity of problems schools face (Bielaczyc & Collins, 1999). The faculty must become committed to sharing leadership with their students in the same way they share it with each other so that students can become an authentic part of the shared vision. Collective ownership and accompanying responsibility are best achieved when leadership is distributed among all group members (Neuman & Simmons, 2000).

Principals have a special role in distributed leadership. First, they need to abandon an approach to leadership based on rules and procedures. Instead, they should ensure that all participate in a shared vision as the source of direction. Second, teachers should not only be invited to participate in the decision-making process, they should be empowered to act upon the shared values they have helped determine. Lack of experience should not be a deterrent. One's lack of leadership experience should serve as an invitation to become involved and learn from others. Principals should make sure that all the members of the teaching staff have an opportunity to receive the necessary training to make good decisions.

Third, principals should be results oriented as well as process oriented. But particular results are not expected. Rather, the principal's role is to help ensure that there are results and that these results come from group deliberations. They should be certain that the deliberation process honors individual inputs to take advantage of diversity and yet is consistent with the collective vision. They have a role to play in helping members understand how promoting the needs and input of each member can be consistent with the covenant made as community members.

Fourth, principals have a special role in posing appropriate questions rather than imposing solutions. Because of the position they occupy, they may be inclined to propose, if not impose, solutions, when their role should be one of ensuring an environment that encourages input from others. In learning communities, it is not only improper to impose one's will, it is inappropriate to allow one's position to skew discussions and decisions in a particular way.

The principal's role is to help the staff learn the particulars of a learning community, promote an atmosphere of care, provide the means by which a vision for the group can be created, ensure that shared goals are addressed, focus on teaching and learning excellence, help determine evaluation strategies consistent with the learning purposes and processes of a community, promote effective collaboration, and effectively involve parents (DuFour, 1999).

Within learning communities collegial relationships among teachers and principals are drastically modified. There are hazards in this new definition of colleagueship. For one thing, it resists important aspects of privacy, individualism, and competition that tend to already be established within the cultural makeup of society. Yet the issue remains regarding how individuality can be maintained within a context of living a coherent, moral life with colleagues that is dedicated to the good of children. Obviously some individuality must be set aside. Personal views must be made public and scrutinized in comparison with the beliefs of others. This, of course, cannot be accomplished within an atmosphere of competition or lack of trust. Nor can it be supported by contradictory personal agendas.

Still, there is likely to be ambivalence between the value of individualism and the need for community. Undoubtedly there will be discomfort whenever it is suggested that teaching practices should become more collectively employed. For many, collegiality is all right so long as it is restricted to positive social interactions but then allows each individual to continue teaching as he or she wishes.

The best way to overcome the obstacles in initiating learning communities is to become involved and allow the situation to play out, all the while noting the benefits of such an undertaking, particularly regarding new insights concerning teaching and modified but improved student achievement. Experience shows that eventually caring relationships evolve and greater effectiveness emerges.

These changes take place particularly when teachers are not required to unduly sacrifice their own thoughts, preferences, and styles (Sergiovanni, 1994). Eventually these individual dimensions of understanding and action become part of the community of mind that creates bonds between community members and binds them to a set of ideas that constitutes a collective conscience (Durkheim, 1964).

The obligations inherent in learning communities do not consist of a set of rules. The desire for some sense of privacy despite the obligation to be united with others and productively interact with them can be employed in different ways, depending on personality, predispositions, and other personal factors. For example, some teachers may wish to employ agreed-upon strategies alone in their classrooms while others may decide to become involved in team teaching. There is room in a learning community for teachers to engage in activities of their own choosing that reflect their own preferences, styles, and needs.

Yet the covenant teachers and administrators share with other community members provides the substance that nourishes and solidifies group commitments and goals through which their personal preferences are played out (Sergiovanni, 1994). In this it is imperative that self-interest not be allowed to dominate. There is clear evidence that self-interest is not a sufficiently powerful motivator to account for a good deal of human behavior. A sense of mission and commitment to professional and social ideals are much more potent motivators. Commonly, humans regularly assess individual urges from a moral perspective and routinely sacrifice self-interest and pleasure for the good of others (Sergiovanni, 1992).

Through their involvement in learning communities teachers can experience considerable intrinsic motivation, because this teaching orientation allows for discovery, exploration, variety, and challenge. It also provides a high degree of involvement with work that is considered important and significant. In addition, motivation is promoted through development of values that bond coworkers together.

Also, in the learning communities autonomy and self-determination are encouraged, replacing the resistance usually experienced where rigid, bureaucratic requirements are in place. Thus, teachers can feel like architects of their own professional lives rather than pawns to the system. These conditions encourage feelings of competence and self-control and enhance feelings of teaching excellence (Sergiovanni, 1990).

In weak school faculties, where teacher isolation is the norm and seniority is highly valued, student passivity is promoted along with a pedagogy based on the transmission of knowledge and lower student achievement expectations. Even strong traditional teacher groups have significant problems. They may be more collegial and less isolating than weak faculties, and share some values and norms. However, characteristics ordinarily do not lead to innovation and school improvement. Instead, these communities enforce traditional notions of student abilities, sort students into academic tracks, grade on the curve, and assign the most experienced teachers to the highest tracks and the least experienced to the lower ones.

In contrast, greater student achievement is associated with professional teacher communities. Within these collegial communities there is a focus on teachers learning along with their students. Professional equity is valued and replaces the control-oriented directives traditionally imposed by the administrative hierarchy. Teachers come to see themselves as lifelong learners. They share their experiences with colleagues, collaborate to improve their practice, and experience collective rather than individual professional success (McLaughlin & Talbert, 2001).

Chapter Eight

Schoolwide Discipline and Outside Communities

Learning communities and democratic discipline have implications for the entire school as well as the community outside the school. Parents in particular have an important role to play. In democratic societies, it is imperative that children receive an education that enables them to live productive lives into which they genuinely incorporate democratic principles and values. In addition, it is logical for this effort to be made not only in the school, but also in homes and the larger community. Not to do so presumes that such aspirations and outcomes have little value, when in fact such efforts are indispensable in preparing children for productive democratic living. This imperative is often ignored when society has misconceptions regarding what kind of an education will lead to responsible democratic citizenship.

It is ironic to assume, as is commonly the case, that education for a responsible life in a democratic society is enhanced through control and punishment. At least democratic purposes are implied in educational rhetoric, even though teaching methods are often coercive and punitive and quite inconsistent with life in democratic communities. It is difficult to believe that educators are deliberately trying to prepare their students to live in a totalitarian state. Yet schools commonly operate as though this was intended.

Excessive control will not promote greater maturity and an ability to live successfully in a democracy. Rather, coercive classroom tactics are much more likely to produce more disruptiveness and rebellion and in some cases extreme violence, which may later find its way into the living style of students who experience excessive coercion at school. It is interesting that children are schooled coercively, and then when they graduate, are assumed to be able to automatically undertake a responsible role in a democratic society.

If schools genuinely try to accentuate democratic processes and provide students with excellent instruction in this regard, it seems wise that training in homes and the surrounding community should be consistent with this. Such efforts require an outreach program in which democratic principles are promoted community-wide. This doesn't seem outlandish as a goal given the value placed on democratic living in society generally, although accomplishing such an ambitious agenda under current conditions appears daunting.

It should be pointed out that an associated problem lies in the fact that many homes and social organizations fail to routinely practice democratic principles. The potential for confusing children is obvious. No doubt they will need the kind of instruction in school that will help them understand the discontinuity that can exist between the democratic principles valued by society and the way they are improperly employed and sometimes ignored by some individuals and groups.

It isn't that society doesn't value democratic ideals. Instead, it is because many citizens appear unconcerned and consequently do not pursue an understanding of what is likely to help or hinder their children in becoming authentic members of democratic communities. Supposedly children will acquire democratic values and attitudes within various control-oriented institutions such as the schools. This, of course, is not true.

It is also erroneously assumed that children can acquire a democratic orientation to life while living under coercive, punishing home conditions. Unfortunately, many parents are under the impression that controlling and punishing children will help them to eventually behave responsibly. However, to live successfully in a democracy, children need to be endowed with freedom at home and have opportunities to gradually become responsible decision makers. If this course is consciously pursued by parents, home life will be dramatically improved and life at school positively impacted.

Such beneficial changes could conceivably take place if parents became more involved in the learning communities in which their children participate at school. The outcome would logically be greater consistency between life at home and at school. It would also tend to promote better family relationships, thus helping to reduce the influence of gangs and other community disruptions. Parents could also be encouraged to form their own learning communities and begin to research and learn more about parenting as well as school operations.

THE ROLE OF PARENTS IN LEARNING COMMUNITIES

Most parents have limited time to spend in their children's classes. However, time they spend there can go far in helping their children acquire an excellent education and improve their parenting skills. Even when opportunities to participate in their children's learning communities are limited, time should still be spent dialoging with children about what is happening in school. These conversations should not focus on achievements, but rather on children's intellectual development and attitudes about school experiences. Parents should encourage their children to explain their learning projects in great detail and make insightful assessments about experiences in their classrooms.

Parents can also become involved in their children's research efforts. This is a far different role than parents traditionally occupy. Most are involved exclusively in making sure their children complete assigned school homework that usually consists of solving lists of repetitive problems, doing exercises of various kinds, reading, and memorizing factual information. In learning communities, student learning is mostly devoted to researching questions and investigating various sources of information to increase understanding and solve problems.

This learning agenda lends itself to parent involvement. Parents can become research partners with their children and assume a role similar to the one their children occupy. Their insights and curiosity can help frame the research they do with their children. They can also share in a leadership role. With proper coordination from school classrooms, parents can help further teachers' intentions of empowering children and helping them to become responsible group learners.

When parents are involved in their children's schooling, attitudes are improved, cooperation is increased, and achievement is enhanced (Becher, 1984; Epstein, 1984; Hayes, Comer & Hamilton-Lee, 1989; Henderson & Berla, 1995). When parents work side by side in learning communities with their children, even more impressive growth can be expected. Lines of communication can be opened between parents and teachers, and in the process parents can become allies instead of adversaries.

When parents are directly involved with their children's learning, meaningful discussions can be held with teachers about substantive aspects of teaching and learning rather than being confined to simple-minded interactions about such subjects commonly addressed as point totals, grades, misbehavior, and missed assignments. Parents can find out what is really happening in the classroom and acquire a more insightful view of the kind of learning the teacher is trying to provide. This equips them to more appropriately interact with their children about learning and provide the kind of support and involvement that will bring about the most fruitful results.

When teachers become better acquainted with parents, they can learn more about their occupations and life experiences, and with this knowledge, help enhance their students' learning. Parents can often provide expertise in a variety of areas where the teacher may have limited experience. Thus, parents can furnish appropriate input regarding more meaningful ways to work on various research projects. These associations also help parents become better acquainted with their children's teachers and consequently become better equipped for meaningful involvement in learning community–oriented education.

Teachers need to understand their students' parents to work with them successfully. Usually parents are interested in assuring that their children succeed academically, and believe teachers have their children's best interests at heart. Sometimes there might be misunderstandings through miscommunications, although some parents may object to what is happening in school, particularly when they believe it is harmful to their children. Sometimes these problems can be avoided through better communications and fuller explanations about what is going on in the classroom.

Parents who are involved in their children's education are significantly more in sync with what takes place in their children's classrooms and more likely to support what happens there. Even so, teachers must realize that different parents may have different expectations of the schools and react in markedly different ways (Walker & Shae, 1995). If teachers prize parent input and utilize it in their classes, dissimilar concerns can become part of an ongoing dialogue and help clear the way for greater understanding and support. When this happens, most of the usual problems never materialize.

Teachers need to be prepared to work with parents who may have either positive or negative views of the school due to biases based on their past experiences. Some parents may be uncooperative and react to the academic difficulties their children suffer. Others may be apathetic and expect the schools to rectify problems exhibited by their children that they themselves have been unsuccessful in solving. Some parents have negative feelings about the schools because of their own unhappy experiences as students. They may conclude that the schools can do nothing to genuinely help their children when they experience difficulties (Manacker, Hurwitz, & Weldon, 1988).

Sometimes parents believe the schools are the source of their children's problems. These parents may, therefore, create ways to avoid interacting with school personnel (Walker & Shae, 1995). Other parents may believe school personnel are the experts and thus excuse themselves from any kind of school involvement (Greenwood & Hickman, 1991; Turnbull & Turnbull, 1997).

Parents can be overwhelmed by the size of their children's schools and the bureaucratic way they are run. They may be uncomfortable with the busy pace as well as the absence of privacy in discussing problems (Lightfoot, 1978). They may also feel alienated because of cultural differences between themselves and school personnel (Swap, 1993). Sometimes the contrast between cultures can pose a threat. For example, Asian-American immigrant parents who are requested to attend conferences with their children's teachers may believe that the purpose of the meeting is for school personnel to "check up on them," and view it as an expression of disrespect (Yao, 1988).

To create a positive atmosphere with parents, teachers must be knowledgeable regarding their students' cultures. Otherwise necessary communications will not take place, and the support of parents will not be forthcoming. Teachers should be certain that the information they have about various cultures is accurate. Sometimes general descriptions are lacking in accuracy and can advance a poor understanding of differences between members of the school community. For example, not all Hispanics adhere to the same cultural norms. Significant differences have also been identified among Asians (Gollnick & Chinn, 1994).

Parents may also resist involvement in school for practical reasons. They may have limited English-speaking ability, no access to transportation, or contrary work hours. Others may not be sufficiently familiar with school practices and procedures or have any idea how they can contribute to their child's education. These parents may react negatively when a face-to-face meeting is requested. They may interpret the purpose of such requests as a focus on poor parenting and become resentful and angry. Obviously interactions with parents should not be restricted to solving problems. There should be plenty of positive expressions about student accomplishments.

Despite potential obstacles, parents' involvement in school can have an enormous impact on their children's academic achievements. All children need the support of their parents in school. This is sustained by parents' having a better understanding of what goes on there along with clear communications with teachers. Epstein (1984, 1987) recommends (1) that parents receive training from the school in child-rearing and parenting along with instruction regarding how to properly supervise, discipline, and guide their children through their school experiences; (2) that communication between parents and the school be continuous and insightful; (3) that parents should be involved in school as volunteers; (4) that parents should be involved with their children's learning activities at home; and (5) that parents should occupy roles in school governance so that monitoring can take place and appropriate recommendations made.

Some states have taken Epstein's suggestions seriously by initiating training programs for parents (Epstein, 1991). For example Illinois (Chapman, 1991) and California (Solomon, 1991) have implemented training programs for parents regarding child-rearing with a focus on promoting better self-concept and preparing children for school. These can be positive experiences so long as parents don't interpret such proposals as an indictment for poor parenting.

As parents become more involved in their children's school experiences, they will recognize that teachers are committed to their children's success and that many of the aversions they have to schooling are inappropriate. For this to be accomplished, teachers must take parents' comments and suggestions seriously. In addition, contact between parents and teachers should be frequent and instructive. This way, problems that develop are not left to fester and become more difficult to solve. When these conditions exist, parents feel that they have a vested interest in the school and are more likely to give their support.

The usual semiannual parent-teacher conferences do not supply sufficient contact between parents and teachers to ensure that communications are meaningful and helpful. With traditional parent-teacher conferences, parents report that teachers tend to be too businesslike, too patronizing, and too inclined to talk down to them (Lindle, 1989). More frequent, meaningful interactions can help eliminate this problem. Parental involvement in learning communities provides far more opportunities for positive associations than the traditional format.

Back-to-school night, which commonly occurs at the beginning of the school year, offers a context in which to inform parents of the nature of learning communities and their role in them. These occasions give parents an opportunity to initiate positive interactions with their children's teachers along with other parents, where clarifications can be made and various opinions forthrightly expressed. Parents have an opportunity in these situations to listen to the concerns and positive responses of others, and to question each other candidly. It is also a time when parent expertise can be expressed, and the potential for using their skills in research projects addressed.

At the beginning of the year, students' actual learning projects will not be known, but it is still a good time to determine the possible use that may be made of parents' background and experience (Christenson & Sheridan, 2001). Teachers should take this opportunity to help parents understand the basic essentials of learning communities as well as their advantages and departures from traditional teaching. Parents should come to understand how their children's needs can be better fulfilled, their understanding and skills enhanced, and their well-being consistently ensured. During the year, the results of student research can be posted on the school website, where parents can track what is being done by all learning groups and consider how they might be of assistance.

In learning communities, parents may serve in a teaching role as well as participate in research. Of course they will have a very limited role as compared to teachers and students. Retired community residents can also become members of learning communities. Some schools have promoted programs that involve retired individuals who function as grandparents.

All adults in learning communities should act as co-learners with students. In this role, they can bring a wealth of knowledge and experience to the group. They can, for example, show students what level of excellence is ordinarily expected in various employment opportunities in the community.

Thus, students can observe excellence firsthand and be helped to become dedicated, sophisticated learners while acquiring a more valid understanding of what is involved in achieving their occupational desires. When adults provide important insights regarding the level of expertise required in various jobs, students can make better occupational choices.

Parents can also help students acquire community service learning opportunities. These experiences should be an integral part of learning communities. Service learning helps deepen students' understanding of community issues as well as extending their sense of community beyond the school. It is an excellent way for students to acquire democratic values within a real context.

Research indicates that service learning experiences have a positive impact on students' intellectual and social/psychological development. They develop a heightened sense of personal and social responsibility, acquire positive attitudes toward adults, become more active in exploring potential careers, develop greater self-esteem, acquire higher levels of moral and ego development, engage in more complex patterns of thought, and achieve greater mastery of skills and conceptual knowledge (Conrad & Hedin, 1991).

One of the most important goals in school is to help students become informed citizens. This involves active involvement in community affairs, becoming informed about issues, and supporting enlightened decisions. Students not only need to know how to get and keep a job, they should also understand how to build a better world. For example, nearly everyone will observe and be negatively affected by discrimination. Also, many will confront dangerous situations such as pollution, drug and alcohol abuse, and gang violence. In addition, children need to understand how the government and other social organizations function and what influences the actions associated officials take.

Schools must create opportunities for youths to address these issues in a more practical setting to help them acquire values such as justice and equity as well as develop a practical knowledge and viable attitudes about various professions, not just pass examinations. Service learning can help them develop democratic values along with an attitude of care, as they learn to make commitments to the communities in which they live. They will become better prepared to help solve significant community problems involving both them and their neighbors now and in the future.

When youths are authentically involved in neighborhood decision making, they learn to think of themselves as contributing community members, particularly when their input is valued. If youths are not taken seriously, they will not take community leaders seriously and may end up appositional. Authentic participation helps youths develop a sense of cooperation in matters that concern them and predisposes them to resist decisions made by governing authorities that ignore their concerns and pay no heed to the views of their constituency.

Great benefits are possible when youths are involved with community leaders. All receive greater insights that can be used for solving problems and develop respect and admiration for each other. Dissimilar membership gives students a reprieve from working exclusively with age-mates, which tends to produce an us-versus-them mentality, making it more difficult to acquire the needed sensitivity and desire to work cooperatively. In this way the detachment ordinarily suffered by youth can be avoided.

Alienated children often harbor resentments when decisions are made by community leaders that impact them, but are enacted without their input. However, when youths have an opportunity to legitimately participate, they feel wanted and needed and their sense of responsibility grows. In this way they can become acquainted with the issues from various perspectives, and eventually realize that problem solving is a very complex process that must involve people from various backgrounds if decisions are to properly represent the views of the entire community.

Before receiving proper instruction and experiences, most youths see solutions to problems in very simplistic, self-serving ways. Often their opinions are governed exclusively by personal wants even when the divergent views of complex societies have to be applied. Involvement in local communities can help them become more sophisticated and comprehensive in their thinking and actions.

When youths are empowered through significant participation in community decision making, they not only develop socially and intellectually, they also acquire resilience with which to face difficult situations in life along with a reduced inclination for violence (Edwards, 2000). Youths want their participation in society to be judged as significant and needful. When this occurs, they not only rebel less, they are less accepting of excesses and violence among their peers. Eventually they see their lives as more meaningful and their contributions to the community more substantial and personally satisfying.

Wise parents and teachers become involved with youths in community affairs both in decision-making roles and in service. Community issues impact families and interact with the concerns of learning communities. Nothing transforms children as much as service activities. Serving others promotes an attitude of care. Children so involved tend to look out for one another to ensure protection from such problems as drug abuse, bullying, and violence (Conrad & Hedin, 1991; Van Hoose & Legrand, 2000). The personal growth thus experienced can establish attitudes about human communities and social responsibility that last a lifetime.

Students who become involved in various community organizations, and who observe the operation of local government, are much more likely to understand the workings of such organizations and make meaningful contributions to society throughout their lives. This kind of effort should be spearheaded by schools where a proper structure exists for not only promoting these kinds of experiences, but also helping students engage in the study of subjects that contribute to understanding and solving social and environmental problems. Schools are ideal places to promote citizenship and social responsibility. However, they will fail to perform this critical role if they continue to emphasize traditional educational objectives and practices.

Imagine the benefit to children who serve in nursing homes, youth organizations, hospitals, agencies for individuals with special needs, and hospices. Children might also become involved in all the occupations of community members. Here they can learn about the world of work from firsthand experience and come closer to determining their own occupational goals. Employees can give students a better idea of the opportunities and constraints associated with different occupations along with providing actual experiences to help them make valid decisions about the kind of work they prefer.

SCHOOLWIDE DISCIPLINE

Classrooms in which democratic learning communities are implemented may be limited in number in a particular school. Sometimes only a single teacher may choose to employ this approach. In this case, students will find inconsistencies between their learning community classroom and the school generally. Consequently teachers should carefully prepare students to understand disparities they may experience.

Part of understanding democratic principles is to truly appreciate contrasting points of view and the necessity of fitting in with whatever educational system is in use. Students could, of course, discuss comparisons during instruction in their democratic learning community. These contrasts can be particularly useful to children as they prepare for life in a complex world that consists of different views of government and social practices among various cultures. It will make them more astute observers of what goes on around them and help them learn to understand the nature of freedom and control as it is exercised in various combinations.

If teachers desire to employ a democratic learning community in their classrooms, their efforts should be coordinated with the school administration. The principal should be aware and give approval so that appropriate support can be given and potential problems avoided. As far as possible, needed resources should be identified that are out of the ordinary, such as transportation required for outreach efforts. More reference material may be needed in the library, and more parents are likely to be coming and going. These requirements need administrative attention.

Then there is the matter of philosophical differences. These need to be carefully delineated along with anticipated teaching-learning practices associated with them. A wise, properly informed principal can be of great assistance in protecting such efforts from criticism within the school. The principal should also be invited to make assessments as time goes by. One critical service the principal might perform is to protect learning communities by excusing students from having to prepare for standardized tests.

Students, of course, may be required by the district or state to take standardized tests, but as much as possible, learning communities need protection from all that accompanies testing efforts. Innovations are never easy, but they should not be categorically prohibited because of this. Rather, well-thought-out innovations should be encouraged. Teachers are much more committed when they are at least partly responsible for the changes made. Considerable benefit comes to students when their teachers are enthusiastic about what they do because they have been involved in making associated changes.

When it comes to discipline, teachers need to ensure that punitive practices are not applied to their students. Even when rule infractions occur outside the classroom, these teachers may wish to have the learning community deal with them. This requires the principal's approval and coordination. In addition, other teachers in the school need assurance that these situations are receiving appropriate attention and not being ignored.

Democratic learning communities may be applied on a schoolwide basis, in which case learning principles and discipline practices can be employed without inherent conflicts. The simplest way to deal with discipline problems outside the classroom is to refer them to a classroom community to which the individual belongs.

Because students will be involved in learning communities in each of their academic classes, each group may have the responsibility for a particular group of students regarding their outside activities. This is likely to be a more satisfactory arrangement than having a disruptive student referred to a school committee with the responsibility of processing discipline problems in the halls, cafeteria, playground, and so on. This approach makes it necessary for each learning community to periodically address potential problems outside the classroom and to deal with specific problems as they arise.

Punitive measures should be discouraged and problems solved through student attempts to prevent problems and address difficulties that require attention. It is unwise for the names of errant students to come up in these discussions. It serves no useful purpose to embarrass them. In discussions, the focus should be upon the value of individuals not embarrassing the group through their bad behavior, along with identifying the personal detriment that comes to those who violate group commitments. These commitments should be reaffirmed in periodic meetings where clarifications can be made about what the group finds objectionable and where group members are encouraged to give input regarding any changes they think are appropriate.

When examining the personal detriment that comes with disappointing group members and violating their trust, each individual should have an opportunity to express how they feel about this. Values can thus be expressed and clarified, and agreements reached with which all are satisfied. Although this process can't guarantee that there will be no misbehavior in school, problems can be greatly reduced. This is particularly true over time. Students will find it increasingly difficult to violate their commitments as the nature of their misbehavior is repeatedly discussed in group meetings, particularly when they know others in the classroom may have observed their unacceptable actions.

PROFESSIONAL LEARNING COMMUNITIES

Teachers need frequent interaction with their peers. In traditional classrooms this hardly ever takes place, except informally in such locations as the faculty room. However, informal discussions in faculty rooms usually don't have the needed focus on teaching and learning, nor are critical topics about learning communities ordinarily brought up with the idea of achieving closure. Teachers are in as much need to enhance their professional growth through learning communities as are their students.

One outgrowth of professional learning communities is a differentiation of leadership tasks. Individual teachers might emerge as a teacher-scholar, teaching researcher, conference coordinator, or an expert in a particular area of interest. Leadership should arise without regard to status or rank. It should be generated by interest and expertise, not by a hierarchal arrangement.

Because of their experience, many teachers may know much more about teaching and learning than the principal does. The principal's leadership role becomes more a matter of encouraging and facilitating the leadership possibilities of others than directly defining what everyone is supposed to do. It isn't even his job to define the agenda in learning community meetings, nor to take the responsibility for getting something done. This responsibility belongs to everyone concerned, even parents who should be involved in such undertakings.

Individuals who lead should be among those who have a greater sense of vision about the possibilities for change in a particular subject regarding teaching and learning, and who have greater commitment for the outcomes along with group functioning and membership. In this configuration, leadership depends on facilitating, brokering, and linking rather than pointing directions (Lieberman, 1996).

Professional learning communities are responsible for finding ways to transform the school culture from traditional organizations governed by externally imposed rules, regulations, and policies to a network of responsible, democratic, inquiring student learning communities. Obviously emphasis must be placed on ways of modifying the school hierarchy so as to better accommodate authentic teaching and learning; empower students through the free exercise of inquiry; maximize growth in knowledge, understanding, and social responsibility; and put the principles of democracy into operation in a climate of reflection and continuous adaptation, despite cynicism and likely attempts by individuals to obstruct others (Hackney & Henderson, 1999).

Students learn best from teachers who are themselves learners. In a learning role, teachers try to find new ways to teach, try them out, share their experiences with other teachers, make refinements, and then try them again. This works well in professional learning communities where the improvement of teaching is assumed to be a lifelong process, and where outstanding teachers learn and grow while researching their craft and communicating what they learn to their colleagues.

Success depends on teachers choosing their own topics for investigation. It must be recognized that it is the learning process that is important, not simply the topics chosen for study, or the outcomes achieved. Just like with students, this is what gives learning its zest (Dodd & Rosenbaum, 1986).

As mentioned earlier, successful professional learning communities depend on the development of the kind of collegiality that embodies professional virtue and a commitment to fulfilling membership obligations. Teaching should engender a strong sense of responsibility. Though teaching provides certain rights and privileges, it also extracts certain obligations and duties. As members of a community, teachers have the right to expect support from members of the profession and school community while at the same time having an obligation to give similar support to others. These are the characteristics that make teachers true colleagues.

This collegiality involves an unwavering commitment to educate the young in the best possible way and should spawn considerable study and research along with extensive interaction with other professional educators. True colleagues experience collegiality through shared goals and purposes. They acquire mutual respect and confidence in the abilities and intentions of those with whom they work. This promotes the growth of professional education communities (Sergiovanni, 1992).

Collegiality will probably not develop unless it is deliberately encouraged. Members must see it as essential to group success and become committed to its growth. It needs to be periodically assessed and appropriate changes made to ensure its continued development. Dysfunctions in interpersonal relationships can be anticipated. These need to be prevented as much as possible, and if they appear, efforts should be made to keep them from escalating.

As members of a professional learning community, teachers must become well acquainted with all aspects of teaching and learning. This can be accomplished through research as well as personal experiences. All the insights acquired by individual teachers should be shared with colleagues. As this is done, agreements can be reached about important principles that should be applied in educating the young.

Obviously teachers should become experts on constructivist learning theory and its applications, along with achieving a sophisticated understanding of conceptual knowledge in their teaching field. They also must learn how to supply students with experiences that satisfy their basic needs and motivate them. Most especially children must be provided a context in which to adequately learn how to govern themselves responsibly. Teachers need to acquire the skills for promoting an atmosphere of care in which strong relationships are fostered. It is essential that acceptable evaluation procedures be employed and that teachers agree with the program. These and other issues constitute the ongoing agenda of professional learning communities where insights can be acquired and commitments reaffirmed.

Chapter Nine

Issues Regarding a Transition to Learning Communities

A number of issues regarding a move to learning communities in schools deserve considerable attention. The first is whether or not the hoped-for outcomes of learning communities are sufficiently superior to those that come from traditional schools. Certainly they must be to justify making such extensive changes. Part of the necessary analysis involves the degree to which students can actually achieve the proposed outcomes of learning communities.

Some individuals might not even agree that achieving these ends is desirable. Thus, having children who are creative, self-governing, and responsible human beings who care about others and who can engage in inquiry learning and solve problems may be considered less desirable than other outcomes. For example, some may not agree that memorizing a vast body of information, most of which will quickly be forgotten, is a waste of time but rather believe that this constitutes the essence of what children should do in school.

Many believe that an educated person is someone who remembers a lot of information such as geography facts. It is common to hear disgruntled expressions from people so inclined when they observe children who are unable to demonstrate their knowledge by naming all of the state capitals. They underscore their disapproval by sharply criticizing teachers and pointing out the sorry state of education.

It is very apparent that there are remarkably different views about what constitutes an appropriate education. There are also those who disagree with implementing learning communities in the schools. Thus, it is necessary to recognize that there are significant differences of opinion regarding education that cannot simply be ignored. However, this does not excuse those responsible for the schools from examining the research to determine which among the various options is most defensible.

The strength of learning communities has considerable research support. At the same time, many aspects of traditional schools are unacceptable. Assuming that the proposed outcomes of learning communities are defensible and desirable, there is still the matter of whether or not children can achieve them. Considerable data have been presented in support of this contention. But it is also clear that some obstacles exist, perhaps the most ominous of which is the conditioning that has taken place in children's prior school experiences.

Generally, children have been conditioned to respond to a whole plethora of expectations in particular ways. For example, they may have come to expect rewards in the form of grades for learning what is expected of them. Students may experience difficulty valuing learning when it isn't rewarded. They will undoubtedly also find it difficult to initiate and responsibly carry through on group research projects. In addition, they will likely find it hard to pursue excellence when they have previously been able to get by and even do well with less than full effort.

The second issue is whether or not schools can be modified sufficiently to accomplish the goals of learning communities. This involves such accepted practices as testing and grading as well as leadership, classroom learning processes, and various school practices such as discipline. Teachers have to be taught the nature of learning communities along with associated implications and come to full agreement regarding them. Associated principles need to be incorporated into teachers' educational philosophies along with learning how to expertly apply them.

All this is likely to involve very radical changes. However, the basic consideration that supports such changes is the fact that preparing students for life in a democratic society is critical, even though it requires substantial changes in converting schools to democratic communities so children can learn appropriate principles and internalize them as a basic constituent of their education. It is difficult not to support such aspirations, particularly when the potential outcomes of various schooling possibilities are carefully examined.

One of the problems for teachers is coming to grips with the idea that traditional teaching not only does not produce such laudatory results, it usually undermines them. It is difficult for educators to consider the possibility that much of what they have previously accomplished in their teaching may be misguided. This is well illustrated by the progressive education movement during the 1930s, which represented a substantial change from curricula based on the transmission of knowledge to those that promoted student choice and self-direction.

Though it had considerable support from educators and substantial efforts were made to implement progressive education, it eventually failed. The suggested reasons for this are varied, but perhaps the primary problem was the inability, or perhaps unwillingness, of teachers to fully employ associated teaching strategies properly. Some scholars suggest that teachers simply lacked the necessary training to fully implement such a radically different educational approach. Taken together, these factors constitute the most likely cause of progressive education's demise (Creman, 1961).

It has also been suggested that educators prefer working with children who are compliant and submissive. In a class of thirty or more students it seems expedient to have children doing the same things rather than expressing their creative urges and helping to govern their own learning activities. Even when children appear incapable of conscientious self-regulation, it may simply be due to teachers' desires for order and control, not the supposed inability of their students to direct their own learning. It could also be in part due to children's inclination to rebel against coercion. When children are disruptive, it is easy for teachers to conclude that they are inherently rebellious and incapable of learning to regulate themselves.

Many individuals claim to believe in democratic principles but fail to fully recognize their appropriateness in various social situations, including school. They speak highly of a democratic society, expressing many of the virtues of such an existence. However, when it comes right down to it, they are out of sync with democratic principles not only in their thinking, but also in their behavior. They often talk about democracy in glowing terms when referring to it generally, but speak disparagingly when referring to particulars. This is especially so in the schools, but is also the case in other situations.

Interestingly there is common acceptance of democratic principles for society at large but no allowance of the same for students, who it is claimed are too immature to be fully empowered. Thus, many teachers speak highly of democratic society but simply cannot visualize democratic principles applied in their classrooms. This can also be found in society generally. For example, some individuals express the need to restrict people of different races or individuals from lower classes whose behavior they consider threatening and inappropriate. It is common to express the necessity of restricting all kinds of behavior that are simply different from that preferred by the person making the judgment.

People often behave contrary to their espoused values without recognizing the discrepancy (Kohlberg, 1976). They may not truly understand the implications of particular values, or they may mindlessly permit their needs to overpower rational thought. For example, everyone has a powerful desire to be in control of what happens to them. They are particularly interested in making sure that all their needs are met. Their need satisfaction can become such an urgent imperative that they exercise excessive control, almost without thinking, to ensure that their desired needs are fulfilled; but they don't realize that such coercive actions will probably keep them from really satisfying their needs.

To these people, their needs justify any actions deemed necessary to satisfy them. Thus, any amount of control seems defensible when need satisfaction appears threatened. Behavior that is contrary to beliefs may well explain why many teachers champion democracy but practice excessive control in the classroom, and why moving to a learning community approach to education may be difficult. Yet the virtue of outcomes associated with democratic learning communities makes it worth the effort.

For many teachers, there is no clear connection between educational practices and their personal philosophies. Also, in many cases, teachers don't have a well-articulated educational philosophy that they can expertly explain in terms of basic concepts and applications. Moreover, some teachers may employ a variety of teaching techniques learned from colleagues that are inconsistent with each other, with the hope that they can alleviate some of the difficulties they may be experiencing in their classrooms. They may rarely consider the inconsistencies between various recommended teaching techniques.

Some teachers may espouse a particular set of principles and practice another. Such was apparently the case in schools visited by the author in which the official written school philosophy was basically humanistic while behaviorism was applied in most classrooms. In these schools, many teachers seemed unaware that a written school philosophy actually existed, and none seemed to care whether or not they followed it. It could perhaps be concluded that the current group of teachers had very little involvement in writing these philosophies, or that they had little interest in using the school philosophy of education to guide their teaching. A well-articulated, consistently applied educational philosophy appeared to be a low priority for these teachers.

It seemed clear in this situation that school administrators had not emphasized the use of educational philosophies to direct instructional programs. Perhaps that is why teachers were unaware of their existence. It is unlikely that no instruction was given to these teachers in their training programs regarding the importance of an educational philosophy. Given this, it isn't particularly easy to ascertain exactly why such inconsistencies exist.

Perhaps the incongruity between educational philosophy and teaching practices occurs because philosophy is given insufficient attention in teacher training, or perhaps it is the way schools are constituted that makes it difficult to consistently employ a well-articulated set of teaching principles. It has long been known that teachers are inclined to teach in the very manner in which they were taught as public school students, despite the fact they received university training directly opposing these practices. This might also be the operating factor.

DETERMINING NECESSARY CHANGES

Nearly four decades ago Daniel and Laurel Tanner (1975) reported that efforts to create change in educational practices had usually been undertaken as expedient and opportunistic responses to the dominant sociopolitical forces rather than stemming from a rationale based upon sound theory and conceptual research. Curriculum reforms had thus been promoted as consensual reactions to emerging crises. The result was an ever-widening gap between theory and practice as reform measures were adopted, modified, discarded, and rediscovered.

In the process, the American public came to expect easy solutions to complex problems. Radical critics and activists rebuffed the application of theory and conceptual research and instead sought sweeping educational reforms based on their visceral impulses and anti-intellectual biases. This was accompanied by narrowly based empirical research that had little bearing on the wider conceptual problems in the field.

The result was for changes to be made based on whatever current demands were most powerful on the sociopolitical scene (Tanner & Tanner, 1975). Little has changed since that analysis was made. These conditions still exist and currently have acquired more strength, given the explicit involvement of the federal government in promoting a traditional approach in the name of educational improvement.

Historically, educational opinion and practice have been sharply divided regarding whether curricula should be based on knowledge, the learner, or society. This has taken place even though a rational approach would be to accept these components as basically interactive and all essential for curriculum development. Instead, each has been independently used as a rallying point for people with disparate opinions (Tanner & Tanner, 1975).

One of the reasons why evaluation of educational principles and practices has been lacking is because most innovations have originated from outside the educational system. Some of these have come from commercial sources, while others have been sponsored by large foundations. Even the U.S. Office of Education has sponsored untested innovations such as performance contracting by offering financial incentives. The federal government's No Child Left Behind initiative is just the latest in this kind of curriculum reform.

Such efforts have created an excessive focus on the monetary aspect of curriculum improvement rather than well-researched, logical aspects. Curriculum improvement has become synonymous with adoption of innovations rather than identification of curriculum problems with appropriate research leading to considered action for improvement (Tanner & Tanner, 1975). The consequence has been the creation of curricula that suffer from imbalance and fragmentation. This is spurred on by society's continual desire for change, for there tends to be dissatisfaction with things as they are.

Such conditions have encouraged educators to institute a plethora of untested modifications. Because innovations have been superficial and rarely attend to substantial concerns, the essence of schooling has remained much the same for many years. Thus, educators have employed flexible schedules, team teaching, and the like with the hope of improving education, but these modifications have very little impact on what really ails education.

Many of these innovations are based on the assumption that teachers should have no responsibility in deciding what should be taught. They are effectively excluded from participation in crucial decisions affecting their work in the classroom. Long ago disparaging results of many of these programs led originators such as the Ford Foundation to concede their mistake regarding teacher involvement and instead decide in favor of having teachers participate in defining problems and developing solutions regarding curriculum and instructional improvement (Ford Foundation, 1972).

Such decisions as the one made by the Ford Foundation were initiated nearly four decades ago, and yet teacher input is still ignored today. Current school managers continue to view teachers as technicians rather than professional educators and ascribe the same set of curricula and evaluation standards to all. However, teachers need to play the role of theoreticians wherein they apply the latest research to their practice rather than technicians who implement standardized curricula without really thinking about the implications of what they are doing.

Some of the problems in society that schools can help address include poor problem determination and solving abilities, poor citizenship, inadequate value development, poor intellectual skills, limited evaluation skills, poor self-concept, deficient social skills, and inadequate sense of care for others. Interestingly, along with students dropping out of school prematurely, these are the same problems for which schools have been criticized for years.

Schools generally fail to properly consider issues such as the ones listed above. Rather than addressing these problems by making them central in curriculum construction, they ignore them. If they are considered at all, they are simply hoped-for outcomes of fact-oriented learning. For example, it is hoped that children will develop social skills, but most classroom experiences actually discourage social contact between students, and it would indeed be rare for teachers to include social skills as part of their critical learning objectives.

Ordinarily, social development is simply allowed to inadvertently take place outside the classroom without teacher input and guidance. Also, in most schools, evaluating character development and the formation of an astute sense of social propriety would indeed be a rarity. The same is true of satisfying children's needs. Students' needs are not usually considered in framing curricula. This scenario could in essence be repeated for other desired outcomes as well.

Before efforts to properly reform education can be undertaken, the above issues must be addressed. All interested parties, including teachers, parents, school administrators, and state education officials, must understand how important these considerations are, that they constitute very critical problems in society, and that schools can help deal with them if education is properly conceptualized and consistently employed in the schools.

It is also important that the entire society appreciates what is at stake and understands that many reform efforts have lacked appropriate purpose and direction. Too often actions are taken without a sufficiently comprehensive framework. Every appropriate aspect of education must be taken into account, and as much as possible, an adequate research base should always be employed. Philosophical questions also must be addressed. These cannot be ignored as if they weren't important or didn't even exist.

Discussions must be held and conclusions reached so that education has consistent, agreeable guiding principles. Thus, a detailed list of educational outcomes must be pursued along with the most effective, consistent educational strategies for achieving them. Issues, such as whether or not children should learn to become responsibly self-governed, need to be carefully examined and the means created for validly determining the impact of innovations.

For changes to be appropriate, educators must focus on fundamental aspects of schooling. One critical issue that has long been excluded from consideration is the nature of learning. It is ironic that such would be the case given the fact that learning is the primary purpose of schooling. A correct understanding of natural learning processes is absolutely essential to framing the entire educational experience. Yet educational practices continue to be pursued whose theoretical support has long ago been abandoned.

For example, it was once thought that subjects such as Latin and mathematics disciplined the mind and that the capabilities thus acquired transferred to other subjects. During the early 1900s Thorndike and other researchers found this was not the case (Thorndike, 1906, 1924; Thorndike & Woodworth, 1901). Yet in subsequent years support continued for the idea that the mind is strengthened through rigorous mental exercises. Most of the curricula employed in the schools were based on that assumption.

Even today, the various subjects are often studied as though this assumption was true. This is particularly the case in the study of mathematics. Thus, mathematical operations are often taught in the absence of real-life contexts and applications. This is done despite the results of the Progressive Education Association's Eight-Year Study, where it was found that success in college was not dependent on students taking the traditional prescribed courses. The students who were most successful in college came from schools with the most nontraditional approaches to instruction. These programs were characterized as unique as well as fostering student self-direction (Aikin, 1942).

Behaviorism has had an enormous influence on the nature of schooling. The primary emphasis of behaviorism is on highly structured learning, specific feedback on learning efforts, and achievement that can be quantitatively measured. From the behaviorist perspective, student learning has to be carefully monitored and rewarded before any improvement can be expected. Behaviorists assume that desirable behavior requires extrinsic reinforcers. Thus, on their own, students would not engage in socially acceptable behavior, nor learn intrinsically. They must be controlled by others.

Curricular applications of behaviorism include an emphasis on managing learning with measurable behavioral objectives and highly controlled instruction rather than outcomes such as intellectual development, artistic representation, social problem solving, creativity, self-direction, and inquiry learning.

Many educational theorists have rejected behaviorism as a valid conception of human learning and have accepted constructivist theory as an accurate description of how people learn. As noted in chapter 6, research has shown that the brain is not a passive consumer of information as behaviorism concludes. Instead, it creates personal interpretations of conceptual knowledge and draws inferences from them. In addition, the brain ignores some information and considers concepts that are more consistent with prior personal conceptions. Thus, understanding depends on the individual constructing personal meaning (Phillips, 2000).

It has been learned that people are very resistant to making changes in what they have organized in their brains. Students won't make changes just because a teacher provides them with a more accurate view of various concepts. They make changes according to their own desires and actually may resist ideas imposed on them. They are far more likely to correct erroneous conceptions after they have personally discovered their ideas to be incorrect than when correct conceptualizations are simply transmitted to them. Inquiry learning experiences tend to be the best way for this to happen (Osborne & Wittrock, 1983). These findings have obvious implications for how education is to be modified and improved.

When children are given access to fundamental knowledge of the world, the process of knowledge construction goes beyond simple personal inquiry. It is, therefore, best if learners are given access to knowledge through personal, self-directed experiences as well as through conceptual knowledge of the subject that may be outside their ordinary experiences. This is necessary if students are to include valued conceptual knowledge from outside their current experience and understanding (Solomon, 1994). This is an entirely different concept of learning than that practiced in the schools or encouraged by behaviorists. Those who make decisions about the schools must address this issue. It cannot simply be ignored. The stakes are too high.

Need satisfaction is another issue that requires deliberate attention in the schools. Many of the problems teachers and administrators experience are those brought on when student needs are ignored or presumed not to exist. Perhaps it is thought that these important sources of student motivation can be temporarily set aside. However, many of the critical outcomes for children are connected to the satisfaction of their needs. For example, the need for autonomy is required for inquiry learning and concept development.

Teachers should make sure that all their students have opportunities to satisfy all of their needs. This, of course, requires substantial modifications in the instructional program. Previous chapters have identified many of the issues that should be addressed by educational decision makers. The usual processes for making innovations in the schools need to be replaced by rational, research-oriented ones. Various philosophical considerations should be examined and their implications illuminated so that all can see what is gained or lost through various curricular approaches.

CHANGES REQUIRED OF STUDENTS

For students to become effectively involved in learning communities, enormous changes are necessary. One of the most formidable obstacles is their previous conditioning in school. Of course, the longer children are exposed to traditional teaching strategies, the more solidified conditioning becomes. This involves a concerted effort by teachers to deprogram them. However, children who have been involved in learning communities since their years in elementary school will have become accustomed to this learning configuration.

The conditioning effect of grades is evident. As pointed out in an earlier chapter, research indicates that students who are given extrinsic rewards such as grades are conditioned by them and eventually come to value the grades more than what they learn to achieve them. This is a particularly potent influence on students if they plan on university training and require excellent grades to qualify for admission.

Currently, college entrance is commonly restricted to students with high GPAs, even though as the Eight-Year Study indicated, the usual academic qualifications for university admissions are not as effective as more creative learning approaches in high school. Yet grades still represent the simplest way to sort students for university admission. However, given the potential detriment of grades, ease of sorting students for college entrance is a woefully inadequate criterion for using them.

In analyzing the nature of conditioning in the schools it is essential to realize that much of what children become is a function of school conditions and practices. Thus, some are labeled as slow learners when in fact they do far less than they are capable of and often show false effort to avoid teachers' wrath. These are learned responses that may arise either inadvertently or from well-planned reinforcement strategies.

Other students become overstrivers and suffer with escalating expectations assumed by themselves or imposed by teachers and parents. These circumstances are usually the result of unintentional conditioning. As a result, children tend to categorize themselves relative to expectations that arise in a variety of ways. Some come about in the early school years, where such things as cleanliness and the kind of clothing worn may be insensitively referred to by teachers. These comments can help children shape their views of themselves and their classmates in both positive and negative ways. The categorizations are very persistent once children have pigeonholed themselves in terms of teachers' labeling and expectations.

In addition, many times teachers define academic standards at levels much below the capabilities of students. Students tend to limit themselves in terms of teacher expectations. Many are capable of a much higher level of excellence than indicated by the standards teachers set. They are also more capable of hard work than teachers believe. Students thus become conditioned by these teacher expectations.

Children's misbehavior can also increase in frequency as a result of punishment. As indicated earlier, rather than promoting compliance as anticipated by teachers, punishment may promote rebellion and a rejection of what teachers want. When teachers impose more potent punishment in consequence of student rebellion, they tend to become increasingly unruly. This is because, unbeknownst to teachers, some students find punishment reinforcing. Eventually these children are considered inherently recalcitrant, as though they were infected with an incurable disease, which it is assumed schools and teachers have no part in creating. Thus, in a number of ways teachers and the school environment are in reality responsible for much of children's conditioning and its consequences. Of course, this can be an impediment to success in learning communities.

Need satisfaction is related to student behavior. As mentioned earlier, schools ordinarily do not satisfy most student needs. This environment causes students to respond in a variety of ways. Those who feel devoid of love will act out in rebellious ways in an effort to acquire attention and acceptance from others. Ordinarily, teachers react by providing less positive and more negative attention. Negative attention is not genuinely satisfying. Thus, students eventually believe their needs will never be satisfied in school. When this happens, even efforts to veritably satisfy their needs may be viewed as insincere.

The bottom line is that student behavior is ordinarily shaped up through conditioning and is often very difficult to modify once these patterns have become established. It is insightful to realize that much conditioning is unintentional. Why would teachers deliberately seek unacceptable student behavior? Of course they don't, but many fail to realize that they are responsible in large measure for student disruptiveness and dissatisfaction. Even when children come from dysfunctional homes and aberrant social conditions, which promote negative school behavior, astute teachers can help modify these behaviors.

Teachers must not only avoid contributing to poor student behavior, they also must know how to help students modify offensive actions that have been shaped up elsewhere. One way to help accomplish this is to properly identify student needs and then help them satisfy them in appropriate ways. Also, the learning environment must be overhauled so that situations that tend to promote misbehavior are eliminated. Learning communities can provide the kind of environment for overcoming many of the above-identified problems.

CHANGES FOR TEACHERS

Teachers can become conditioned in similar fashion to their students. They, of course, have been conditioned as students themselves. For most teachers this frames the way they teach. As described earlier, it is easy for them to teach as they were taught without thinking much about the implications. In addition, it is common for teachers to fail to apply the principles they learned as part of their teacher training programs. This conditioning process is strengthened by the fact that modifying themselves may constitute an admission that they are lacking in some way. It is not known if this is a conscious response in an effort to avoid threats to personal self-concept, or if it constitutes a lack of awareness regarding these inconsistencies.

Teachers' inability to change may not only be impeded by an unwillingness to admit questionable teaching practices, it may also be a function of mindlessly maintaining the status quo. Teachers who have taught in a particular way for a number of years may be understandably resistant to change. They may have a lot of materials prepared to support their teaching that cannot be used with new practices. The time and effort taken to prepare these materials may make change, even for worthy purposes, very difficult. It seems to take compelling reasons to change under these circumstances, and even then teachers must agree that such modifications are imperative. It is easy for them to convince themselves that they are not.

There is also the matter of teachers' philosophies. In many cases they may not be well defined and are minimally incorporated into their teaching practices. Some teachers may have limited commitment to any particular philosophy and rather practice their craft inconsistently. Consequently there may be little inclination to adopt a particular set of teaching principles. Such a course of action may appear to them to limit their flexibility.

Many teachers consider flexibility far more important than consistency. It is essential to realize that these two orientations are very contradictory and constitute one of the most formidable obstacles to change. Teachers may fail to realize that there is considerable flexibility within a particular philosophical teaching orientation. Instead, they prefer flexibility that allows for changing basic principles even though there may be considerable discontinuity and conflict in doing so. Unfortunately, the inconsistency and resultant chaos may not be recognized as a significant detrimental contributor to class disruptions and ineffective learning.

Principled teaching helps students to predict what is likely to take place from day to day. They cannot effectively function when drastic changes in basic principles are made repeatedly. For example, suppose a teacher starts out allowing students considerable autonomy only to follow this up with strict control. A few days later greater autonomy may again be employed, followed soon after with greater control as circumstances in the classroom appear to merit these changes. Obviously, students would be unable to reliably function under such conditions and consequently become more likely to either mentally drop out or rebel.

Repeated changing of principles is sometimes recommended by theorists regarding classroom discipline techniques. For example, Wolfgang and Glickman (1980) suggest such a shifting approach in which entirely different discipline theories are applied in the classroom depending on the student behavior exhibited at a particular time. Thus, if teachers start out by using a nonintervention approach such as Gordon's Teacher Effectiveness Training or Bern's Interaction Analysis and find students continue to be unruly, they suggest that an interactional approach like Reality Therapy/Choice Theory be used instead. If additional control is believed necessary, an even more controlling theory like behavior modification or Assertive Discipline would be employed.

The teacher could also start by using behavior modification, changing to Reality Therapy/Choice Theory as conditions in the classroom appear to dictate, and then shifting to Teacher Effectiveness Training or Interaction Analysis as the amount of student unruliness decreases. Wolfgang and Glickman also indicate that teachers could start with an interaction approach and move either to intervention theories or nonintervention theories as the situation seems to demand.

Other individuals recommend an eclectic approach to discipline. For example, Charles (1992) suggests that teachers select components of various discipline models that suit them best and recombine them into an "effective approach that is satisfactory to all." Charles indicates that this recombination is necessary because one approach may work well with one student whereas another approach works better with others. He believes that combining different approaches helps teachers discipline students in terms of changing circumstances. However, it should be noted that the various discipline theories are fundamentally different in terms of basic characteristics and applications. Combining them so that there is consistency would be an impossible task, and applying them would be very confusing to students.

The defense commonly offered for using eclectic and shifting discipline consists of the following:

1. Some theories work better than others depending on children's ages, personal and social aptitudes, home and social environments, ethnic and racial background, or school situations. These elements constitute considerable complexity and to be properly managed, require the use of a full range of discipline theories. Charles (1992) indicates that while behavior modification theory may work better with young children and with developmentally disabled students, other techniques such as Assertive Discipline may be needed with older children and youngsters with more severe behavioral disorders. He further claims that Assertive Discipline may control misbehavior at all levels but may be too cumbersome for primary grades. It may also prevent students from gaining a proper value orientation because it focuses exclusively on students' obedience, making its replacement with other methods imperative.
2. Some teachers may find it difficult to use some techniques successfully with certain groups of students. For example, teachers may be able to employ Reality Therapy/Choice Theory only as long as students do not become too mischievous. In this case, the teacher may need more teacher-directed discipline.
3. Some students may be so hard to handle initially that the teacher may need to control more vigorously at first and then implement different tactics as students become more able to govern themselves.
4. When the discipline technique used doesn't work well, it makes sense to change to some other technique.

Teachers who have a well-organized and carefully articulated set of values to which they are committed usually prefer a theory-based approach to discipline. Ordinarily the principles these teachers apply professionally are the same ones that govern their private lives. To them it makes more sense to consistently apply a defensible set of principles they have carefully considered and adopted than opt for a broad range of discipline techniques with disparate principles and guidelines. They find sufficient flexibility within a particular discipline theory to deal with most problems in the classroom. They may use various strategies depending on circumstances, but all of these efforts are consistent with a single set of principles and anticipated outcomes. Democratic Discipline in Learning Communities is an example of a theory-based approach.

Teachers who apply a theory-based instructional approach counter eclecticism with the following arguments:

1. Those who advocate periodic shifting between discipline theories suggest such changes are necessary because of different or changed circumstances in the classroom. These may include children's growth and development or their inclinations to be more or less disruptive. Thus, younger children are considered less able intellectually to respond to discipline techniques that emphasize self-determination. These youngsters are thought less able to accurately express their personal thoughts and feelings and to engage in the kind of communications needed in some discipline approaches. However, these problems have not been proven to exist. Children in elementary school are appropriately responsive to any of the discipline techniques.

2. Sometimes a different discipline approach seems necessary because the one currently in use has not eliminated student misbehavior. It is assumed that changing classroom conditions or altered student inclinations have promoted more misbehavior, which makes it necessary to make changes. However, there is no evidence to support using a particular theory in any specific set of circumstances. In fact, most discipline theories are routinely and effectively used in a wide variety of classroom situations as well as in other settings. Thus, behavior modification has been used in mental hospitals and successfully applied to children with autism, individuals with social and behavioral disorders, and individuals with a host of everyday problems such as smoking and eating disorders.

   Reality Therapy/Choice Theory has been applied in treating people with all types of mental illness, counseling people who are socially maladaptive, and helping inmates in penal institutions regulate their behavior. Both behavior modification and Reality Therapy/Choice Theory have been employed in a variety of special school situations as well as regular classrooms at all levels. Other theories have also been applied in a variety of situations. There should be no doubt that various discipline approaches are suitable for sustained use in the classroom in a variety of situations and conditions.

3. It is unlikely that teachers will learn a number of different discipline approaches well enough to apply them all with sufficient prowess. Each requires considerable skill, particularly those that depend on a high level of interpersonal expertise such as Reality Therapy/Choice Theory, Teacher Effectiveness Training, Logical Consequences, Judicious Discipline, and Democratic Discipline in Learning Communities. Also, most teachers would experience difficulty switching between discipline approaches because of differences in their application, assumptions, and expected results. For example, some theories support student compliance with teacher expectations while others promote self-regulation. Also, the educational philosophies of many teachers, were they carefully defined and articulated, would prevent them from applying such a divergent array of discipline tactics.

4. Using multiple discipline theories would also be confusing to students. In implementing the different models, the one attribute that would be in a constant state of flux is autonomy. It is impossible for teachers to validly determine what level of student autonomy is most appropriate for a particular situation, given the variety of student inclinations and behavior. No available research indicates when it is appropriate to switch methods or which discipline approach should be the next one used in supposed changing conditions. There is also no research that indicates that periodically switching discipline methods works at all.

In addition, when the amount of control employed is made to depend on how responsibly students use their freedom, any effort to increase control will be seen by students as undermining their desire to become more self-determined. It will also sabotage the teacher's credibility. To students, it will appear as if their teachers either don't know what they are doing, or that they are going back on their word.

Because many teachers have been conditioned to value flexibility over a theory-based approach to discipline, it will be necessary to provide clarification and help them understand the hazards of such strategies. Learning communities are based on a single set of principles that require valid implementation. Instructional or discipline approaches that incorporate disparate principles are unacceptable. When employing democratic principles in the classroom, there is no place for curricula determined exclusively by the teacher or outside agencies or any approach that utilizes coercive practices.

Some educators feel that students should first be exposed to teaching tactics that emphasize control, and then later democratic principles can be applied as students become more responsible learners. However, coercive practices do not help students to learn how to responsibly direct their own learning. In fact, they work against student independence. It is only when students are consistently involved in self-regulation that they will learn to accountably govern their own behavior.

For teachers to adopt a learning community approach to instruction, it is necessary to be converted to the use of democratic principles in their teaching. This seems like a simple thing to do, but it is not. The tradition in teaching is based on coercive practices with little or no confidence in students' ability to live responsibly in a democratic society. Each person has a long history of control tactics applied to them in the schools. Thus, changing to a learning community approach to teaching not only requires student deprogramming, but also a commitment from teachers to use democratic principles in their teaching.

It is also necessary for teachers to learn how to apply these principles. This is where many teachers find difficulty. When they attempt to put democratic principles into action, they often find that students don't react as anticipated. Furthermore, they likely will continue to behave as though no changes have been made. They cannot learn in an instant how to react to an entirely different approach to learning.

Thus, teachers have to give their students time to adjust and in the meantime become more skilled in creating fully functioning democratic learning communities. Because specific teaching behaviors are not identified, teachers must create most of their own strategies. But, of course, whatever they employ must be consistent with democratic principles.

To create authentic democratic learning communities, most teachers will need to change personal dispositions. It seems to be human nature to control others, particularly when an individual is in a position to do so. Teachers are particularly vulnerable to controlling students excessively because of the positions they occupy. Children are novices and obviously require guidance. But what kind of direction should they be provided? Given their experiences, many students may be inclined to balk at even well-meant teachers' instructions. Under such conditions, teachers are all the more inclined to react coercively. Obviously this must be resisted.

Teachers must also learn to be more accepting of a variety of viewpoints. Nearly everyone has come to believe that reality is consistent with their personal view of the world. Yet there are differences of opinion about most matters confronting us that are based on personal experiences. While seeking commitment to a single viewpoint as they work with others in learning communities, teachers are inclined to try to convince their associates they are right and contrary viewpoints in error.

This mind-set predisposes every individual to try to get others to change their opinions so that they are consistent with his or her own. Teachers so inclined are less likely to be accepting of learning strategies at variance with their beliefs. Insisting on a single course of action for students is inconsistent with life in learning communities or in democratic societies.

Teachers also have to abandon any inclination they may have to punish disruptive students. To do so, they must become very familiar with appropriate research. An enormous amount of information is available that contradicts punitive teaching practices. This information must be understood and applied appropriately. Teachers should also engage in their own classroom research projects.

CHANGES FOR ADMINISTRATORS

For learning communities to work effectively, administrative practices must be adjusted. The usual administrative model is top-down and control oriented. Directives are normally given with little or no input from teachers, parents, or students. Often these mandates have a political orientation rather than a logical or professional one. Usually they satisfy administrative concerns without regard to pedagogical requirements. Thus, students are often viewed as something to be processed and controlled rather than educated. And the potential long-range negative effects of such administrative practices are rarely considered.

Ordinarily management principles are applied in schools rather than insightful leadership. Management involves efforts to get people to do things they would ordinarily resist, while leadership helps to empower all individuals to pursue a course that is satisfying as well as beneficial. Managers usually employ rewards and punishments. Ordinarily they seek goals that make sense to them without regard to others' viewpoints. They categorically deny others an opportunity for shared leadership. Thus, it is rare for teachers to become involved in leadership responsibilities. Yet when learning communities are implemented, leadership must be shared with teachers.

Not only are there learning communities involving groups of students, there are also learning communities involving teachers, administrators, and parents. In all learning communities, leadership should be shared. Individuals should occupy leadership positions depending on preparation and skills as well as needs and desires. The administrative role is to make sure that all participants share in the leadership function. This becomes a benefit not only to the individual; the whole group profits. Proper leadership provides a format for greater development of participants in working with others as well as supplying far more insightful information about how and what to learn. Greater insights are thus possible regarding the learning directions to pursue as well as how to solve problems the group faces.

Administrators need to believe that both teachers and students are capable of making appropriate decisions and achieving excellence in whatever they undertake. Any evidence to the contrary should not lead to controlling over-

tures. Rather, the administrators' leadership responsibility is to allow sufficient time for development to take place and then to encourage improvement
along the lines individuals choose.

Obviously critical issues should be examined by all members of a learning community and challenges addressed to achieve excellence. But the degree to which this can be expected has to be left up to the individuals involved. Thus, in a state of cooperation and commitment, everyone in a learning community should help define goals for themselves while contributing as
best they can to the well-being of all group members.

References

Abrams, L., & Haney, W. (2004). Accountability and the grade 9 to 10 transition: The impact on attrition and retention rates. In G. Orfield (Ed.), *Dropouts in America: Confronting the graduation rate crisis* (pp. 181–205). Cambridge, MA: Harvard Education Press.

Aikin, W. M. (1942). *The story of the eight-year study*. New York: Harper & Row.

Albert, L. (1989). *Cooperative discipline: How to manage your classroom and promote self-esteem*. Circle Pines, MN: American Guidance Service.

Albert, L. (2003a). *A teacher's guide to cooperative discipline*. Circle Pines, MN: American Guidance Service.

Albert, L. (2003b). *Cooperative discipline*. Circle Pines, MN: American Guidance Service.

Amabile, T. M., Hennessey, B. A., & Grossman, B. S. (1986). Social influences on creativity: The effects of contracted-for reward. *Journal of Personality and Social Psychology, 50*, 14–23.

Apple, M., & Beane, T. (1995). *Democratic schools*. Alexandria, VA: Association for Supervision and Curriculum Development.

Applegate, J. H., Flora, V. R., & Lasely, T. J. (1980). New teachers seek support: Some people are supportive and others aren't. *Educational Leadership, 38*, 74–76.

Armstrong, T. (1998). *Awakening genius in the classroom*. Alexandria, VA: Association for Supervision and Curriculum Development.

Aronson, E., & Carlsmith, J. M. (1962). Performance expectancy as a determinant of actual performance. *Journal of Abnormal and Social Psychology, 65*, 178–182.

Ashton, P. J., & Webb, R. B. (1986). *Making a difference: Teachers' sense of efficacy and student achievement*. New York: Longman.

Athanases, S. Z. (1997). The promise and challenges of educational portfolios: Theses from the book chapters. In J. Barton and A. Collins (Eds.), *Portfolio assessment: A handbook for educators*. Menlo Park, CA: Addison-Wesley Publishing Company.

Balsam, P. D., & Bondy, A. S. (1983). The negative side effects of reward. *Journal of Applied Behavior Analysis, 16*, 283–296.

Banks, J. A. (2003). Multicultural education: Characteristics and goals. In J. A. Banks & C. A. M. Banks (Eds.), *Multicultural education: Issues and perspectives* (4th ed., pp. 3–30). New York: John Wiley & Sons.

Barth, R. (1990). *Improving schools from within*. San Francisco: Jossey-Bass.

Basinger, D. (1997). Fighting grade inflation: A misguided effort? *College Teaching, 45*, 88–91.

Bates, P. B., & Kunzmann, R. (2004). Two faces of wisdom: Wisdom as a general theory of knowledge and judgment about excellence in mind and virtue vs. wisdom as everyday realization in people and products. *Human Development, 47*, 290–299.

Bates, P. B., & Saudinger, U. M. (2000). Wisdom: A metaphysical (pragmatic) to orchestrate mind and virtue toward excellence. *American Psychologist, 44,* 122–236.

Baummeister, R. F. (1996, Summer). Should schools try to boost self-esteem? *American Educator, 22,* 14–19.

Beaver, W. (1997, July). Declining college standards: It's not the courses, it's the grades. *The College Board Review, 181,* 2–7+.

Becher, R. M. (1984). *Parent involvement: A review of research and principles of successful practice.* Washington, DC: National Institute of Education.

Beck, L. G. (1992). Meeting the challenge of the future: The place of a caring ethic in educational administration. *American Journal of Education, 100* (4), 454–496.

Berne, E. (1964). *Games people play.* New York: Ballantine Books.

Berne, E. (1966). *Principles of group treatment.* New York: Oxford University Press.

Bestor, A. (1956). *The restoration of learning.* New York: Alfred A. Knopf.

Beyer, L. A. (1998). *Uncontrolled students eventually become unmanageable: The politics of classroom discipline* (pp. 51–81). In R. E. Butchart & B. McEwan, *Classroom discipline in American schools: Problems and possibilities for democratic education.* Albany: State University of New York Press.

Biehler, R., & Snowman, J. (1982). *Psychology applied to teaching.* Boston: Houghton Mifflin.

Bielaczyc, K., & Collins, A. (1999). Learning communities in classrooms: Advancing knowledge for a lifetime. *NASSP Bulletin, 83* (604), 4–10.

Biggs M. (2008a). Grade inflation and the professionalism of the professorate. In L. H. Hunt (Ed.), *Grade inflation: Academic standards in higher education* (pp. 109–120). New York: State University of New York Press.

Biggs, M. (2008b). Fissures in the foundation: Why grade conflation could happen. In L. H. Hunt (Ed.), *Grade inflation: Academic standards in higher education* (pp. 121–152). New York: State University of New York Press.

Bledsoe, J. C., Brown, I. D., & Strickland, A. D. (1971). Factors related to pupil observation reports of teachers and attitudes toward their teacher. *Journal of Educational Research, 65* (3), 119–126.

Bohn, A. P., & Sleeter, C. E. (2000). Multicultural education and the standards movement: A report from the field. *Phi Delta Kappan, 82* (2), 156–159.

Bok, S. (1979). *Lying: Moral choice in public and private life.* New York: Vintage.

Bracey, G. W. (2001). The 11th Bracey report on the condition of public education. *Phi Delta Kappan, 83* (2), 157–169.

Brandt, R. (1992). On building learning communities: A conversation with Hank Levin. *Educational Leadership, 50* (1), 19–23.

Bromley, D. G., Crow, M. L., & Gibson, M. S. (1978). Grade inflation: Trends, causes, and implications. *Phi Delta Kappan, 59* (10), 694–697.

Brophy, J. (1998). *Motivating students to learn.* Boston: McGraw-Hill.

Brown, A. L. (1994). The advancement of learning. *Educational Researcher, 23* (8), 4–12.

Brown, A. L., & Campione, J. C. (1994). Guided discovery in a community of learners. In K. McGilly (Ed.), *Classroom lessons: Integrating cognitive theory and classroom practice.* Cambridge, MA: MIT Press.

Bruner, J. S. (1971). The process of education revisited. *Phi Delta Kappan, 53,* 21.

Bull, B. L. (1990). The limits of teacher professionalism. In J. I. Goodlad, R. Soder, & K. A. Sirotnik (Eds.), *The moral dimensions of teaching.* San Francisco: Jossey-Bass.

Butchart, R. E. (1998a). Introduction. In R. E. Butchart & B. McEwan (Eds.), *Classroom discipline in American schools: Problems and possibilities for democratic education* (pp. 1–16). Albany: State University of New York Press.

Butchart, R. E. (1998b). Punishments, penalties, prizes and procedures: A history of discipline in U.S. schools. In R. E. Butchart & B. McEwan, *Classroom discipline in American schools: Problems and possibilities for democratic education* (pp. 19–49). Albany: State University of New York Press.

Butler, R. (1992). What young people want to know when: Effects of mastery and ability goals on interest in different kinds of social comparisons. *Journal of Personality and Social Psychology, 62,* 934–943.

Bybee, R. (Ed.). (1985). *Science Technology Society: 1985 Yearbook of the National Science Teachers Association*. Washington, DC: National Science Teachers Association.

Calfee, R. C., & Perfumo, P. (1993). Student portfolios: Opportunities for revolution in assessment. *Journal of Reading, 36* (7), 532–537.

Canter, L., & Canter, M. (2001). *Assertive discipline: A take-charge approach for today's educator*. Seal Beach, CA: Canter and Associates.

Chamberlain, D., et al. (1942). *Did they succeed in college?* New York: Harper & Row.

Chapman, W. (1991). The Illinois experience: State grants to improve schools through parent involvement. *Phi Delta Kappan, 72* (5), 355–358.

Charles, C. M. (1992). *Building classroom discipline: From models to practice* (4th ed.). New York: Longman.

Charles, C. M. (2000). *The synergetic classroom*. Boston: Allyn and Bacon.

Christenson, S. L., & Sheridan, S. M. (2001). *Schools and families: Creating essential connections for learning*. New York: Guilford Publications.

Claxton, G. (2008). Advanced creativity? In A. Craft, H. Gardner, & G. Claxton (Eds.), *Creativity, wisdom, and trusteeship: Exploring the role of education* (pp. 35–48). Thousand Oaks, CA: Corwin Press.

Claxton, G., Craft, A., & Gardner, H. (2008). Concluding thoughts: Good thinking—education for wise creativity. In A. Craft, H. Gardner, & G. Claxton (Eds.), *Creativity, wisdom, and trusteeship: Exploring the role of education* (pp. 169–176). Thousand Oaks, CA: Corwin Press.

Clifford, M. (1984). Thoughts on a theory of constructive failure. *Educational Psychologist, 19*, 108–120.

Clinchy, E. (2001). Needed: A new educational civil rights movement. *Phi Delta Kappan, 82* (7), 493–498.

Cloud, J. (2003, October 27). Inside the new SAT. *Time, 162* (17), 48–56.

Coats, W. D., & Swierenga, L. (1972). Student perceptions of teachers—A four analysis study. *Journal of Educational Research, 65* (8), 357–360.

Cohen, P. A. (1984). College grades and adult achievement: A research synthesis. *Research in Higher Education, 20* (3), 281–293.

Coleman, D. L. (2002). *Fixing Columbine: The challenge to American liberalism*. Durham, NC: Carolina Academic Press.

Coloroso, B. (2002). *Kids are worth it! Giving your child the gift of inner discipline*. New York: HarperCollins.

Coloroso, B. (2003). *The bully, the bullied, and the bystander: How parents and teachers can break the cycle of violence*. New York: HarperCollins.

Combs, A. W. (1962). A perceptual view of the adequate personality. In A. W. Combs (Chairman), *Perceiving, behaving, becoming: A new focus for education: 1962 yearbook* (pp. 50–64).Washington, DC: Association for Supervision and Curriculum Development.

Condray, J. (1977). Enemies of exploration: Self-initiated versus other-initiated learning. *Journal of Personality and Social Psychology, 35*, 459–477.

Confrey, J. (1990). What constructivism implies for teaching. In R. Davis (Ed.), *Constructivist views on the teaching and learning of mathematics* (p. 109). Reston, VA: National Council of Teachers of Mathematics.

Conrad, D., & Hedin, D. (1991). School-based community service: What we know from research and theory. *Phi Delta Kappan, 72*, 543–549.

Coombe, K. (1999). Ethics and the learning community. In J. Retallic, B. Cocklin, & K. Coombe (Eds.), *Learning communities in education: Issues, strategies and contexts*. New York: Routledge.

Cooper, H. (1989). *Homework*. White Plains, NY: Longman.

Covington, M. V. (1992). *Making the grade: A self-worth perspective on motivation and school reform*. New York: Cambridge University Press.

Covington, M. V., & Beery, R. G. (1976). *Self-worth and school learning*. New York: Holt, Rinehart and Winston.

Craft, A. (2008). Tensions in creativity and education. In A. Craft, H. Gardner, & G. Claxton (Eds.), *Creativity, wisdom, and trusteeship: Exploring the role of education* (pp. 16–34). Thousand Oaks, CA: Corwin Press.

Craske, M. (1985). Improving persistence through observational learning and attribution retraining. *British Journal of Educational Psychology, 55,* 138–147.

Crawford, B., Krajcik, J., & Marx, R. (1999). Elements of a community of learners in a middle school science classroom. *Science Education, 83* (6), 701–723.

Creman, L. (1961). *The transformation of the school.* Knopf.

Cristofoli, D. (1992). A new definition of leadership. *Snapshots: A fax newsletter, 2* (2), 12.

Cronback, L. (1965). *Educational psychology.* New York: Harcourt, Brace & World.

Cross, K. P. (1985). The rising tide of school reform reports. *Phi Delta Kappan, 66,* 167–172.

Csikszentmihalyi, M. (1990). *Flow: The psychology of optimal experience.* New York: Harper & Row.

Curwin, R. L., & Mendler, A. N. (1988). *Discipline with dignity.* Washington, DC: Association for Supervision and Curriculum Development.

Darling-Hammond, L. (1993). Reframing the school reform agenda: Developing the capacity for school transformation. *Phi Delta Kappan, 74,* 753–761.

Darling-Hammond, L. (1997). *The right to learn: A blueprint for creating schools that work.* San Francisco: Jossey-Bass.

Darling-Hammond, L. (2007). Standards, accountability and school reform. In C. E. Sleeter (Ed.), *Facing accountability in education: democracy and equity at risk* (pp. 78–111). New York: Teachers College Press.

Darling-Hammond, L., Wise, A. E., & Pease, S. R. (1983). Teacher evaluation in the organizational context: A review of the literature. *Review of Educational Research, 53,* 285–297.

Deci, E., Koestner, R., & Ryan, R. (1999). A meta-analytic review of experiments examining the effects of extrinsic rewards on intrinsic motivation. *Psychological Bulletin, 125* (6), 627–668.

Deci, E., & Ryan, R. (1985). *Intrinsic motivation and self-determination in human behavior.* New York: Plenum.

Deci, E., & Ryan, R. (1991). A motivational approach to self: Integration in personality. In R. Diensbier (Ed.), *Nebraska symposium on motivation: Vol 38. Perspectives on Motivation* (pp. 237–288). Lincoln: University of Nebraska.

Dewey, J. (1916). *Democracy and education.* New York: Macmillan.

Dewey, J. (1934). Comments and criticisms by some educational leaders in our universities. In *The activity movement, thirty-third yearbook of the National Society of the study of Education, part II* (chap. 5). Bloomington, IL: Public School Publishing Company.

Dewey J. (1964). My pedagogic creed. In R. D. Archambault (Ed.), *John Dewey on Education.* New York: The Modern Library.

Dodd, A. W., & Rosenbaum, E. (January, 1986). Learning communities for curriculum and staff development. *Phi Delta Kappan,* 380–384.

Dreikurs, R. (1968). *Psychology in the classroom: A manual for teachers* (2nd ed.). New York: Harper & Row.

Dreikurs, R., & Grey, L. (1968). *A new approach to discipline: Logical consequences.* New York: Hawthorne Books.

Dreikurs, R., Grunwald, B. B., & Pepper, F. C. (1982). *Maintaining sanity in the classroom: Classroom management techniques* (2nd ed.). New York: Harper & Row.

Drews, E. M. (1963). Profile of creativity. *National Education Association Journal, 26,* 26–28.

DuFour, R. P. (1999). Help wanted: Principals who can lead professional learning communities. *National Association of Secondary School Principals Bulletin, 83* (604), 12–17.

Durkheim, E. (1964). *The division of labor in society* (G. Simpson, trans.) New York: Free Press (originally published in 1893).

Ebers, E., & Streefland, L. (2000). Collaborative learning and the construction of common knowledge. *European Journal of Psychology in Education, 15* (4), 479–490.

Edwards, C. H. (2000). Moral classroom communities and the development of resiliency. *Contemporary Education, 71* (4), 38–41.

Einstein, A. (1950). *Out of my later years* (p. 32). New York: Philosophical Library, Inc.

Englander, M. E. (1986). *Strategies for classroom discipline*. New York: Praeger.

Engle, R. A., & Conant, F. R. (2002). Guiding principles of fostering productive disciplinary engagement: Explaining an emergent argument in a community of learners classroom. *Cognition and Instruction, 20* (4), 399–484.

Epstein, J. L. (1984). *Effects on parents of teacher practices in parent involvement*. Baltimore: Johns Hopkins University, Center for Social Organizations of Schools.

Epstein, J. L. (1987). What principals should know about parent involvement. *Principal, 66* (3), 6–9.

Epstein, J. L. (1991). Paths to partnerships: What we can learn from federal, state, district and school initiatives. *Phi Delta Kappan, 72* (5), 345–349.

Epstein, J. L., & Harackiewicz, J. (1992). Winning is not enough: The effects of competition and achievement orientation on intrinsic interest. *Personality and Social Psychology Bulletin, 18*, 129–138.

Fabes, R. A., Futz, J., Eisenberg, N., May-Plumlee, T., & Christopher, F. S. (1989). Effects of rewards on children's prosocial motivation: A socialization study. *Developmental Psychology, 25*, 509–515.

Fensham, P. (1992). Science and technology. In P. W. Jackson (Ed.) *Handbook of research in teaching* (p. 108). New York: Macmillan.

Fenstermacher, G. D. (1990). Some moral considerations on teaching as a profession. In J. I. Goodlad, R. Soder, & K. A. Sirotnik (Eds.), *The moral dimensions of teaching* (pp. 130–151). San Francisco: Jossey-Bass.

Finkelhor, D., Mitchell, K. J., & Wolak, J. (2000). *Online victimization: A report on the nation's youth*. Alexandria, VA: National Center for Missing and Exploited Children; Durham, NC: Crimes Against Children Research Center.

Ford Foundation, Annual Report (1972). *A foundation goes to school*. New York: The Ford Foundation.

Freedman, J. L., Cunningham, J. A., & Krismer, S. (1992). Inferred values and the reverse-incentive effect in induced compliance. *Journal of Personality and Social Psychology, 62*, 357–368.

Freeman, D. J., Kuhn, T. M., Porter, A. C., Floden, R. E., Schmidt, W. H., & Schwille, J. R. (1983). Do textbooks and tests define a natural curriculum in elementary school mathematics? *Elementary School Journal, 83* (5), 501–513.

Gamoran, A., & Berends, M. (1987). The effects of stratification in secondary schools: Synthesis of survey and ethnographic research. *Review of Educational Research, 57* (4), 415–435.

Gardner, H. (1991). *The unschooled mind: How children think and how schools should teach*. New York: Basic Books.

Gardner, H. (1994). Multiple intelligences: A theory in practice. *Teachers College Record 95*(4), 576–583.

Gardner, H. (2008). Creativity, wisdom, and trusteeship. In A. Craft, H. Gardner, & G. Claxton (Eds.), *Creativity, wisdom, and trusteeship: Exploring the role of education* (pp. 49–65). Thousand Oaks, CA: Corwin Press.

Gathercoal, F. (1990). *Judicious discipline* (2nd ed.). San Francisco, CA: Caddo Gap Press.

Gathercoal, F. (2001). *Judicious discipline* (5th ed.). San Francisco, CA: Caddo Gap Press.

Glasser, W. (1984). *Control theory: A new explanation of how we control our lives*. New York: Harper & Row.

Glasser, W. (1986). *Control theory in the classroom*. New York: Harper & Row.

Glasser, W. (1990). *The quality school: Managing students without coercion*. New York: Harper & Row.

Glasser, W. (1992). *The quality school*. New York: Harper & Row.

Glasser, W. (1998). *Choice theory: A new psychology of personal freedom*. New York: Harper Collins.

Glasser, W. (2005). *Every student can succeed*. Chatsworth, CA: William Glasser.

Glickman, C. D. (1993). *Renewing America's schools: A guide for school-based action*. San Francisco: Jossey-Bass.

Goldberg, M. D., & Cornell, D. G. (1998). The influence of intrinsic motivation and self-concept on academic achievement in school and third grade students. *Journal for the Education of the Gifted, 21* (2), 179–205.

Goldman, G. (1985). The betrayal of the gatekeepers: Grade inflation. *The Journal of General Education, 37*(2), 97–121.

Gollnick, D. M., & Chinn, P. C. (1994). *Multicultural education in a pluralistic society* (4th ed.). Upper Saddle River, NJ: Merrill / Prentice Hall.

Good, T. L., & Brophy, J. E. (1986). *Educational psychology* (3rd ed.). White Plains, NY: Longman.

Goodlad, J. I. (1984). A place called school: Prospects for the future. New York: McGraw-Hill.

Goodlad, J. I. (1994). Retrospect and prospect. In J. I. Goodlad & P. Keating (Eds.), *Access to knowledge: The continuing agenda for our nation's schools* (pp. 329–344). New York: College Entrance Examination Board.

Goodlad, J. I. (2000). Education and democracy. *Phi Delta Kappan, 82* (1), 86–89.

Goodlad, J. I. (2002). Kadzu, rabbits, and school reform. *Phi Delta Kappan, 84* (1), 19.

Gordon, J. A. (1998). Caring through control. *Journal of a Just and Caring Education, 4* (4), 418–440.

Gordon, T. (1989). *Discipline that works: Promoting self-discipline in children.* New York: Penguin Books.

Gose, B. (1997). Efforts to curb grade inflation get an F from many critics. *The Chronicle of Higher Education, 43,* A41–A42.

Goss v. Lopez, 419 U.S. 565 (1975).

Green, M. (1988). *The dialectic of freedom.* New York: Teachers College Press.

Greenburg, M. T., Kusche, C. A., & Spelz, M. (1991). Emotional regulation, self-control, and psychopathology: The role of relationships in early childhood. In D. Cicchetti & S. Toth (Eds.), *Rochester symposium on developmental pathology: Vol. 2. Internalizing and externalizing expressions of dysfunction* (pp. 21–55). Hillsdale, NJ: Erlbaum.

Greenwood, G. E., & Hickman, C. W. (1991). Research and practice in parent involvement: Implications for teacher education. *The Elementary School Journal, 91* (3), 279–288.

Griffin, G. A. (1991). *Toward a community of learning: The preparation and continuing education of teachers.* East Lansing, MI: The Holmes Group's National Curriculum Committee.

Hackney, C. E. & Henderson, J. G. (1999). Educating social leaders for inquiry-based democrative learning communities. Educational Horizions, Winter, 67–73.

Haerr, C. (2006). The first days of school. In T. S. Poetter, J. C. Wegwert, & C. Haerr (Eds.), *No child left behind and the illusion of reform* (pp. 77–90). New York: University Press of America.

Hammons, C. (2006). Home schooling: The nation's fastest growing education sector. In P. E. Peterson (Ed.), *Choice and competition in American education* (pp. 243–254). Lanham, MD: Roman & Littlefield.

Harackiewicz, J. M., & Manderlink, G. (1984). A process analysis of the effects of performance-contingent rewards on intrinsic motivation. *Journal of Experimental Social Psychology, 20,* 531–551.

Harris, T. A. (1967). *I'm OK—you're OK.* New York: Avon Books.

Haste, H. (2008). Good thinking: The creative and competent mind. In A. Craft, H. Gardner, & G. Claxton (Eds.), *Creativity, wisdom, and trusteeship: Exploring the role of education* (pp. 96–104). Thousand Oaks, CA: Corwin Press.

Hayes, N. M., Comer, J. P., & Hamilton-Lee, M. (1989). School climate enhancement through parent involvement. *Journal of School Psychology, 27,* 87–90.

Heckhausen, H. (1991). *Motivation and action* (2nd ed.). New York: Springer-Verlag.

Henderson, A. T., & Berla, N. (1995). *A new generation of evidence: The family is critical to student achievement.* Washington, DC: Center for Law and Education.

Hennessey, B. A. (2000). Rewards and creativity. In C. Sunstone & J. M. Harackiewicz (Eds.), *Intrinsic and extrinsic motivation: The search for optimal motivation and performance* (pp. 53–78). San Diego: Academic Press.

Henry, S. E., & Abowitz, K. (1998). Interpreting Glasser's Control Theory: Problems that emerge from innate needs and predetermined ends. In R. E. Butchart & B. McEwan (Eds.), *Classroom discipline in American schools: Problems and possibilities for democratic education*. Albany: State University of New York Press.

Hiatt, M., & Diana, B. (2001). School learning communities: A vision for organic school reform. *School Community Journal, 11* (2), 93–112.

Hoffa, H. (1963, February). The artist views creativity: Conforming and creativity. *Journal of Education, 145*, 51–53.

Horney, K. (1973). Culture and neurosis. In T. Milton (Ed.), *Theories of psycho pathology and personality* (2nd ed., pp. 161–162). Philadelphia: W. B. Saunders.

Howell, W. G. (2006). School choice in No Child Left Behind. In P. E. Peterson (Ed.), *Choice and competition in American education* (pp. 255–264). Lanham, MD: Rowman & Littlefield.

Hunt, L. H. (2008). Afterword: Focusing on the big picture. In L. H. Hunt (Ed.), *Grade inflation: Academic standards in higher education* (pp. 201–215). New York: State University of New York Press.

Hutchins, R. M. (1936). *The higher learning in America* (pp. 82–85). New Haven, CT: Yale University Press.

Hyman, I. A., & Perone, D. C. (1998). The other side of school violence: Educator politics that may contribute to students' misbehavior. *Journal of Student Psychology, 36* (1), 7–27.

Jackson, P. W. (1968). *Life in classrooms*. Austin, TX: Holt, Rinehart and Winston.

Jalongo, M. R. (1991). *Creating learning communities: The role of the teacher in the 21st century*. Bloomington, Indiana: National Education Service.

Johnson, D. W., & Johnson R. T. (1991). *Learning together and alone: Cooperative, competitive, and individualistic learning* (3rd ed.). Englewood Cliffs, NJ: Prentice-Hall.

Johnson, S. M. (1990). *Teachers at work: Achieving success in our schools*. New York: Basic Books.

Johnson, V. E. (2003). Grade inflation: A crisis in college education. New York: Springer.

Jones, B. F. (1988). Toward redefining models of curriculum and instruction for students at-risk. In B. Z. Presseisen (Ed.), *At-risk students and thinking: Perspectives from research* (pp. 76-103). Washington, DC: National Education Association and Research for Better Schools.

Jones, F. H. (1987a). *Positive classroom discipline*. New York: McGraw-Hill.

Jones, F. H. (1987b). *Positive classroom instruction*. New York: McGraw-Hill.

Jones, F. H. (2001). *Fred Jones' tools for teachers*. Santa Cruz, CA: Fredric H. Jones & Associates.

Juola, A. (1980). Grade inflation in higher education—1979: Is it over? (ED 189 129).

Kagan, S. (2001). Teaching for character and community. *Educational Leadership, 59* (2), 50–55.

Kagan, S., Scott, S., & Kagan, S. (2003). *Win-Win Discipline course workbook*. San Clemente, CA: Kagan Publishing.

Kamber, R. (2008a). Understanding grade inflation. In L. H. Hunt (Ed.), *Grade inflation: Academic standards in higher education*. New York: State University of New York Press.

Kamber, R. (2008b). Combating grade inflation: Obstacles and opportunities. In L. H. Hunt (Ed.), *Grade inflation: Academic standards in higher education* (pp. 171–189). New York: State University of New York Press.

Kanter, R. M. (1987). *Men and women of the corporation*. New York: Basic Books.

Katz, S. R. (1997). Presumed guilty: How schools criminalize Latino youth. *Social Justice, 24* (4), 77–95.

Kellerman, B. (1984). Leadership as a political act. In B. Kellerman (Ed.), *Leadership: Multidisciplinary perspective*. Englewood Cliffs, NJ: Prentice-Hall.

Kelly, E. C. (1962). The fully functioning self. In A. W. Combs (Chairman), *Perceiving, behaving, becoming: A new focus for education: 1962 yearbook* (pp. 9–20).Washington, DC: Association for Supervision and Curriculum Development.

Kennedy, M. M. (1987). *Inexact sciences: Professional education and the development of expertise*. East Lansing, Mich.: The National Center for Research on Teacher Education.

Klerman, G., Laver, P., Rice, J., Reich, T., Antacid, J., Andersen, N., Keller, M., & Hirshfeld, R. (1985). Birth cohorts trends in rates of major depressive disorders among relatives of patients with affective disorders. *Archives of General Psychiatry, 42*, 689–693.

Kohlberg, L. (1976). Moral stages and moralization: The cognitive-developmental approach. In T. Lickona (Ed.), *Moral development and behavior*. New York: Holt, Rinehart & Winston.

Kohn, A. (1992). *No contest: The case against competition*. Boston: Houghton Mifflin.

Kohn, A. (1993). *Punished by rewards: The trouble with gold stars, incentive plans, A's, praise, and other bribes*. Boston: Houghton Mifflin.

Kohn, A. (1996). *Beyond discipline: From compliance to community*. Alexandria, VA: Association for Supervision and Curriculum Development.

Kohn, A. (1998). Only for my kid: How privileged parents undermine school reform. *Phi Delta Kappan, 79*, 569–577.

Kohn, A. (1999a). Constant frustration and occasional violence: The legacy of American high schools. *American School Board Journal, 186* (9), 20–24.

Kohn, A. (1999b). The costs of overemphasizing achievement. *School Administrator, 56* (10), 40–46.

Kohn, A. (2006). *The homework myth: Why our kids get too much of a bad thing*. Cambridge, MA: DaCapo Press.

Kounin, J. S. (1970a). *Discipline and group management in classrooms*. New York: Holt, Rinehart & Winston.

Kounin, J. S. (1970b). Observing and delineating techniques of managing behavior in classrooms. *Journal of Research and Development in Education, 4* (1), 62–72.

Kounin, J. S., & Gump, P. V. (1961). The comparative influence of punitive and non-punitive teachers upon children's concepts of school misconduct. *Journal of Educational Psychology, 52*, 44–49.

Kounin, J. S., & Gump, P. V. (1974). Signal systems of lesson settings and the task related behavior of pre-school children. *Journal of Educational Psychology, 66*, 554–562.

Kouzma, N. M., & Kennedy, G. A. (2002). Homework, stress, and mood disturbance in senior high school students. *Psychological Reports, 91*, 193–198.

Kraus, W. A. (1984). *Collaboration in organization: Alternatives to hierarchy*. New York: Human Sciences Press.

Lal, S. R., Lal, D., & Achilles, C. M. (1993). *Handbook on gangs in schools: Strategies to reduce gang-related activities*. Thousand Oaks, CA: Corwin Press.

Landau, B. M. (2004). *The art of classroom management: Building equitable learning communities* (2nd ed.). Upper Saddle River, NJ; Columbus, OH: Pearson; Merrill / Prentice Hall.

Laska, J., & Juarez, T. (1992). *Grading and marking in American schools: Two centuries of debate*. Springville, IL: Charles C. Thomas.

Lepper, M., & Greene D. (Eds.). (1978). *The hidden costs of reward: New perspectives on psychology of human motivation*. Hillsdale, NJ: Erlbaum.

Lepper, M. R., Greene, D., & Nisbett, R. E. (1973). Undermining children's intrinsic interest with extrinsic rewards: A test of over-justification hypothesis. *Journal of Personality and Social Psychology, 28*, 129–137.

Lewis, B. (1991). *The kids guide to social action*. Minneapolis: Free Spirit.

Lieberman, A. (1996). Creating intentional learning communities. *Educational Leadership, 54*(3), 51–55.

Lieberman, A., & Miller, L. (2008). Developing capacities. In A. Lieberman & L. Miller (Eds.), *Teachers in professional communities: Improving teaching and learning* (pp. 18–28). New York: Teachers College Press.

Lightfoot, S. L. (1978). *Worlds apart: Relationships between families and schools*. New York: Basic Books.

Lindle, J. C. (1989). What do parents want from principals and teachers? *Educational Leadership, 47* (2), 12–14.

Lipman, M. (1991). *Thinking in education*. New York: Cambridge University Press.

Lorber, M. A. (1996). *Objectives, methods and evaluation for secondary teaching*. Boston: Allyn and Bacon.

Lortie, D. C. (1975). *Schoolteacher: A sociological study.* Chicago: University of Chicago Press.

Losen, D. L. (2004). Graduation rate accountability under the No Child Left Behind Act and the disparate impact on students of color. In G. Orfield (Ed.), *Dropouts in America: Confronting the graduation rate crisis* (pp. 41–56). Cambridge, MA: Harvard Education Press.

Madaus, G., Russell, M., & Higgins, J. (2009). *Paradoxes of high stakes testing.* Charlotte, NC: Information Age Publishing.

Manacker, J., Hurwitz, E., & Weldon, W. (1988). Parent-teacher cooperation in schools serving the urban poor. *Clearing House, 62,* 108–112.

Marshall, M. (2001). *Discipline without stress, punishment or rewards: How teachers and parents promote responsibility and learning.* Los Alamos, CA: Piper Press.

Maslow, A. (1968). *Toward a psychology of being* (2nd ed.). New York: Van Nostrand.

Matthews, M. R. (2000). Appraising constructivism in science and mathematics education. In D. C. Phillips (Ed.), *Constructivism in education: Opinions and second opinions on controversial issues: Part I.* 99th yearbook of the National Society for the Study of Education (pp. 161–192). Chicago: University of Chicago Press.

May, R. (1977). *The meaning of anxiety* (Rev. ed.). New York: Norton.

McHenry, I. (2000). Conflict in schools: Fertile ground for moral growth. *Phi Delta Kappan, 82* (3), 223–227.

McLaughlin, M. W., & Talbert, J. E. (2001). *Professional communities and the work of high school teaching.* Chicago: University of Chicago Press.

McNeil, L. M. (1988a). Contradictions of control, part 1: Administrators and teachers. *Phi Delta Kappan, 69* (5), 333–339.

McNeil, L. M. (1988b). Contradictions of control, part 2: Teachers, students, and curriculum. *Phi Delta Kappan, 69* (6), 433–438.

McNeil, L. M. (2000). Creating new inequalities: Contradictions of reform. *Phi Delta Kappan, 81* (10), 729–734.

Meier, D. (2002). *In schools we trust: Creating communities of learning in an era of testing and standardization.* Boston: Beacon Press.

Merrow, J. (2001). Undermining standards. *Phi Delta Kappan, 83* (9), 653–659.

Meyers, E. A. (1968). *Education in the perspective of history.* New York: Harper Brothers.

Milton, O., Pollio, H. R., & Eison, J. A. (1986). *Making sense of college grades.* San Francisco: Jossey Bass.

Mintzberg, H. (1987). Crafting strategy. *Harvard Business Review,* July–August, 66–75.

Moriarty, B., Douglas, G., Punch, K., & Hattie, J. (1995). The importance of self-efficacy as a mediating variable between learning environments and achievement. *British Journal of Educational Psychology, 65,* 73–84.

Nagle, B. (1998). A proposal for dealing with grade inflation: The relative performance index. *Journal of Education in Business, 74* (1), 40–43.

Nathan, J., & Kielsmeier, J. (1991). The sleeping giant of school reform. *Phi Delta Kappan, 72,* 729–742.

National Commission on Teaching and America's Future (NCTAF). (1996). *What matters most: Teaching and America's future.* New York: Darling-Hammond.

Nelsen, J. (1996). *Positive discipline.* New York: Ballantine.

Nelsen, J., & Lott, L. (2000). *Positive discipline for teenagers: Empower your teens and yourself through kind and firm parenting.* Roseville, CA: Prima.

Nelsen, J., Lott, L., & Glen, H. (1993). *Positive discipline in the classroom.* Rocklin, CA: Prima.

Neuman, M., & Simmons, W. (2000). Leadership for student learning. *Phi Delta Kappan,* September, 9–12.

Newman, F. M., Marks, H. M., & Gamoran, A. (1995, April). *Authentic pedagogy and student performance.* Paper presented at the meeting of the American Education Research Association, San Francisco.

Noddings, N. (1986). Fidelity in teaching, teacher education and research for teaching. *Harvard Educational Review, 56* (4), 496–510.

Noddings, N. (2002). *Educating moral people: A caring alternative to character education.* New York: Teacher's College Press.

Oakes, J. (1992, March 4). *Preparing a match: Professionalism and effective equitable opportunity structures.* Seven Oaks School Division Symposium Series. Winnipeg, Manitoba.

Osborne, R. J., & Wittrock, M. C. (1983). Learning science: A generative process. *Science Education, 67,* 489–508.

Paik, H., & Comstock, G. (1994). The effects of television violence on antisocial behavior: A meta-analysis. *Communication Research, 21* (4), 515–546.

Penfield, W. (1952). Memory mechanism. *A.M.A. Archives of Neurology and Psychiatry, 67,* 178–198.

Pettijohn, T. F. (1995). Correlations among students' grade point averages and American College Test scores. *Psychological Reports, 76,* 336–338.

Phillips, D. C. (2000). An opinionated account of the constructivist landscape. In D. C. Phillips (Ed.), *Constructivism in education: Opinions and second opinions on controversial issues: Part I.* 99th Yearbook of the National Society for the Study of Education. Chicago: University of Chicago Press.

Pinata, R. C. (1999). *Enhanced relationships between children and teachers.* Washington, DC: American Psychological Association.

Poetter, T. S. (2006). The impact of NCLB on curriculum, teaching, and assessment. In T. S. Poetter, J. C. Wegwert, & C. Haerr (Eds.), *No child left behind and the illusion of reform.* New York: University Press of America.

Popham, W. J. (1999). Why standardized tests don't measure educational quality. *Educational Leadership, 56* (6), 8–15.

Poplin, M., & Weres, J. (1992) *Voices from the inside: A report on schooling from inside the classroom.* Claremont, CA: Institute for Education in Transformation, Claremont Graduate School.

Power, F. C., & Higgins-D'Alessandro, A. (2008). The just community approach to moral education and the moral atmosphere of the school. In L. P. Nucci & D. Narvaez (Eds.), *Handbook of moral and character education* (pp. 240–247). New York: Routledge.

Prawat, R. S. (April, 1992). From individual differences to learning communities—Our changing focus. *Educational Leadership,* 9–13.

Raywid, M. A. (1993). Community: An alternative school accomplishment. In G. A. Smith (Ed.), *Public schools that work: Creating community.* New York: Routledge.

Reeve, J., & Deci, E. (1996). Elements of the competitive situation that affect intrinsic motivation. *Personality and Social Psychology Bulletin, 22,* 24–33.

Reich, T., Van Eerdewegh, P., Rice, J., Mullaney, J., Klerman, G., & Endcott, J. (1987). The family transmission of primary depressive disorder. *Journal of Psychiatric Research, 21,* 613–624.

Resnick, L. (1987). Learning in school and out. *Educational Researcher, 16,* 13–20.

Resnick, L. (1990). *Literacy in school and out.* Daedalus, *119* (2), 169–185.

Robins, L., Helzer, J., Weissman, M., Orvaschel, H., Gruenberg, E., Burke, J., & Regier, D. (1984). Lifetime prevalence of specific psychiatric disorder in three sites. *Archives of General Psychiatry, 41,* 949–958.

Rodereck, M. (1994). Grade retention and school drop out: Investigating the association. *American Educational Research Journal, 31,* 729–759.

Rogers, C. (1969). *Freedom to learn.* Columbus, OH: Charles E. Merrill.

Rohrkemper, M., & Corno, L. (1988). Success and failure on classroom tasks: Adaptive learning and classroom teaching. *Elementary School Journal, 88,* 299–312.

Rosenberg, J. (1965). *Society and the adolescent self-image.* Princeton, NJ: Princeton University Press.

Rubin, L. J. (1963, March). Creativity and the curriculum. *Phi Delta Kappan, 44,* 438–440.

Russell, J. (2007). *How children become moral selves: Building character and promoting citizenship education.* Portland, OR: Sussex Academic Press.

Ryan, R., & Deci, E. L. (2000). Intrinsic and extrinsic motivation: Classic definitions and new directions. *Contemporary Educational Psychology, 25,* 54–67.

Sax, L. (2005). *Why gender matters: What parents and teachers need to know about the emerging science of sex differences*. New York: Doubleday.

Scardamalia, M., & Bereiter, C. (1992). Text-based and knowledge-based questioning by children. *Cognition and Instruction, 9* (3), 177–199.

Schalock, D. (1979). Research on teacher selection. In D. C. Berliner (Ed.), *Review of research in education* (Vol. 7). Washington, DC: American Educational Research Association.

Schoenfeld, A. H. (1988). When good teaching leads to bad results: The disasters of "well taught" mathematics courses. *Educational Psychology, 23* (2), 145–166.

Schon, D. (1983). *The reflective practitioner: How professionals think in action*. New York: Basic Books.

Schwartz, D. L., & Lin, X. (2001). Computers, productive agency, and the effort toward sharing meaning. *Journal of Computing in Higher Education, 12* (2), 3–33.

Seligman, M. E. P. (1995). *The optimistic child*. New York: Harper Collins.

Sergiovanni, T. J. (1990). *Value-added leadership: How to get extraordinary performance in schools*. San Diego, CA: Harcourt Brace Janovich.

Sergiovanni, T. J. (1992). *Moral leadership: Getting to the heart of school improvement*. San Francisco: Jossey-Bass.

Sergiovanni, T. J. (1994). *Building community in school*. San Francisco: Jossey-Bass.

Sergiovanni, T. J. (1995). *The principalship: A reflective practice perspective* (3rd ed.). Boston: Allyn & Bacon.

Sergiovanni, T. J. (1999). The story of community. In J. Retallic, B. Cocklin, & K. Coombe (Eds.), *Learning communities in education: Issues, strategies, and contexts* (pp. 9–25). New York: Routledge.

Sergiovanni, T. J. (2000). *The life-world of leadership: Creating culture, community, and personal meaning in our schools*. San Francisco: Jossey-Bass.

Shavelson, R. J. (1985). Schemata and teaching routines. Paper presented at the annual meeting of the American Educational Research Association, Chicago.

Shulman, L. (1987). Knowledge and teaching: Foundations of the new reform. *Harvard Educational Review, 57* (1), 1–22.

Siegel, L. (1998). Should the Internet be censored? No! No! No! No! *Update on Law-Related Education, 22* (2), 119–130.

Skinner, B. F. (1953). *Science and human behavior*. Boston: Houghton Mifflin.

Smith, F. (2001). Just a matter of time. *Phi Delta Kappan, 82* (8), 573–576.

Smith, J. O., & Price, R. A. (1996). Attribution theory and developmental students as passive learners. *Journal of Developmental Education, 19* (3), 2–4.

Solomon, J. (1994). The rise and fall of constructivism. *Studies in Science Education, 23*, 1–19.

Solomon, Z. P. (1991). California's policy on parent involvement: State leadership for local initiatives. *Phi Delta Kappan, 72* (5), 359–362.

Steinberg, L. D. (1996). *Beyond the classroom*. New York: Simon & Schuster.

Strike, K. A. (2008). School community and moral education. In L. P. Nucci & D. Narvaez (Eds.), *Handbook of moral and character education* (pp. 117–133). New York: Routledge.

Sullivan, A. J. (1963). The right to fail: Creativity versus conservatism. *Journal of Higher Education, 34* (4), 191–195.

Swap, S. M. (1993). *Developing home-school partnerships: From concepts to practice*. New York: Teachers College Press.

Sykes, C. (1995). *Dumbing down our kids*. New York: Martins Press.

Tan, D. L. (1991). Grades as predictors of college and career success. *Journal of College Admissions, 132* (Summer), 12–15.

Tanner, D., & Tanner, L. (1975). *Curriculum development: Theory into practice*. New York: Macmillan Publishing Co.

Taylor, B. (1998). Should the Internet be censored? Yes! Yes! Yes! *Update on Law-Related Education, 22* (2), 13–15.

Taylor, C. (1985). *Hegel and modern society*. Cambridge: Cambridge University Press.

Tennyson, W., & Strom, S. (1986). Beyond professional standards: Developing responsibleness. *Journal of Counseling and Development, 64*, 298–302.

Thompson, K. M., & Braaten-Antrim, R. (1998). Youth maltreatment and gang involvement. *Journal of Interpersonal Violence, 13* (3), 328–345.

Thorndike, E. L. (1906). *The principles of teaching.* New York: A. G. Seiler.

Thorndike, E. L. (1924). Mental discipline in high school subjects. *Journal of Educational Psychology, 15,* 1–22, 83–98.

Thorndike, E. L., & Woodworth, R. S. (1901). The influence of improvement in one mental function upon efficiency of other functions. *Psychological Review, 8,* 247–261, 384–395, 553–564.

Tinker v. Des Moines Independent School District 393, U.S. 503 (1969).

Torrance, E. P. (1962). *Guiding creative talent.* Englewood Cliffs, NJ: Prentice-Hall.

Turnbull, A. P., & Turnbull, H. R. (1997). *Families, professionals, and exceptionalities: A special partnership* (3rd ed.). Upper Saddle River, NJ: Merrill / Prentice Hall.

Van Hoose, J., & Legrand, P. (2000). It takes parents, the whole village, and school to raise children. *Middle School Journal, 31* (3), 32–37.

Walker, J. E., & Shae, T. M. (1995). *Behavior management: A practical approach for educators* (6th ed.). Upper Saddle River, NJ: Merrill / Prentice Hall.

Walker, J. E, & Shea, T. M. (1999). *Behavior management: A practical approach for educators* (7th ed.). Upper Saddle River, NJ: Merrill / Prentice Hall.

Walker-Barnes, C. J., & Mason, C. A. (2001). Perceptions of risk factors for female gang involvement among African American and Hispanic women. *Youth and Society, 32* (3), 303–336.

Walsh, A., & Beyer, J. A. (1987). Violent crime, sociopathy and love deprivation among adolescent delinquents. *Journal of Moral Education, 22* (87), 705–717.

Watkins, C. (2005). *Classrooms as learning communities: What's in it for schools?* New York: Routledge.

Watson-Ellam, L. (1997). Video games: Playing on a violent playground. In J. R. Epp & A. M. Watkinson (Eds.), *Systemic violence in education: Promise broken* (pp. 72–93). New York: State University of New York Press.

Weiner, B., & Kukla, A. (1970). An attributional analysis of achievement motivation. *Journal of Abnormal and Social Psychology, 15,* 1–20.

Wiggins, G. (1989). *A true test: Toward more authentic and equitable measurement.* Phi Delta Kappan, *70* (8), 703–713.

Wilson, S. W., & Peterson, P. L. (1997). *Theories of learning and teaching: What do they mean for educators?* Working paper, Benchmarks for schools. Washington, DC: Department of Education, Office of Educational Research and Improvement.

Wolfgang, C. H., & Glickman, C. D. (1980). *Solving discipline problems: Strategies for classroom teachers.* Boston: Allyn and Bacon.

Wynne, E. A. (1995). The moral dimensions of teaching. In A. C. Ornstein (Ed.), *Teaching: Theory into practice* (pp. 189–202). Boston: Allyn & Bacon.

Yao, E. (1988). Working effectively with Asian immigrant parents. *Phi Delta Kappan, 70* (3), 223–225.

Younge, G. D., & Sassenrath, J. M. (1968). Student personality correlates of teacher ratings. *Journal of Educational Psychology, 59* (1), 44–52.

Yukel, G. A. (1989). *Leadership in organizations* (2nd ed.). Englewood Cliffs, NJ: Prentice-Hall.

Zahorick, J. A. (1970). The effect of planning on teaching. *Elementary School Journal, 71,* 143–151.

Index

About the Author

Clifford H. Edwards is a former professor of science education whose thirty-five-year professional career was spent at Illinois State University and Brigham Young University. He is the author of books and articles primarily in the areas of curriculum and student discipline.

Breinigsville, PA USA
15 December 2010
251520BV00003B/1/P